CIRCULATING LITERACY

CIRCULATING LITERACY

Writing Instruction in American Periodicals 1880–1910

Alicia Brazeau

Southern Illinois University Press
Carbondale

Southern Illinois University Press
www.siupress.com

Copyright © 2016 by the Board of Trustees,
Southern Illinois University
All rights reserved
Printed in the United States of America

19 18 17 16   4 3 2 1

Cover illustration: *The Muses in the Sacred Wood*, by Maurice Dennis; doverpictura.com

Library of Congress Cataloging-in-Publication Data

Names: Brazeau, Alicia, author.
Title: Circulating literacy : writing instruction in American periodicals, 1880–1910 / Alicia Brazeau.
Description: Carbondale : Southern Illinois University Press, 2016. | Includes bibliographical references and index.
Identifiers: LCCN 2016013857 | ISBN 9780809335442 (paperback) | ISBN 9780809335459 (ebook)
Subjects: LCSH: American periodicals—History. | Women's periodicals, American—History. | Periodicals in education—United States—History. | Authorship—Study and teaching—United States—History. | Literacy—United States—History. | Women—Education—United States—History. | Self-culture—United States—History. | Books and reading—United States—History. | BISAC: LANGUAGE ARTS & DISCIPLINES / Literacy. | LANGUAGE ARTS & DISCIPLINES / Study & Teaching.
Classification: LCC P53.475 .B729 2016 | DDC 808/.0420973—dc23 LC record available at https://lccn.loc.gov/2016013857

Printed on recycled paper. ♻

Contents

List of Illustrations   vii

Introduction: Literacy by Subscription   1

1. Literacy Identities: Defining Magazine Writers   23
2. Buying and Selling Literacy: The *Ladies' Home Journal*   49
3. Joining the Club: Clubwomen, Magazine Readers, and Scholars   83
4. Special Invitation to Write: Magazine Readers as Contributors   119

Conclusion: Subscribing to a Professional Writing Community   151

Notes   169
Works Cited   175
Index   189

Illustrations

May 1906 cover for the *Ladies' Home Journal* 29

Margaret Hamilton Welch's "Club Women and Club Work" 36

"Men Who Write for Us" 40

April 1905 cover for the *Ladies' Home Journal* 51

Profile from the *Ladies' Home Journal* 68

"Nobody is really so superior as to be too good to marry" 85

Welch's "Club Women and Club Work" 95

Ohio Farmer feature 129

CIRCULATING LITERACY

Introduction: Literacy by Subscription

In 1900, 238,000 persons were enrolled in college courses in the United States. Three years later, a single magazine, the *Ladies' Home Journal*, could claim 1 million subscribers and even more readers. At the dawn of the twentieth century, in the midst of a literacy crisis that has received a great deal of attention from literacy scholars such as Graff and Gordon and Gordon, and at the same time that required composition courses were first being incorporated at institutions such as Harvard, Yale, and the University of Michigan, an incontrovertible fact was that far more people were reading magazines than were sitting in college composition classrooms. Despite this, however, our histories of literacy and composition in the United States have almost wholly ignored popular periodicals and their place in the literate lives of such a large population. If, as compositionists, we accept that at least one of our fundamental disciplinary goals is to understand and historicize the ways that people have learned to write and enter into a community of readers, then we must also critically consider the limits we have placed on historical study and the populations we have documented. Most histories of composition and rhetorical studies have focused exclusively on academic institutions and English and composition departments in particular, despite repeated arguments suggesting the value of widening our historical purview (Gere, Susan Miller, Gold).

Such a sustained focus on upper-level institutional education has meant that histories of composition, especially those covering the first part of the twentieth century, have limited themselves to an incredibly small and homogenous percentage of the U.S. population. Likewise, more general histories of literacy, while considering larger populations as well as education at the primary and secondary levels, have tended to restrict their studies to census reports, schools, and tax and employment documents. In *The Literacy Myth: Literacy and Social Structure in the Nineteenth-Century City*, Harvey Graff stresses that his numerical approach allows him to provide the necessary empirical basis to properly understand qualitative discussions of literacy history. In *Literacy in America: Historic Journey and Contemporary Solutions*, Edward E. Gordon and Elaine H. Gordon likewise draw from a wide range of materials, linking numerical data with autobiographical materials to consider the place of reading in the lives of individuals. In this way, both Graff and Gordon and Gordon use their histories to move beyond institutional ideologies, common myths about literacy, and strictly numerical records to gain a better understanding of how actual nineteenth-century people made use of literacy skills.

Although many newspapers and periodicals at this time certainly continued to propagate what Graff has called the "literacy myth," they represent a complex site of study in that they offered multiple perspectives on literacy and, more important, articulated their own definitions of literacy for their readers. Regardless of the kinds of books they frequently attempted to persuade readers they ought to be reading, the popularity of the magazines is evidence of what nineteenth-century Americans truly were reading, and as such, they remain important artifacts of the literate lives of a wide population. While valuable, histories concentrating on university texts and pedagogies, and other institutional academic sites, need to be joined by complementary and contradictory histories of other sites of literacy learning—sites that tell the story of readers and writers not included in the college classroom.

This is not to suggest that scholars have wholly ignored the history of literacy and rhetorical learning in nonacademic settings; to the contrary, in "Kitchen Tables and Rented Rooms: The Extracurriculum of Composition," Anne Ruggles Gere argues that composition historians should extend beyond the academy and professional settings to incorporate the diverse contexts where literacy learning happens. Work such as that done by Gere (1997), Susan Miller (1998), and Shirley Wilson Logan (2008) all embrace this call and touch on "everyday" sites of literacy education in late nineteenth- and early twentieth-century America. Histories such as these offer new perspectives on the cultural, local literacy practices that shaped the lives of nineteenth-century Americans.

This book joins discussions on the "extracurriculum" of composition at the turn of the century by examining popular magazines as sites of literacy instruction. Periodicals are an especially useful tool for study because of their incredible popularity at that time; thanks to improvements in publication technology and cheap postage, periodicals circulated widely and in many cases were a more easily attainable and affordable reading source than books. Significantly, they were popular in all parts of the country—not just in major eastern cities—and were able to reach audiences that had little to no access to the higher education addressed in histories of the composition classroom. Indeed, memoirs written in the late nineteenth century by rural teachers such as Irene Hardy, teachers in impoverished and isolated communities such as Mary Stone and Katherine Petit, and missionary teachers at reservation schools such as Gertrude Golden all note how much they had valued magazines in their own homes and how eager their students were for greater access to popular magazines.[1] Here, teachers and students suggest that periodicals were commonly viewed as both a form of entertainment and a tool of literacy learning—one that extended or supplemented formal education. A survey of periodical archives for this time period demonstrates that this idea is reinforced in the journals, which make frequent reference to readers' self-improvement and study, and, as I explore in the following chapters, where the editors engage in explicit literacy instruction with correspondents.

Literacy and Education at the Turn of the Century

Throughout the book, I am concerned not only with how popular magazines connect with the understanding of late nineteenth- and early twentieth-century composition education visible in our current histories, but also with how these magazines responded to a perceived literacy crisis and a corresponding national preoccupation with education. In the first column of the "Home Study" department in *Harper's Bazar*,[2] for instance, E. B. Cutting outlines the value of education in general and the goals of the "home study club" in particular. Urging readers to begin to form local groups and inviting readers already belonging to established clubs to correspond with the periodical, Cutting makes clear that the purpose of the department is to establish a fellowship of students in the "realm of books." In surveying possible study topics, Cutting's proposal suggests that education, self-directed or otherwise, has patriotic and social consequences, that it leads to self-improvement (personal and literate), and that it is a social activity that forms connections among women—Christian, middle-class women, by implication. The educational paradigm outlined in this initial prospectus echoes the primary goals that appear in dominant nineteenth- and early twentieth-century narratives of literacy and education. These narratives, as numerous literacy scholars have pointed out, often relied on assumed connections among literacy, moral and civic virtue, and social mobility. Literacy education was as much about adopting the values and habits that the student would need to participate in a middle-class, capitalistic culture as it was about the acquisition of reading and writing skills—or, rather, it was based on the belief that skill in the latter enhanced the former.

As histories such as Graff's, Gordon and Gordon's, and Jessica Enoch's examine, the end of the nineteenth century and the beginning of the twentieth century were marked by a national preoccupation with literacy and education. Like literacy crises at any historical moment, this one emerged inextricably linked to social, political, moral, and economic concerns. In *Literacy in America*, Gordon and Gordon consider the attitudinal shift prompting turn-of-the-century Americans to consider basic literacy as necessary in their personal lives and for the livelihood of their communities. Gordon and Gordon attribute the appearance of this particular perspective on literacy to increased immigration, industrialization, and urbanization (263). The immigration boom at this time—it is estimated that over 28 million immigrants arrived between 1880 and 1930—meant that cities, especially eastern cities, experienced not only increasing populations but also changing ethnic and linguistic demographics. Basic education in literacy was perceived by many political and educational leaders as the best way to help members of these new urban populations assimilate. Correspondingly, leaders cast the cultural threat posed by foreign populations as a crisis of illiteracy. Although late nineteenth-century narratives and propaganda draw a connection between the "problem" of immigration and low rates of literacy, however, such a connection is not necessarily supported by evidence. Graff notes how literacy histories have commonly focused on the association made between rising immigration and fears for literacy but uses an empirical approach to assert that "despite common notions that many immigrants to North America were the dregs of their societies of origin and were rooted in cultures of poverty, . . . their levels of literacy were well above average for those places" (*Literacy Myth* xviii).

Graff likewise warns that the connections made between industrialization and literacy need to be considered carefully. Business and political leaders at this time certainly advocated literacy education for the new industrial workforce as a means of instilling the virtues and habits required in an economy of mass production. Horace Mann, among others, argued that basic education taught discipline, hard work, punctuality, and respect for authority. In the *Fifth Annual Report of the Massachusetts Board of Education*, Mann seeks to offer evidence for the argument that education leads to clean, moral workers and asserts that literacy education benefited the workers in the form of wage increases. Both Graff and Gordon and Gordon, however, make equally clear that Mann's perspective, while common, was far from universal. Business leaders continued to worry that education could also foster feelings of resentment among the working class about their current social order and result in radical social and political awareness. Moreover, Graff makes clear that working-class perspectives also revealed an "awareness of the contradictions of educational promotion and programs" that assumed a direct and unambiguous connection between increased literacy and personal economic welfare (*Literacy Myth* 212). Nonetheless, this perspective that literacy was the key to economic security and advancement for individuals, and was consequently vital to the financial and social welfare of the larger community, remained predominant throughout the Progressive Era.

Because basic education was seen as a fundamental element of social (and economic) mobility, instruction in literacy needed to be carried out carefully. If, as many nineteenth-century discourses on literacy suggest, literacy acquired independently of proper instruction and supervision posed a potential social and political threat (Graff, "Literacy Myth at Thirty"), then it was important that education seek to inculcate in students the right (white, pan-Protestant) moral and social values. Teachers, therefore, as Graff discusses and Nan Johnson in *Nineteenth-Century Rhetoric in North America*, David Wallace Adams in *Education for Extinction*, and Jessica Enoch in *Refiguring Rhetorical Education* also note, were required to be models of Christian, middle-class attitudes and values and were responsible for their instillation and restraint in young students. As a 1900 article, "The Training of Teachers for Indian Schools," states so succinctly, "the teacher is the maker and protector of civilization" (Dyke 696). Even outside of discussions of education at the primary and secondary levels, however, the goals for basic literacy instruction stressed the overall good of the nation (Graff, Enoch). In a wide range of popular periodical articles at the time, illiteracy was consistently linked with crime, poverty, and immorality.

Although critiquing the unequal opportunities for education in the southern states, a contributor to the *Ohio Farmer* in the "Current Comment" column of 1901 nevertheless articulates mainstream fears that illiterate voters would be detrimental to local and national governments:

> The ballot in the hands of an ignorant, depraved people is a dangerous power. The only safety in a republican form of government lies in the intelligence and virtue of the voters. The state should require the ability to read and write and then provide the opportunity to every man to secure the education. (350)

This kind of discourse was neither uncommon nor linked solely to African Americans; applied by turns to immigrants, Native Americans, and impoverished communities generally, the connection among morality, social stability, and literacy appears frequently. These moral and social goals are clearly visible in pedagogies governing reading in particular, where it was argued that a course of reading taught time management, mental discipline, and the development of sensitivity to a text's aesthetic and didactic features, and that reading aloud was connected with religious performance (Carr, Carr, and Schultz).

This moral perspective on literacy, moreover, worked to bolster the growing common school movement through the middle and late nineteenth century. This movement, which began primarily in New England states and was promoted by educationalists such as Horace Mann, joined with discussion on illiteracy to assert that government-funded public schools would provide the foundation for a moral, stable workforce. These supporters, as Graff explains,

> stressed schooling for social stability and the assertion of appropriate hegemonic functions.... This view emphasized aggregate social goals—the reduction of crime and disorder, the instillation of proper moral values and codes of conduct, and, to a more limited extent, increased economic productivity. (*Literacy Myth* 22)

Tax-supported, mandatory public schooling slowly came into being as each state individually passed compulsory education laws. By 1918, all states had officially agreed on such laws, but the extent to which they were enforced varied greatly. Graff suggests that most real opposition to the common school movement was over by the mid-nineteenth century.

Although legally mandated public schools existed in all states by the early twentieth century, the requirements set by these schools were not uniform, attendance fluctuated, and overall enrollment did not increase between 1880 and 1890. As Gordon and Gordon make clear, at the turn of the century, for the nation as a whole, there were profound disparities in the schooling that was actually available to any given American. . . . [and] there were significant regional differences in attitudes toward literacy education and establishing schools. Further, there were major racial, ethnic, and religious disparities in access to literacy and schooling and in what the schools were designed to accomplish for their students. (263)

For writers such as the contributor to the *Ohio Farmer*, such educational disparities along racial and ethnic lines only reinforced anxieties about immigrant and African American voters in southern states and eastern cities. For the farming periodicals, in particular, the resolution to such anxieties involved promoting better access to education. As compulsory education laws were more regularly enforced in the early decades of the twentieth century, attendance and enrollment steadily increased, and the national literacy rate rose as well, according to U.S. Census records.

Changes in the rates of literacy listed in the national census are complex, however, and they are governed as much by an actual increase in the percentage of the population able to read and write as by changes in the way that literacy is tested and what counts as literacy. Graff indicates that early census records relied on self-identification and asked heads of households how many adults could read and write their names, while later records also included the literacy of children. Moreover, what counts as literacy and the meanings attached to literacy vary by individual and change over time. Graff argues that

> the meaning of literacy in mid-nineteenth century urban society can only be understood in context; it can be established neither arbitrarily nor abstractly nor uniformly for all members of the population. It cannot be determined realistically without reference to the structures of demands, needs, and uses for literacy skills, which themselves vary and change. (*Literacy Myth* 292)

The definitions for literacy visible in popular magazines at the turn of the century, and therefore the understanding of literacy that I use throughout this book, fall in line with other dominant institutional discourses casting literacy as a moral and economic imperative and as a corollary to Christian, middle-class work and social habits. Indeed, as such a predominant part of late nineteenth-century print culture, magazines were, in many respects, responsible for the continued promotion of such attitudes toward literacy.

While it is impossible to know the specific contexts of actual readers, equally important for my consideration is the contexts the magazines envisioned for the subscribers. In particular, however, I shall make clear how periodicals constructed their own definitions of literacy for their audiences. Here, what counted as advanced literacy required that readers have the skills to participate in a community of readers and writers outlined by the magazine, and that they use literacy practices both to reinforce social relationships and to promote basic and advanced literacy in others.

Periodicals and Progressive Education

While popular women's and farming magazines certainly catered to a mainstream audience and may not, at first glance, seem a likely place for considering writing instruction, they were nonetheless among the primary fixtures in the literate lives of turn-of-the-century Americans and were a resource to which many would have had access. The content of these magazines ranged widely, as today, but religiously oriented publications, children's magazines, women's magazines, literary periodicals, and farming magazines and newspapers were among the most popular. As is still true, popular magazines brought together multiple goals: educating and informing readers on diverse topics (ranging from household products to reading habits to social and moral debates), entertaining readers, and appealing to readers as consumers. By the beginning of the twentieth century, the last two goals dominated, but most magazines still retained a didactic intent, though not necessarily a part of every department or section. It is obvious in the magazines I investigate that readers and editors are preoccupied with education and literacy; discussions of the schooling of readers' children, the possibility (or lack thereof) of a college education and even extension programs for their readers, and the resulting need for readers to acquire literacy skills not learned in school fill the pages of many popular publications, in particular the *Ladies' Home Journal, Harper's Bazar,* and farm journals. For these magazines, the content and availability of formal education is linked to the literacy practices editors argue their reading audiences need to acquire through interaction with their magazines. Specifically, these magazines advocate a new set of literacy practices and argue that their audiences need to learn them because such skills are not taught in schools but are nonetheless important in the lives of their readers.

Given that the magazines I investigate sought to reflect the experiences of their audiences and to build an intimate relationship among readers, it is not surprising that editors should spend so much time discussing literacy and education—issues they could easily assume were important to readers. Attempting to connect with a family-based reading audience, editors of the *Bazar*, the *Journal*, *Maine Farmer*, and *Ohio Farmer* concentrated on issues governing the schooling of children and the possibility of a college education for both sons and daughters. The *Bazar* and the *Journal*, especially, debated the value of college education for female readers, reflecting and responding to broader cultural arguments about the purpose of higher education for women. Farming publications, similarly, responded to circulating rural concerns, visible in the Country Life movement, about the importance of reforms of rural schools. However, mainstream periodicals such as the women's and farming magazines on which I concentrate did more than just reproduce and expand discussions of what education should entail for rural children, young women, and men invested in agriculture; they also situated such discussions within the context of the magazine's specific values and interests—and, by implication, the interests and values editors illustrated were specific to the audience community.

Moreover, despite obvious, superficial differences among this collection of magazines, they all operated on Progressive Era ideals for education and its connection to individual and community improvement. Of course, what might be called Progressive ideals were not necessarily uniform or connected to a singular reform activity or movement. Nancy S. Dye, in her introduction to *Gender, Class, Race, and Reform in the Progressive Era*, characterizes Progressivism as

> a complex, sometimes contradictory amalgam of social criticism, popular protest, political restructuring, economic regulation, and social welfare legislation ... [that] embodied a vast array of responses to changes taking place in American society at the turn of the twentieth century. (1)

Progressive-inspired debates over education in the late nineteenth and early twentieth centuries, however, generally focused on the need for reform and standardization of schools; the necessity of increasing opportunities for education among poor, immigrant, rural, and ethnic populations; and the ability of schools to improve the nation by fostering a moral, educated population with middle-class "American" values, as historians such as Dye, William L. Sherman and Paul Theobald, Amy M. Goodburn, and Lynn D. Gordon describe. Such beliefs are overtly visible throughout the varied discussions of education that appear in the *Bazar*, the *Journal*, *Maine*, and *Ohio*. For Edward Bok, an immigrant who had had limited access to formal education in his youth, the advancement of standardized education for the nation was a matter of personal conviction and the inspiration for a national magazine that would operate as an educational resource for and about middle-class culture and domestic life. For the *Bazar*, discussions of education stemmed directly from the magazine's connection to the women's club movement and as a result were often tacitly connected to the social reform ideals of turn-of-the-century women's organizations. For farm journals, discussions of school and literacy learning were connected to their mission of developing rural life and the agricultural profession in line with the publications' promotion of the Progressivist-inspired Country Life movement. In this way, each of these periodicals deployed Progressive beliefs about literacy specific to their particular audience, but all emphasized how education for readers would influence their families, local communities, and nation.

Although a great deal of scholarship has been devoted to exploring nineteenth-century magazines and their immense popularity, of all the periodicals I examine in the following chapters, only the *Ladies' Home Journal* has received sustained scholarly attention. Scanlon in *Inarticulate Longings* and Thompson in *Education for Ladies, 1830 to 1860* both examine nineteenth-century women's magazines and their contribution to discourse on gender, social roles, and, for Thompson, education. Thompson examines the common arguments about women's education that appeared in periodicals during these years, asserting overall that popular magazines reflected the conflicting attitudes already present in mainstream culture toward women's proper sphere and educational goals and opportunities. Thompson's discussion is valuable in its recognition of a range of attitudes; however, Thompson's perspective treats these texts as "reflections" of culture only and does not consider how magazine print culture (and individual contributors and reader-correspondents) *participated* in the formation, addition, promotion, and revision of the narratives governing education in general and literacy in particular. Although she is concerned with *Godey's Lady's Book*, which was published earlier in the century, rather than the *Ladies' Home Journal*, Nicole Tonkovich also gives a great deal of critical attention to education and popular periodicals. In her discussion of the editor, Sarah Hale, Tonkovich illustrates how Hale promoted education for women, making clear, however, that education was to be adapted to the female gender.

This perspective is equally visible in the *Ladies' Home Journal* and *Harper's Bazar*, where editors articulate how advanced education would be useful to their female readers. While the *Journal* gives greater emphasis to the merits of domestic professionalism as an outcome for education and the *Bazar* concentrates more on social reform and community work as goals for education, both publications offer a range of views on how higher education and literacy pursuits will allow readers to live more fulfilling lives. Surveying the lives of women who have attended college, Grace W. Soper's "Occupations of Women College Graduates," for instance, suggests a range of purposes for and outcomes of education for women. Acknowledging old arguments against higher education for women, articles such as Soper's are quick to make clear that education need not interfere with family and domestic life, arguing that the educated woman is "guarded by a training which restrains her from unadvised matrimonial measures.... and the result of happy marriages is one of the best features of the higher education of women" (18). In this same theme, Soper makes clear that higher education, in addition to allowing women to take on teaching jobs, primarily, and enter other professions if they choose, can train women to better help their professional husbands: "society receives a double benefit when the scientist or professional man is assisted by a wife who adds to the zeal of a loving woman the well-trained powers of the student" (18).

As I explore in the following chapters, both the *Bazar* and the *Journal* hint at the possible, more liberal, range of possibilities for women's education that includes employment or shared work with their husbands but are simultaneously careful to connect their discussions of formal education with more traditional concerns with the welfare of the family. For *Bazar*, as well, the welfare of the community was an important purpose for women's education, which the magazine, in line with Progressive rhetoric, portrayed as a natural extension of "women's work." Amy M. Goodburn, in "Girls' Literacy in the Progressive Era: Female and American Indian Identity at the Genoa Indian School," finds a similar impulse in her examination of the educations offered to young women and American Indians, noting that "Progressive educations sought to broaden the program and function of schools to include direct concern for health, vocation, and the quality of family and community life" (80). In this way, the *Bazar* and the *Journal* used Progressive rhetoric to blend more traditional arguments about women's domestic sphere of influence with newer ideas about the possibilities of education for female readers. Editors and writers in these journals do not entirely dismantle beliefs about "separate spheres," but rather use and extend ideals about women's unique role in the family and culture. Concentrating women's experiences at single-sex and coeducational colleges between 1890 and 1910, Lynn Gordon likewise finds that "female separatism, social activism, and belief in a special mission for educated women characterized their activities" (1). For both the *Bazar* and the *Journal*, while certain editors—such as Bok—were more conservative, still the range of activities suggested for readers in various departments of the magazines was surprisingly broad, resulting in a text that held broad appeal for audiences with a range of values.

In their emphasis on the possibilities for self-betterment offered by higher education, however, both the *Bazar* and the *Journal* demonstrated an understanding of gender reliant on middle- and upper-class economies. A 1905 *Journal* article, "A College Girl's Experience as a Wife," assures readers that after graduating, she has found fulfillment in running a home and, moreover, that higher education had prepared her to be the wife of a like-minded, civically interested husband. She addresses reader questions such as "don't you find your mind becoming atrophied with your monotonous housework?" Her solution, however, is overtly class-based: she hired a washerwoman, accepted a post as the head of the domestic science department "at a leading university," and then hired more students to also help her at home. Katharine Roich, in "The College-Bred Woman in Her Home" (1899), arrives at the same conclusion as the "College Girl": she acknowledges that it might be difficult to transition from college to the home but assures readers that "the most serious difficulty in this new work is likely to arise from the lack of competent servants who can relieve the young housekeeper of care, and even of drudgery" (14). Both Roich and "College Girl" make clear, too, that in fact higher education is necessary for a middle-class homemaker to possess, both so that she can succeed in the domestic realm and so that she need not be tied too closely to it. Beyond advising her readers to hire "competent servants" to spare them from drudgery, "College Girl" makes the argument that critical thinking skills honed in the college classroom will allow women to approach domestic work intellectually and then become "an authority on it in [the] community" (42). For both Roich and "College Girl," then, education offers the possibility to leave the home, or at least leave behind the less appealing aspects of domestic work, in pursuit of community work or a career. In such a way, the *Bazar* and the *Journal* present a gendered and class-based argument for education that reflects Progressive ideals, but they do not maintain a consistent purpose for women's education throughout articles or across the period I studied. In leaving a singular or specific purpose for learning unresolved—apart from making clear that it will improve rather than impede domestic fulfillment—the *Bazar* and the *Journal* leave room for readers' own interpretations, which was no doubt part of the marketing strategy.

In the end, surprisingly, it is the farming publications that are both the most socially and politically empowering in their discussions of education and the most limiting, as demonstrated in chapter 4. Changes in agricultural technology and a growing movement, visible in farm Granges and farm journals, to advance farming as a scientific profession contributed to what Frank Luther Mott, in *A History of American Magazines*, refers to as the "farmer's movement of the 1870s" (148). The Granger movement, which began in 1867 with the organization of the Patrons of Husbandry, grew by 1873 to represent five thousand Granges with three hundred thousand members (149). Farm periodicals grew along with Granges and doggedly promoted Grange meetings, work, and ideals, urging readers to view their Granges as not only professional organizations but also educational institutions. When farm editors considered education, then, they not only centered their articles on local schools and state-funded universities and agricultural colleges, but also analyzed how the funding, subjects, and pedagogical methods of these institutions prepared students to enter agricultural communities and participate in nonacademic educational sites such as Granges and agricultural journals.

Considering the history of reform in rural schools, William L. Sherman and Paul Theobald, in "Progressive Era Rural Reform: Creating Standard Schools in the Midwest," cite the Country Life Commission President Roosevelt created in 1908 to address the "rural problem"; surveying rural populations, commissioners found that educational opportunities were consistently linked with the welfare of rural communities, and "as a consequence, most of the reforming done under the auspices of the Country Life movement was focused on the rural school" (84). Rose-Marie Weber finds a similar connection between discussions of education and its applicability to farm life in "Even in the Midst of Work: Reading among Turn-of-the-Century Farmers' Wives," her exploration of some of the first university extension courses in the 1890s. Weber asserts that documents that outline the literacy practices of women's reading courses also

> present an elaborated perspective on the value of reading and the ways its benefits could be enacted in rural settings. This perspective is in turn embedded in a national policy to keep agriculture viable and make farming a more rational and satisfying way of life. (293)

While the journals often appear to assume a male writer or contributor, women contributed to the agricultural press as well—notably, Laura Ingalls Wilder was a poultry writer for the *St. Louis Star* and later the *Ruralist*. Ultimately, the farm publications considered here all sublimate the question of gender to the greater mission of advancing rural life, a purpose for education to which editors and contributors insisted readers needed to aspire. Editors and contributors to agricultural publications such as *Maine* and *Ohio* were uniform, and noticeably uncompromising, in their assertion that the welfare of rural life depended on the education offered in schools, agricultural organizations, and the farm press.

Moreover, in articulating the value of education and literacy in readers' lives, farm periodicals begin to suggest that formal education alone was inadequate. In "The Education of Our Boys" (1884), the writer argues for the value of agricultural colleges over traditional universities, claiming:

> It is strange that farmers do not appreciate the superior advantages of a college course arranged and a college equipped especially for their benefit. It is high time farmers declare their independence of the tyranny of the old courses of study. Our sons can be better educated, and at less cost of time and money, at the agricultural or technological colleges, than at the universities, where scientific courses are esteemed inferior to the classical. (S.N.B. 1)

He echoes other farm journals in insisting that farmers now need to be able to write for Grange work and farm publications and further argues that practical experience is the best preparation for such writing:

> In the expressive, concise language of these orations, we have proof that the accuracy of thought and expression, which must be exercised in every day's work, in the laboratory and class-room and work on the farm, lead to as elegant and forcible use of language as can be acquired by the old classical courses, which have long been claimed as essentials to good writing and forcible oratory. (S.N.B. 1)

The idea that agricultural work experience inspires the most valuable contributions to farm magazines recurs throughout farming publications and connects with more overt critiques of the literacy education offered in schools. Importantly, similar but less emphatic beliefs are also visible in the *Bazar* and the *Journal*, where editors demonstrate the value of women's clubs and organizations, as well as the magazines themselves, in supplementing and expanding the education readers had received in school.

On the surface, variations among the publications on the precise purposes of education for readers correlate with differences of gender and place. For discussions of education reflected what editors saw as possibilities for readers in their own lives and in ways they would influence culture at large, so these magazines tell us something about the different kinds of opportunities available to turn-of-the-century men and women. Still, these publications are alike in their contention that education will elevate individuals and their communities, and that formal schooling has failed to offer their audiences instruction in the specific kinds of literacy practices the magazines wish to promote. In an article simply titled "Writing" (1881), James M. Taylor laments that schools spend a great deal of time on composition: "from childhood up through years in the school-room it is practiced almost daily. And yet how few there are who can express their ideas on paper correctly!" (302). Both the women's and the farm magazines feature articles on letter writing, tailoring their instruction to particular situations and purposes they imagine their readers face, hinting that students do not spend enough time learning to compose the kinds of letters they will send as adults. Taylor is even more direct; he argues, in agreement with the overall tenor of other farm journals, that current pedagogies are to blame:

> The fault lies in the failure to make their knowledge practical. Teaching others to parse and analyze is not teaching to write the English language correctly. Experience proves this.... In like manner there are any number of our best grammarians, if thorough knowledge of the technicalities of that branch as now generally taught is a test, who would feel bewildered if required to write a notice ten lines in length for publication. (302)

As I analyze more deeply in chapter 4, for Taylor and other writers in farm periodicals, the ability to participate in Grange work and compose publishable agricultural articles is the mark of true literacy for farming professionals.

In their history of the growth of the common schools, *The Rise of Literacy and the Common School in the United States*, Lee Soltow and Edward Stevens review attendance data, focusing specifically on rural parts of Ohio, to assert that "teachers were willing to classify their students as literate by the time they enrolled in grammar, and this tells us that students were generally classified as literate by the time they were twelve to fourteen years of age" (113). For the *Bazar*, the *Journal*, and farming publications, however, what would count as literacy for their readers could not be defined by enrollment in grammar or by attaining a certain number of years in school. As the later chapters explore, magazines articulated their own definitions of literacy as it applied to their designated audiences and outlined a set of literacy practices. What is important to the discussion here, however, is that magazines offered instruction in particular literacy habits to their readers precisely because they did not believe that time spent in academic institutions provided students with these kinds of literacy practices. Farm journals and two of the most popular women's periodicals—the *Bazar* and the *Journal*—sought to supplement the writing instruction offered in schools by teaching readers new practices that editors argued were meaningful in readers' lives. In doing so, they not only questioned the primacy of schools as the most important educational institutions but also created and promoted new constructions of advanced literacy.

Literacy Learning by Subscription

In the chapters that follow, then, I trace readers' and editors' treatments of literacy in popular periodicals, illustrating how magazines moved beyond general discussions of reading and writing to prompt readers to participate in new literacy constructions. These periodicals sought to outline the form, practices, and values of advanced literacy in their audience communities. They not only provided instruction in reading and writing techniques but also offered readers opportunities for participation in the literacy experiences advertised by editors. In addition to material written by magazine editors, each of the magazines I investigate presents a diverse collage of information and perspectives on literacy, writing, and education, including reader-submitted articles and poetry; advertisements for schools, educational programs, and "reading courses" or college extension programs; and correspondence column discussions of topics that touch on writing and learning. My discussion, however, centers specifically on long-running columns and features that contribute to what I argue is the magazine's overall agenda for literacy. Nonetheless, the items discussed in the following chapters did not stand alone, but rather appeared alongside a collection of other discussions and advertisements.

I focus specifically on *Harper's Bazar* and the *Ladies' Home Journal* as examples both of exceptionally popular women's magazines and of magazines that catered to two somewhat different populations of American women, one presumed to be younger, more urban and affluent, and the other more domestic and, according to its editor, quintessentially middle-class. The *Journal* is especially useful in that in addition to having a vast circulation—Edward Bok calculated that one in six people in the United States were *Journal* readers during his editorship—the magazine was influential in terms of editorial style and marketing strategy. I also consider a number of farm periodicals, publications that strove to remain specific to their local state communities but collectively represented a type of magazine growing in popularity at the turn of the century. Three magazines that I emphasize most, *Michigan Farmer*, *Ohio Farmer*, and *Maine Farmer*, were state-specific and are important in that they remained successful longer than most agricultural periodicals.³ These publications, unlike the *Bazar* and the *Journal*, were aimed at a family audience but more pointedly targeted men in rural communities; given that 40 percent of U.S. citizens lived on farms at the beginning of the twentieth century, the audiences of farm journals represent an important and understudied population of readers. In addition, while much work has been done in exploring the social, commercial, and gender values of women's magazines in general and the *Ladies' Home Journal* in particular, women's periodicals have been largely overlooked as sites of literacy learning. The interactive features of both *Harper's Bazar* and *Ladies' Home Journal*—the "Home Study Club," the correspondence columns, and "Just among Ourselves"—have not received much critical attention either. More important, farming magazines have not been studied at all in the context of composition and literacy. Given their popularity at this time and the fact that they were designed to be used as teaching tools in the home, popular publications such as the *Journal*, the *Bazar*, and farm journals provide an important contribution to any discussion of popular turn-of-the-century magazines and literacy.

While on the surface it is easy to view *Harper's Bazar* as a fashion text that would have had little in common with texts on farming techniques, such as *Maine* or *Ohio*, or even a domestic-helper text like the *Journal* in their fundamental sense of purpose, their approaches, and, as I consider at greater length in later chapters, the makeup of their audiences, this collection of magazines shares much in common. In particular, and most strikingly, all envisioned a distinctly pedagogical purpose for their publication that was inherently connected to their editors' beliefs that a target audience, whether women or rural populations, desired new literacy possibilities in response to changing cultural narratives about their roles. It would be an oversimplification to suggest that these three types of magazines were the only sites of such literacy and pedagogical work at the turn of the century, especially since all of the magazines in this collection assume a white and generally middle- to upper-middle-class audience. Indeed, other publications targeting or naming specific identity groups, particularly those that address immigrant and minority groups generally left out of the *Journal* and *Bazar*, present possibilities for literacy work. Though she does not consider literacy and composition specifically, Noliwe M. Rooks in *Ladies Pages: African American Women's Magazines and the Culture That Made Them* uncovers often-ignored publications, analyzing how the press allowed African American women to explore and expand identities and communication networks. Likewise,

Sally M. Miller in *The Ethnic Press* in the United States points to the work yet to be done in historicizing the immigrant press. Both Miller and Rooks suggest areas and types of publications that were important to the literate lives of large populations in turn-of-the-century America and subsequently present rich potential for considerations of literacy learning and identity. The collection of periodicals I address here, then, is representative of part of this range of publications and is especially apt because of how visible these magazines were and how well they succeeded in gathering subscribers.

Examining the *Bazar*, the *Journal*, *Maine*, and *Ohio* together, moreover, illustrates how these publications deployed three distinct but complementary approaches to literacy and identity, blending aspirations, values, and fears that resonated with a wide readership. All of these periodicals sought to cultivate a broader appeal by incorporating a variety of departments with different purposes and different subaudiences, simultaneously dispersing and complicating the publication's general literacy trend. While the *Farmers* overtly catered to an agricultural audience concerned with farming practices, these periodicals also circulated among urban audiences and contained sections designed to appeal to children, gardeners, and women interested in domestic concerns. Likewise, although the *Bazar* editors suggested that they sought a younger, more Progressive reader, both the *Bazar* and the *Journal* purposely blended Progressive and conservative, domestic and public ideals in their columns to ensure that many readers would find common ground with the publication. This hybridity of approach, which blended departments catering to a range of interests into a single text and blended both old and new ideals, particularly about women's roles, allowed this collection of magazines to reach a wider audience.

Comparing the differing roles editors prompt readers and writers to adopt in the *Bazar*, the *Journal*, and farm periodicals, chapter 1 demonstrates how this collection of magazines shares a common strategy: constructing a literacy identity for readers to assume in their reading and writing. I consider how editors work to connect their illustration of the social, professional, and class identity of the audience in general with a set of lifestyle-specific reading and writing practices. I ultimately argue that these magazines construct their definitions of literacy around the roles they imagine readers will need to assume as writers, persuading readers that magazine-approved definitions and identities will be meaningful in their communities.

Chapters 2 and 3 concentrate on the nationally circulating women's journals, demonstrating how the *Journal* and the *Bazar*, though their editors asserted they were writing for all American women, deployed two distinct illustrations of literacy values for communities of women and two very different definitions of advanced literacy and identity. Chapter 2 outlines how the *Journal* and its editor, Edward Bok, cast women as consumers and sellers of literacy. I consider the roles the magazine played both in helping women become critical reader-consumers and in teaching readers the necessary practices of writing for publication. Demonstrating that the magazine encouraged women to understand literacy in distinctly economic terms, but also taught them to be critical of their buying and selling choices, I assert that the *Journal* offered readers a departmentalized vision of literacy identity. Turning to the *Bazar*, chapter 3 explores the magazine's relationship with the women's club movement and argues that editors introduced readers into the literacy practices of these clubs through features such as "The Home Study Club." Ultimately, the *Bazar* urged its readers to adopt habits of reading and writing that emphasize communal relationships among women and prompted readers to assume the role of a mentor or contributor to a club community. In this way, the *Bazar* moved beyond the *Journal* to demonstrate that literacy identities for women not only were adaptable to different "departments" but also would allow women to join and create meaningful communities.

Farm journals, the subject of chapter 4, were likewise preoccupied with the value of literacy as a tool for shaping and empowering a community. In this chapter, I examine the imperative articulated by farm publications for farmers to contribute articles to the agricultural press, so that they could more fully participate in the formation of agriculture as a scientific profession. While pulling from a collection of farm journals, I center my argument on two in particular, the *Ohio Farmer* and the *Maine Farmer*, which, in addition to celebrating reader contributions and arguing for the value of writing produced by farmers, offered readers more explicit instruction in writing than other periodicals. Arguing that advanced literacy was defined not by mechanical correctness, but by the ability of a writer to convey intelligent and clear ideas, these publications guided readers into textual roles as mentors in a community of professionals.

Throughout these chapters, I am working from an understanding of literacy practices as social constructions, as representing a set of domain-specific ways of reading and writing. Scholarship such as that of Barton and Hamilton (2000), Swales (1990), Ivanic (1998), and Gee (1990) articulates an understanding of literacy that focuses on participants' learning, negotiating, and revising particular reading and writing practices within discourse communities. Barton and Hamilton, in particular, concentrate on the social and ideological significance of domain-specific literacy practices, asserting that considering literacy from the perspectives of practices "offers a powerful way of conceptualizing the link between the activities of reading and writing and the social structures in which they are embedded and which they help shape" (7). All of these scholars argue for the importance of critically analyzing the connection between literacy practices and the values, social relationships, and power structures that accompany them.

Throughout my consideration of the *Bazar*, the *Journal*, and the farm magazines, then, I examine how practices recommended by editors connect to larger social ideals and relationships magazines wished to promote. In chapters 2 and 3, especially, editors' sense of audience obviously engaged questions of gender and class. The *Ladies' Home Journal* and *Harper's Bazar* were part of a publishing industry that increasingly catered to white, middle-class, female consumers, as Lee Joliffe notes in her discussion of nineteenth-century women's magazines. As popular and influential publications, these magazines both created and reinforced gender norms and conceptions of domesticity. In addition to their gender-specific notions of audience, all of these magazines believed that they were speaking to a specific class of readers and consequently constructed vivid illustrations of the beliefs, values, experiences, and resources of such an audience. In my considerations of identity and literacy, central to chapter 1, and throughout my discussion of editors' illustrations of their readers, I am drawing additionally on the conception of social class and cultural capital articulated by Pierre Bourdieu; I am concerned not with the actual economic makeup of the audience, but with editors' constructions of the tastes, values, and power relationships of the presumed audience community.

Additionally, in considering the multiple goals and practices visible in both the women's and farming magazines, my approach is to consider them using Deborah Brandt's conception of sponsors of literacy. A great deal of recent contemporary and historical literacy work focuses on specific "sites of literacy"—both institutional and extra-institutional places where individuals take part in literacy events. At the same time, Brandt in *Literacy in American Lives* works equally from the perspective that people build up and practice literacy through participation with others in specific contexts. In particular, she puts forth the idea of literacy sponsors—agents that can be real or abstract who support, restrict, enable, and shape literacy. Brandt sees these sponsors as "delivery systems" of ideologies of literacy and as also helping illustrate the range of relationships and influences present at scenes of literacy. Both of these theoretical approaches to literacy and space—pointing to both sponsors and local sites of literacy—make clear that while it is important to consider literacy in terms of larger cultural, ideological constructs, it is equally important to consider how these constructs work in conjunction with the goals and conditions of the individuals taking part in the literacy practice.

Moreover, because the individuals participating in the magazines included in this project are not all equally represented in the texts of the magazines—editors are obviously more vocal in their discussions of the literacy goals and habits of the magazine, but these publications also feature the writing of contributors and readers submitting letters to correspondence columns—I treat these texts as sites of textual and ideological hybridity. In their examination of nineteenth-century composition textbooks, Carr, Carr, and Schultz argue that such texts cannot be read as single-author documents or understood as presenting a monolithic ideological perspective. Rather, they maintain that composition textbooks need to be seen as complex hybrids that make use of multiple forms, sources, influences, and practices, and as hybrids, they were meant to be used in multiple, even divergent, ways. I would argue that popular magazines in general, and certainly the collection on which this book concentrates, are hybrids as well. Although put together by a single editor with a specific vision for the magazine as a whole, the individual articles, departments, and advertisements vary in tone, agenda, and at times sociopolitical stance. Thus my reading focuses on each magazine as a hybrid—as a place that blends mass culture with home life; simultaneously values domestic, popular, and academic learning; and negotiates multiple goals, ideologies, and practices at once.

Although she is not focused on theorizing contemporary understandings of literacy, Catherine Hobbs, in her introduction to *Nineteenth-Century Women Learn to Write*, offers a way of reading historical literacy practices that centers on participants acting within specific literate domains or communities. Specifically, she makes clear that in investigating the diverse spaces in which women participated in reading and writing, she is not concerned with literacy as defined by "only the technical skills of reading and writing but the tactical—or rhetorical—knowledge of how to employ those skills in the context of one or more communities" (1). Hobbs proposes instead the term "effective literacy" to describe the work done by the subjects of her collection, defining it as "a level of literacy that enables the user to act to effect change, in her own life and in society" (1). For Hobbs, this might mean that women, such as Sojourner Truth, who lacked "technical skills of reading and writing" but nonetheless possessed a rhetorical presence, could be effectively literate. The men and women who interacted with *Harper's*, the *Journal*, and the farming magazines—however much they might have worried about grammatical mistakes or insufficient schooling—were certainly schooled in the basic technical skills of writing; nonetheless, Hobbs's concept of effective literacy is useful because of the emphasis placed on users' ability to connect with a community and to perceive a purpose for their writing.

Ultimately, all of these magazines are concerned with specific experiences of reading and writing and are seeking to help their readers participate in a community, whether it is a club or a profession. The magazines I examine are ultimately concerned with how effectively their readers are expressing themselves in writing—and for *Harper's* and farming magazines especially, this concern springs from the editors' insistence that readers become contributors to their own communities. More important, however, while it is possible only to guess at the kinds of goals actual magazine readers might have established for themselves, editors' conceptions of both a purpose and community for the writing of their reading audience is visible throughout their discussions of literacy and education—and forms the basis for editors' attempts to persuade readers to adopt certain literacy strategies.

Popular periodicals, then, represent a site that in some ways is disconnected from the traditional purview of historical composition work—and offer the possibility, as Gere contends in looking at women's clubs, of considering a relationship between the university and "outside" culture that can disrupt professionalization narratives, expand what counts as a site of composition education, and illuminate how pedagogy is enacted when there is no present "teacher." In this, they can expand disciplinary histories of what has influenced the field's ideologies and pedagogies; they can also expand our sense of how institutional practices and values have circulated outside the academy and among different populations and inform our understanding of literacy and how to engage it.

1.

Literacy Identities: Defining Magazine Writers

We present this week the portraits of nine of the men who write for The Ohio Farmer, knowing that our readers will be better able to appreciate their writing when they are thus made acquainted with them.

—"Some of Our Contributors," *Ohio Farmer*, 1900

A contributor to the 1844 *Maine Farmer*, complaining of the inadequate education offered in schools, explained that it was important for teachers to account for and incorporate the skills and experiences of their students, as they "must know how to adapt [their] instructions to the several capacities and circumstances of [their] scholars" ("For the Farmer" 1). *Harper's Bazar* echoed *Maine*, claiming that education needed to suit the experiences and interests of female students. And Edward Bok, desiring to expand a promising periodical into a trend-setting business, believed that he needed to understand the ideals and material realities of American women in order to connect with them in *Ladies' Home Journal*. In spite of wide gulfs in terms of publication goals, content, and pedagogical strategy that will be apparent in later chapters, *Harper's Bazar*, *Ladies' Home Journal*, and farming journals all operated not only on the belief that writers need to learn to understand and consider their audiences, but also on the conviction that teachers, and magazine editors, must understand the skills and contexts of their students. All emphasize the importance of contribution, arguing that advanced literacy was defined by the ability to contribute to a community. Operating on different but equally specific definitions of literacy, the *Bazar*, the *Journal*, and farming periodicals ultimately articulate not just practices but also literacy communities and identities for their readers.

Expansive literacy histories like those of de Castell and Luke, Graff, and Gordon and Gordon have provided us with both a broad perspective on literacy rates at the turn of the century and more nuanced critiques of the diverse factors, such as employment and housing trends, school reforms, and publishing costs, that contributed to the reading and writing experiences of Americans. They also agree that during the late nineteenth century, Americans were preoccupied with the perceived threats posed by illiteracy in poor and immigrant populations and, in turn, focused efforts on increasing national literacy rates, especially by educating children. Scholars such as Jessica Enoch, David Wallace Adams, and Jacqueline Jones Royster articulate how African American and American Indian populations, in particular, served as focal points for this literacy crisis, the subjects of a benevolent mission to foster morality and middle-class, white citizenship through literacy. Given how regularly this national preoccupation with illiteracy appears in our histories, and indeed in archives of nineteenth-century newspapers and journals, it is perhaps surprising that between 1880 and 1910 few articles discussing illiteracy appear in the magazines I investigated. Articles discussing the education of readers' children appear often enough, especially in *Ladies' Home Journal* where the magazine addresses its mothers and in the farming journals where writers are concerned with specific local school issues, but even these articles presuppose that children will learn to read and write well enough; it is the overall quality (and cost) of their education that is on debate. In fact, the only place where these periodicals consider the literacy worries so well historicized by scholars is in a few articles that work to reinforce the literacy practices endorsed by the magazines and, often, to disassemble literacy myths, arguing that that there is no connection between illiteracy and criminality.

I examine these magazines' treatment of literacy and morality later, but it is first important to consider *why* a collection of popular periodicals, one in particular with an unprecedented national circulation, that *are* concerned about the education and reading and writing practices of their audiences do not devote appreciable space to discussing the lack of literacy in others. It is possible, of course, that Edward Bok, so devoted to the domestic issues facing his middle-class mothers and inclined to avoid controversy, simply did not deem illiteracy a topic relevant for his audience. Likewise, it is conceivable that a collection of eastern and middle-eastern state-specific journals devoted almost exclusively to rural issues would be more interested in how educational trends and laws would affect their district schools than national literacy rates.

However, I argue that the reason the *Journal*, the *Bazar*, and farming journals do not give attention to discussions (or threats) of illiteracy among poor, urban populations is that these magazines operate almost exclusively on definitions of literacy specific to their own audiences. For the readers of the *Bazar* and the *Journal*, education was extremely important, but basic reading and writing abilities were not at question. Although each journal uses a slightly different definition, which I outline in chapters 2, 3, and 4, none suggests that literacy for its readers can be evidenced by the basic ability to write a name or read a paper; rather, these magazines seek to introduce their readers to specific literacy practices and demonstrate how these practices will enable them to participate in specific communities of readers—whether in women's clubs (*Harper's Bazar*) or in the periodical or agricultural press (*Ladies' Home Journal*, *Maine Farmer*, and *Ohio Farmer*). What is significant about this practice of articulating and describing a set of lifestyle-specific literacy practices, however, is that in doing so, these magazines create and support literacy identities for their reading audiences. Literacy identities, I contend, were honed by editors to facilitate readers' participation not only with the magazine but also with the discourse communities invoked and promoted by the magazine.

Literacy Practices and Identities

It is obvious, in *Journal* columns on reading critically, in every *Harper's* outline for clubwomen, and in each article offering advice to the contributors to the agricultural press, that these popular journals all wish to educate their readers in specific literate habits; it is equally obvious that editors believe they know the audiences to whom they are speaking and understand the values and goals for reading and writing in their readers' lives. The illustrations of literacy editors provide are best understood in the context of the social and ideological framework the magazines construct, in particular their depiction of their readers as representing a class of men and women who share common experiences, values, and resources.

In this chapter, I analyze these magazines' definitions of literacy in correlation with their construction of their audiences' collective identity, arguing that each magazine's treatment of literacy and audience illustrates the construction of a literacy identity for readers. The magazines I examine are ultimately concerned with how effectively their prospective writers are able to contribute to a community of readers. Importantly, the communities identified by the magazines—whether they were women's clubs in the *Bazar*, periodical publishers in the *Journal*, or an agricultural profession—were consciously established and defined by editors within the contexts of their magazines. In working so hard to describe for readers the social domains in which they need to read and write, editors convey how particular literacy practices connect magazine readers to the values and goals of communities of which they (should) feel a part. What these three types of magazines offer us are three different kinds of literacy or discourse communities—rural/agricultural, young urban women, and adult married women and mothers—and three corresponding conceptions of the literacy skills and values editors insist accompany these domains. In spite of the apparent differences in literacy domains, however, all are united in their corresponding fixation on identity; they all assert that in becoming a contributor, writers assume a certain identity—a construction the magazines work to define and promote. Editors directly link the identity and goals ascribed to their audiences with the reading and writing practices they are advocating, offering for their readers a kind of literacy identity—an illustration of a set of lifestyle-specific reading and writing practices that allow participants to enter communities with whom they identify.

The farming journals, the *Bazar*, and the *Journal* construct a literacy identity for their readers by first establishing a collective audience identity and describing a collection of interests and goals associated with that audience, and then arguing for a specific set of reading and writing practices that will allow readers to fulfill those goals. *Harper's Bazar* illustrates its readers as educated women engaging in an active social life with other women, asserting that such women are interested in further developing relationships with other women and in learning more about literature, history, and culture. The *Journal*, at the same time, although sometimes addressing "girls"—and always by name—speaks to its readers as wives and mothers, focusing on the audience's perceived desire to be better buyers and caretakers of a household and to find enjoyment in reading. Farming periodicals, finally, construct their readers' identity on their profession and location; even more explicit and emphatic than the women's magazines, the farming journals demand that readers take an interest in the scientific exploration of agriculture and seek to contribute to the professional development of other farmers and the improvement of community lives.

I do not mean to suggest that these magazines, all of which contained a wide range of departments, addressed myriad topics, and acknowledged large reading audiences, focused exclusively on the goals and interests I discuss above, or that, throughout each magazine as a whole, editors did not offer a more complex and varied reading of their audience's identity. I am saying only that in the articles and columns I have addressed—in the places where readers are offered explicit advice in reading and writing practices— editors concentrate on women as members of intimate clubs with a social interest, on women as readers and writers of literature for pleasure, and on men as professionals developing an agricultural field. What is striking about all three illustrations is that they convey change and emergence into new possible roles in new communities. Both the *Bazar* and the *Journal* reflect the shifting, and multiple, roles for women at the turn of the century in their promotion of two different ways for women to develop a conservative but modern identity in literacy. Likewise, farm journals navigated opposing conceptions of rural life and arguments for the proper place of farmers in a new economy to support a literacy identity that would allow writers to effect change. All three types of periodicals crafted a literacy identity for readers in what editors saw as a time of shifting and uncertain roles.

Not surprisingly, then, editors' illustrations of audience identity are wrapped in their assumptions about economic and social class and their portrayal of the characteristics of various social groups. Despite differences in tone and goals, all of these magazines focus incredibly closely on their audiences as constituting a specific class of the national population and correspondingly devote effort to illustrating how certain reading and writing practices fit in with their own constructions of the values and tastes of that class. It is not possible, of course, to know exactly who was reading each periodical, and it is likely, especially with such popular magazines as *Harper's* and the *Journal*, which would have circulated well beyond the subscriber list, that readers came from diverse economic backgrounds. In fact, in the *Journal*, in "Just among Ourselves," readers talk about their habit of passing magazines to friends and donating old issues. Bok, moreover, in "The Magazine with a Million," outlines the circulation of the magazine, census records of the literate population, and surveys the *Journal* conducted about magazine sharing; he reports that "each copy of the *Journal* is, on average, read by seven persons during its life" (16). In addition, taking readers through his calculating process, Bok asserts that as "a safely conservative estimate,"

> with twenty-five millions of people possible of becoming interested in the magazine, we reach the figure that one out of every five persons met with in every part of the United States is either a subscriber or a reader of *The Ladies' Home Journal*. (16)

Although they enjoyed much smaller circulations than the *Journal*, periodicals such as *Maine Farmer* and *Ohio Farmer* were not read solely by farmers, as their names suggest, but rather circulated among both men and women, and among persons in a range of professions and locations. Nonetheless, each editor constructs a relatively homogenous, class-based audience identity—all of them claiming to be writing for "middle-class" readers—and connects certain literacy practices with that identity.

The understanding of class that I am working from here is not tied directly to readers' presumed income, but rather is based on Pierre Bourdieu's definition of classes as "sets of agents who occupy similar positions and who, being placed in similar conditions and submitted to similar types of conditioning, have every chance of having similar dispositions and interests, and thus of producing similar practices and adopting similar stances" (231). Throughout discussions of education, women's clubs, publishing, and writing for the press, editors articulate a set of conditions, dispositions, and goals for their audience, arguing that readers require certain literacy practices to participate in a like-minded community.

Numerous studies have reflected on the connection between literacy and identity, nearly all of them focused on contemporary writers, particularly in classrooms or online (Ivanic, Williams, Thomas, boyd, Rose). In "Literacy and Identity: Examining Metaphors in History and Contemporary Research," Elizabeth Birr Moje and Allan Luke outline and categorize the many approaches to literacy and identity used in recent scholarship, arguing that scholars need to be as critical of their definition of identity as they are of their conception of literacy. They are justifiably wary of the implications of what they term "identity-as-difference" approaches—approaches that focus on economic, racial, or ethnic groups, theorizing "how people are distinguished from one another by virtue of their group membership and on how ways of knowing, doing, or believing held or practiced by a group shape the individual as a member of that group" (419–20). Their concern is that "such identity perspectives are often considered essentialist, reducing people to phenotype, country of origin, sexual orientation, and other qualities of difference" (421).

While "identity-as-difference" certainly poses challenges for theorizing and studying the literate activities of individual writers, this conception of identity does resonate with the literacy identity constructions provided by magazines, which, although arguably attempting to offer readers the authority to contribute to women's clubs and periodical publications, nonetheless did present their audiences with a predefined identity construction.

Literacy Identities

May 1906 cover for the *Ladies' Home Journal*.
Ladies' Home Journal 23.6 (May 1906). Copy of image
made available by Oberlin College Library.

In her exploration of student writers negotiating discoursal identities in *Writing and Identity: The Discoursal Construction of Identity in Academic Writing*, Ivanic asserts that "writing is an act of identity in which people align themselves with socio-culturally shaped possibilities for self-hood, playing their part in reproducing or challenging dominant practices and discourses, and the values, beliefs and interests which they embody" (32). In my analysis of the literacy identities formulated in the *Bazar*, the *Journal*, and farm magazines, I examine how these turn-of-the-century magazines went about creating and deploying "socio-culturally shaped possibilities for self-hood."

"Reading People": Becoming a Woman of the Magazine Community

Although Bok claims in his autobiography that when he assumed the role of editor at the *Journal*, he knew nothing about women's thoughts and preferences, he quickly establishes in his column "At Home with the Editor" that he has learned a great deal about the talents, values, and concerns of his readership through their letters to him.[1] In fact, Bok did know something about the subscribers to his magazine: he asked readers to complete a survey in the first "At Home" issue, and the Curtis Publishing Company kept records of the income rates of subscribers and ultimately formed the first market research department of any publishing house. Bok used information about his readers in constructing magazine advertisements but also allowed it to shape magazine content. Both the *Journal* and the *Bazar*, in featuring a great deal of pictures and image content and in employing more women on their editorial boards than most magazines, projected an illustration of the American woman and sold it to readers as a representation of themselves. Editors further connected assumptions about audience identity to discussions of education and reading and writing habits, ultimately offering readers an illustration of themselves as readers and writers.

Although she is examining women's magazines in the late 1970s, Martha A. Starr considers how periodical content can both reflect and work to construct gendered identities in "Consumption, Identity, and the Sociocultural Constitution of 'Preferences': Reading Women's Magazines." Starr contends that two magazines in particular, *Working Woman* and *Working Mother*, worked to construct an identity for the "working woman": "in *describing* how women could stylize and conceptualize themselves to find meaning, fulfillment, and social worth through work, they were also participating in the process of *defining* conventions of what the working woman would be like" (297; italics in the original). For the *Journal* and the *Bazar*, in addition to being obviously gendered for their female audiences, the identity constructions they promote are also overtly connected to the magazines' treatment of consumption and class. Although both magazines outline a literacy identity that emphasizes social relationships, the *Bazar* presents readers as clubwomen contributing to an intimate community of women, while the *Journal* offers two separate subject positions: readers as consumers and writers as saleswomen.

It is obvious that the literacy-based activities editors are recommending for readers are contingent on a series of overt assumptions about the experiences and resources of their audiences. While both the *Bazar* and the *Journal* acknowledge that their readers may require insight into the practices of women's clubs and literary publishing, they also clearly assume a high level of literacy among their readers. For both women's journals, it is a given that readers have completed and moved beyond a basic education; if readers have not been able to attend college themselves, it is assumed that they are discussing the possibility for their daughters. The *Journal* concentrates more on its readers as being responsible for a household and children, while the *Bazar* considers a more decidedly urban population and focuses less on its readers' presumed domestic responsibilities—in part because numerous places make mention of their audiences' natural inclination to hire domestic help. However, both journals take for granted that their readers are interested in pursuing some form of self-education and have the money, time, and local resources—such as libraries and bookstores—to do so. The *Bazar* clearly imagines that its readers have the leisure time both to take part in a women's club and to do the kind of reading and reflection the "Home Study" column imagines is necessary for participation in club work. Likewise, while Bok acknowledges the idea of a large and economically diverse readership, he simultaneously asserts that, partially through the *Journal* itself, his readers have the resources to educate themselves and that they are alike in their desires for improving the home and their own minds.

In his regular column, "At Home with the Editor," in which he discusses correspondence and ongoing *Journal* themes and issues, Bok provides his own loose definition of a "middle-class" audience, making clear that while he believes this class may include a wide range of incomes (excluding only absolute poverty), it is united in the deeper ideals of family, home, and charity. Admitting that he "cannot hope to reach" the "wretched poor of the world," he simultaneously asserts that

> the peculiar character of the *Journal* brings it within the homes of all classes, and it is not strange that where so many topics are discussed, a responsive chord is often touched, now with the fashionable city woman of society, then with the lonely woman on the frontier or in remote village. (April 1891, 10)

Given that the *Journal* always claims to speak to "the American woman," the magazine thus tacitly situates all loyal *Journal* readers as both middle-class and representatives of an official American womanhood and excludes the "wretched poor" from this identity.

The *Bazar*, likewise, ignores women not included in its illustration of an intelligent, socially active American womanhood. Articles such as Katharine Roich's "College-Bred Woman in Her Home" acknowledge the challenges facing educated women beginning household management. Roich, in agreement with the overall tenor of both the *Journal* and the *Bazar*, asserts that readers unsatisfied with a life of domestic work hire outside help and begin to approach household management as an intellectual endeavor: reading and writing to magazines such as the *Journal* and the *Bazar*, and taking responsibility for the reading practices of their family. More frequently, the *Bazar* suggests that readers either hire servants or study ways of running households more efficiently so that they continue to possess the time available for activities such as study clubs. For the *Bazar*, then, reading and writing practices are tied not to consumption, but to their readers' social lives and their relationships with other women, as the periodical urges women to assume the role of clubwomen in their literate lives. In chapter 3, I demonstrate how the *Bazar* as a whole and E. B. Cutting in particular, in "Our Home Study Club," introduced the magazine audience to the practices of women's clubs, guiding them in the reading and writing techniques used by clubwomen and offering explicit outlines of study for individual readers and clubs. Alongside Cutting's study advice and syllabi in the "Study Club," however, Margaret Hamilton Welch, in the "Club Women and Club Work" column, not only discusses national club news but also defines what women's clubs do and who clubwomen are. In this way, the *Bazar* offers a reflection of the American clubwoman and, as Starr finds in magazines such as *Working Woman* in the 1970s, takes part in constructing her literacy identity, mentoring readers in assuming this particular role in their own reading and writing both by teaching them the literacy practices necessary for club work and by promoting an image of the ideal clubwoman.

The basic formula for the "Club Women" column consists of Welch's general discussion of relevant club issues, mention of national conventions, and a profile of either an individual club or a woman. This profile, which often includes images of the club members and meeting place, advertises the construction and activities of clubs. The accompanying images may depict members reading together, as in an 1897 issue, where two members of the New Century Club of Philadelphia are depicted in a home library, or the February 1899 issue, which includes a photograph of the directors of the Brooklyn Woman's Club sitting together with books open. More pointedly, the profiles of leading clubwomen, such as that of Matilda Williams Howard in the October 1897 issue, outline their influence among other women and the importance of the work done for and by the club. Of Howard, in particular, Welch points out that

> her service as corresponding secretary through her exceptionally long term of office is recognized as of great value to the society. Possessed of marked literary ability which found expression in much published work, both prose and poetry.... Her reports were as full of practical interest as they were models of purity of diction. Her penmanship was remarkable in its clearness and legibility, her minutes of her last meeting as secretary showing no trace of a tremulous hand. (862)

Welch further describes how members of Howard's club honored her by creating an album, each member contributing a page in "her own handwriting" (862). Profiles of individual clubwomen often make note of literary and rhetorical work, highlighting secretarial and speaking abilities, but also always linking these skills to Welch's overall description of that woman's appearance, manner, and position in her community. The December 1898 description of Miss Irwin Martin, whose photograph appears in the column, makes clear that she

> is a Colonial Dame, and was for some time recording secretary of the New York City Chapter of the Daughters of the American Revolution. With a distinct charm of manner and high intelligence she unites a special ability as presiding officer, having a distinguished and elegant bearing, and speaking with great ease and aptness. (1133)

Moreover, Welch frames all the discussions in "Club Women and Club Work" as the story of the actions and experiences of individual women constituting small communities. Thus, when discussing the activities of clubs, Welch pointedly attributes decisions and actions to individual women, often citing a list of the officers of every club mentioned in each issue. So, for instance, in the February 1899 issue highlighting the Brooklyn Woman's Club, Welch does not simply state that the group debated the use of the word "club" in its title, but further indicates that "objections were raised to its use because of the attitude of society, but Mrs. Burleigh advocated retaining the word" (98). Welch's outlines of other club decisions, actions, and descriptions follow suit: the names of individual women appear throughout the discussion to such an extent that Welch almost seems to go out of her way to include the names of clubwomen and sometimes even their words.[2] In this way, the work and literacy practices of women's clubs, so thoroughly described in both "Club Women" and "Home Study Club," are associated with the names and faces of women that fit the description of the audience to which the *Bazar* was writing and was urging readers to become.

Significantly, too, even in their reading and writing outside of clubs, women are encouraged to continue to act as clubwomen. Thus discussions of general reading in the *Bazar* are often framed as a social interaction between author and reader, with the magazine urging readers to assume the same well-mannered and socially oriented role in their reading as they would in a club. In fact, Margaret Sangster, the magazine's chief editor, compares serious reading with social interactions, advising that "in the first place, girls, do not overlook the fact that a certain formality should be observed in making the acquaintance of a new book" ("My Girls" 32). The method of reading used by *Bazar* subscribers should also connect with their sense of polite conventions:

> If the author has written a preface, politeness requires you to read it; otherwise you will be in the position of a boorish person who forces her way into a drawing-room after she had been courteously requested to linger a moment in the vestibule. (32)

Sangster further recommends that readers commit authors and publishers to memory, as they would new acquaintances at a party, for

> if you demand of an unlettered person some information about the novel he read last week, preferring the very natural inquiries, who wrote it, or by whom is it published, he will probably reply, "I'm sure I don't know. I did not notice." Reading people never show this inadvertence. (32)

For the *Bazar*, the difference between "reading people" and "unlettered" people is not the ability to read a book, but rather the practice of following specific conventions in approaching that book and the ability to discuss that book with others; if *Bazar* readers are to be characterized by their desire to connect intimately with other women, then the reading practices they adopt need to contribute to this desire. Likewise, in "The Busy Woman's Reading," Mary R. Baldwin invites readers to imagine themselves in the profile offered of the "busy woman" considering reading selections: "she often stands before her opportunities wondering how she could grasp and hold them, while longing to use them toward satisfying the cravings of her mind and heart" (164). Baldwin ultimately recommends that readers read established literary classics and respected criticism, framing this practice not in terms of texts, but as an interaction with a "great mind," assuring readers that spending "a half-hour each day with a leader of thought and a master of expression will save one from the mistake of following one's own misdirected inclinations" (164).

Always, the *Bazar* suggests that readers will want to share their reading experiences with other women and stresses editors' recognition of the fact that they are already speaking to "reading people" as though women who enjoy reading and discussing that reading belong to a common class, as the editor indicates in "Novel-Readers," claiming that "if one could separate novel-readers from the rest of humanity, as a class, one would say there was no other corresponding number of people that received so much enjoyment from existence as they" (466). The editor goes on to assert that, "of course, as it is well known, there are exceptions to every rule, and so there are individuals of the race to whom the novel is a bore, and that not because they are illiterate," assuring that readers "who do love novels" share a common bond in their ability to connect to one another through shared enjoyment of particular stories and characters. Here, too, reading practices are linked to the formation of social relationships, especially among women, and to an assumed audience identity of intelligent clubwomen.

For the *Journal*, conversely, the reading practices discussed by the magazine focus less on social relationships and instead speak to the audience's perceived identity as middle-income wives and mothers in charge of maintaining a household. Bok worked to demonstrate that women were the natural consumers of the household as well and, as I discuss in chapter 2, also helped readers understand how they could be consumers and producers of texts in the market. While the magazine contained articles that instructed readers on the practices and rhetorical values of editors and publishers, illuminating for interested *Journal* readers their role as novice writers, most *Journal* articles situated women as responsible, critical consumers—of commercial products and of reading material. Francesca Berry, in "Designing the Reader's Interior: Subjectivity and the Woman's Magazine in Early Twentieth-Century France," examines shifts in the construction of feminine identity that played out in women's magazines and in discussions of the domestic interior. Berry asserts that magazines such as *Feminina* made use of "innovative representational strategies to appeal to the reader's sense of self or even selves" and concludes that, while feminine subjectivity remained a site of negotiation for magazine readers, nonetheless, "*Feminina* encouraged its readers to communicate a self educated in the nuances of personal taste linked to the feminine toilette" (74). Berry focuses her analysis on the periodical's discussions of design and decoration and illustrations of readers' display of self, and in this way, like Starr, she touches on consumption,

SHALL CLUB WOMEN REORGANIZE?

OPINIONS OF LEADING CLUB WOMEN FOR AND AGAINST THIS RADICAL STEP

TALK of reorganization of the General Federation of Women's Clubs filled the air of the club world following the biennial at Denver eighteen months ago. Club women asked over and over again the questions: "Is the General Federation unwieldy? Can its work be done through the State federations? Is reorganization needed?" All this diffuse talk crystallized, at the council meeting at Philadelphia, in the creation of a committee of fifteen, which asks for reports from all State federations and federated clubs, in order that the wish of the membership may be known. These reports will be carefully collated and considered, and their gist presented next spring at the biennial meeting at Milwaukee. Realizing the great interest which club women take in this important question, the BAZAR has asked the opinion of a number of well-known club women whose personal connection with the federation gives their kleis special weight. Naturally Mrs. J. C. Croly, founder of the General Federation as she was, and of one or two others of the club women's movement in this country, was the first person sought.

"I OBJECT," said Mrs. Croly, promptly, "to the word reorganization. The General Federation does not need reorganization. It may need adjustment to its development, as any successful movement may as it enlarges its scope and increases its area of activity.

"A pivotal point is that relating to the State chairmen of correspondence. When the General Federation was organized, no single State federation existed; none had been thought of. A State chairman of correspondence was a necessity for territorial expansion. There was nothing but the General Federation for a centre, and the State chairman for a medium between it and the circumference of the local clubs. When State federations were organized, the State chairman, who had at first been appointed by the board of directors, was elected by the State; later she was made an independent officer and superior to the State president. This was undoubtedly a mistake, as it created a possibility for friction, always an undesirable condition, and one that should be avoided in any organization. Please emphasize that I do not say a necessity for friction, but a possibility.

"Later in the history of the federation another mistake was made, which was making the State chairmen of correspondence practically the elective body of the General

MRS. J. C. CROLY.
Honorary Vice-President General Federation Women's Clubs.

anybody. All that the federation wants is an income for working expenses, and that certainly ought to be supplied."

MRS. ALICE IVES BREED, of Lynn, Massachusetts, ex-vice-president of the federation, wrote informally, and more from her general knowledge of the subject than from any recent careful study of it.

"While the G. F. W. C. is big and more or less unwieldy, yet I have always believed and still believe in the direct representation of the individual club. That, to me, has always been one of the most commendable features in our organization, and I should regret to see it eliminated. Some of those who advocate the doing away of the individual representation say, by way of argument, that the federation is like a great political organization, in which nation comes first, then State, then the individual. This is absurd! The cases are not parallel at all. I believe in the democracy of our G. F. W. C. as it now stand. Some changes and modifications may be necessary, and these I believe in as they are needed and come about naturally. When the per capita tax was first suggested, it struck me favorably—provided it could be carried out. I realized, however, that there would be opposition. It will be difficult, I fear, to effect reorganization and please nearly all of our club women."

MRS. LOUISE DICKINSON SHERMAN, president of the Chicago Woman's Club, says: "Judging from the action of the Chicago Woman's Club, and from that taken at the recent meeting at Quincy of the State federation, I think a wise plan of reorganization will be accepted, not, however, without opposition. At present, too little is known about it. The proposal comes with almost a shock to most of the clubs, and the first instinct is against any change. The fact, however, that good reasons for this change—the unwieldiness of the body, the duplication of work, etc.—exist appeals to thinking minds, but sentiment clings to the close relation between the individual club and the General Federation. In my own judgment, reorganization must logically come, but it should not be forced at all. Unless the plan formulated by the committee of fifteen be satisfactory and desirable, and every way acceptable to a large majority at the next biennial meeting, it should not be adopted. Evolution will bring it in the proper time."

MRS. ELLA HOES NEVILLE, president of the Wisconsin Federation, says: "I think we are all agreed that the time has come when reorganization of the General Federation has become a necessity, the only question being how shall it be done? If only State federations make up the general society, will individual clubs lose their personal interest in the larger organization? I do not think so. As our State federations are composed of clubs, the clubs being made up of individual members, a natural sequence would bring about a General Federation formed of State organizations. There is a lack of unity in the present arrangement by which a few of the clubs of each State, not all, belong to the parent society. Without unity the federation is weakened, and loses in force and helpfulness. But the question of necessity for reorganization requires no argument; there can be but one mind regarding it. That this shall be done by the admission only of State federations seems the only reasonable solution.

"When the General Federation shall be composed of State federations only, how are the expenses to be met? A per capita tax seems the most equitable and just arrangement. A club of six hundred members and one of a dozen should not be assessed at the same rate. If the

State collected from each club a General Federation per capita tax in addition to the annual State tax, and that sum was paid to the General Federation as the State dues, it would simplify matters, and be more just than the double dues which States and clubs now pay. The assessment I should like to see made as little as necessity would permit, so that small clubs might not be embarrassed by it. In Wisconsin the majority of our clubs are the small study clubs of from a dozen to twenty-five members, meeting usually at the homes of their members, and managed without a treasury. These clubs form a valuable part of our strength, and they in turn derive more help and inspiration from union with the federation than do the larger clubs. These I should first consider in any plan for a per capita tax. The suggestion from Pennsylvania, that the sum be fixed at ten cents, is, in my opinion, too much, that of three cents, proposed by Massachusetts, being better, all things considered. Representation will simplify itself if settled on the ratio of the number of members in each State paying taxes, delegates to be chosen either at the annual State convention or appointed by the executive board. This latter plan would better divide the honor among the clubs, but probably would not give as good satisfaction. With the reorganization of the general society by admission only of State federations, and the settlement of the question of representation and taxation, that of State chairman will adjust itself. In the new plan there would be no necessity for any officer other than the president and one other elected by the State, and called by such name as may hereafter be decided upon, to stand between the two organizations. This arrangement would be more helpful and pleasanter, speaking from a grand stand-point."

THE committee of the Massachusetts Federation, the first to present a definite plan, offers a new constitution for the general society which meets squarely the important issues which have influenced the movement towards reorganization. It provides, first of all, that the General Federation shall consist solely of State federations and kindred organizations. The State chairman point is thus disposed of: "The committees of correspondence in the several States, appointed by the G. F. W. C. shall cease to exist, and their work shall be performed by federation committees appointed by the executive boards of the State federations." Under another article it is directed that the State president shall be the head of all G. F. W. C. interests in the State, and shall lend the State delegation at biennials, and that the federation chairmen shall be vice-chairmen of the delegation. In the matter of finance, an article provides that the State federations and other federated organizations shall be responsible for the financial support of the General Federation, and the latter shall cease to levy a per capita tax upon individual clubs. To secure this income the State federation, besides the payment of its annual State tax, shall annually

MRS. ELLA HOES NEVILLE.
President Wisconsin State Federation.

Federation at its biennial meeting. That a State chairman should be a member of a nominating committee of the General Federation was, and is, in my opinion, unparliamentary and improper. I am in favor of a modification or amendment of the constitution which shall adjust this matter. It is not a difficult problem. One obvious solution is to abolish the office entirely in States where State federations exist, or continue it in those States, as well as in those that have not yet federated locally, purely in an organizing capacity, for which, in the beginning, the office was created.

"Concerning club representation, I would not have individual clubs withdrawn from the federation. Some modification clause regulating proportionate representation is perhaps needed, but the direct link between the federation and the club should not be severed. The federation does not exist merely to govern and control; it exists to inspire, to suggest, to help, to where said develop where widening and development are needed, to centralize where energy is diffuse and non-efficient. First, last, and all of the time I am against any movement which shuts out individual clubs from direct representation. As to the per capita tax, it is on the same principle as the government tax of two cents upon legal documents. It provides an income and does not hurt

MRS. LOUISE DICKINSON SHERMAN.
President Chicago Woman's Club.

levy a general tax of three cents per capita upon the membership of all federated clubs in the State. The plan contemplates several official changes. The general officers will remain as at present, but club presidents will cease to be vice-presidents of the general society. The presidents of State federations shall be ex officio members of the governing board of the General Federation. It remains to be seen whether the New York State Federation will wish to duplicate any provisions that have been set forth in the Massachusetts women.

MARGARET HAMILTON WELCH.

Margaret Hamilton Welch's "Club Women and Club Work" column, which features significant figures in club debates. *Harper's Bazar* 32.44 (November 1899), 934. Copy of image made available by Oberlin College Library.

taste, and identity. Ultimately, the *Journal*, much as *Feminina* did with decorational choices, represents its readership as articulating its consumer identity through the selective choice of reading material.

"Mr. Mabie's Literary Talks" offer the most consistent representation of the *Journal* readership as consuming readers. Mabie demonstrates, for instance, the differences between those who embark on a course of reading without forethought and those, like his readers, who learn to make critical selections. He offers descriptions of uncritical readers who

> read the books which come their way instead of putting themselves in the way of getting the right books. They buy and borrow without thought or plan because they do not understand that reading ought to be a resource as well as a recreation. (May 1902, 17)

Concluding that "the chief difference between men does not lie in the difference of opportunity but in difference of ability to recognize an opportunity when it appears," Mabie teaches his readers how to "recognize" literary opportunities, working on the assumption that as *Journal* readers they are already savvy consumers (17). He warns *Journal* women about the population of readers "without critical judgment" who have negatively influenced the literary market, which they must now navigate by making more responsible selections, describing "an immense constituency of uneducated readers, without critical judgment, ignorant of the standards of art and bent on entertainment simply, [that] has come into existence and has made the trade of writing books . . . extremely profitable" (Oct. 1903, 15). Mabie makes clear that being an intelligent consumer can be challenging, as even "the most expert judges are often misled by a novelty of thought or form which simulates originality" (15), but implies, in suggesting how his readers might avoid such mistakes, that his readers are capable of becoming "expert judges" of the literary marketplace. In this respect, Mabie situates *Journal* readers as representing intelligent literary consumers and yet always in need of the magazine's services to become a better consumer. In *A Magazine of Her Own? Desire and Domesticity in the Woman's Magazine, 1800–1914*, Margaret Beetham examines magazines as vehicles for constructing definitions of femininity, arguing that it is

> always represented in magazines as fractured, not least because it is simultaneously *assumed as given and still to be achieved*. Becoming the woman you are is a difficult project for which the magazine has characteristically provided recipes, patterns, narratives and models of the self. (17; italics added)

In just such a way the *Journal* illustrates female readers as already embodying a consumer self, but also as continuously interacting with the magazine to further define that role.

In addition, Mabie speaks, at times pointedly, to the fact that his readers, as educated consumers, have many opportunities and much "capital" that should frame the role they take as household consumers and managers of the family library and children's reading; he identifies the "great unused educational capital" of "men and women of culture and some leisure" that might be put to use in educating younger, less well-read individuals (Sept. 1903, 15).[3] Mabie urges such readers to consider leading reading groups for young people so that "one or more persons whose education has been in advance of those about them turn their capital to the advantage of their less fortunate neighbors" (15); he then offers *Journal* readers a few guidelines in leading such groups, presuming members of his readership to be those with some of that "capital." In this way, too, the *Journal*, like the *Bazar*, links the identity its audience assumes as readers and writers with the assumption of cultural capital.

Contributing to the Profession: Farmer Writers

Farming periodicals are equally concerned with their readers' ability to communicate effectively; for these magazines, the literacy identity offered to readers is equally concerned with social relationships but focuses further on writers as active contributors to their professional community. In his extensive survey of nineteenth-century magazines, *A History of American Magazines, 1865–1885*, Frank Luther Mott connects the growth in the number of farming periodicals, and their popularity, with the rise of farmers' Granges in the 1870s. In particular, he attributes the growth of the agricultural press to increased public interest in exploring new farming technologies. Michael Allen Chambers, in his dissertation, *Traditional Values and Progressive Desires: Tensions of Identity in the Rhetoric of the Granger Movement in Illinois, 1870–1875*, also notes the close connection between farm periodicals and farm organizations, the Granges in particular, linking Granger rhetoric on scientific farming and rural identities with the rhetoric visible in agricultural publications (40).

Maine, *Ohio*, and the other farm journals certainly situate themselves as extensions of other agricultural organizations. They exhort readers to participate in their periodicals as they would in their local Granges and, in doing so, suggest that as writers for the agricultural press they take on the same identity they already possess as active Grange members. Thus editors at farm journals such as *Maine* and *Ohio* frame the act of composing an article for the magazine as parallel to speaking to the Grange: the goals for communication are the same, and the language used ought to be similar as well; their readers possess the skills and knowledge necessary for participating in Grange work and should transfer these same skills to the task of submitting an article. The editors make clear, moreover, that they should use the resources made available to them through the Grange—newspapers or letters, reading material for meetings, and books from Grange-based libraries—as material for writing to the *Farmer*s. Ultimately, as writers, readers are asked to assume the identity of a professional farmer engaging in "talk over the fence" with other professionals.

Numerous articles in the magazines report on Grange meetings and outline the ideal values and attitudes of Grange farmers—values and attitudes repeated in articles aimed at writing for the press. In "The Educational and Social Responsibilities of the Grange," S. J. Hawes reminds readers that true Grange members take an active role in meetings, rhetorically positioning herself and the reader as members of the same professional community: "if we take only a little time between the stated meetings to study, read and think about the subjects that are presented, we shall find that we are interested and better prepared to understand and discuss them" (8). She further argues that members have a responsibility to act as speakers and teachers, admonishing reluctant readers:

> When our Worthy Lecturer expects us to be prepared to read a paper on any given subject, we do not think of trying to avoid it. Instead, we try to express ourselves to the best of our ability, knowing that our friends will be lenient in their criticism. (8)

Hawes and others assert that the Grange is in large part an educational organization and further urge readers to become knowledgeable speakers and teachers in the Granger movement, roles editors also ask them to take on as writers. G. P. Lewis, in the *American Agriculturalist*, for example, defends the instructive benefits of the agricultural press, asserting that "the observations and experience of many intelligent, practical farmers, who have hitherto remained silent, would be a valuable addition to our agricultural literature, and of incalculable benefit to their co-laborers" ("Farmers Should Write" 371).

To further encourage reluctant writers—and promote the visibility of farmers who have taken up the role of contributor—farm journals pair representations of Grange farmers with descriptions of journal contributors, making clear that the two were, in fact, the same. The *Ohio Farmer* boasts

"Men Who Write for Us," which appeared in *Ohio Farmer*, providing readers with profiles of notable writers. Later issues featured more contributors, including women. *Ohio Farmer* 98.15 (October 11, 1900), 1; copyright © 2016, Penton Media, 121033:0116SH. Copy of image made available by the History, Philosophy, and Newspaper Library of the University of Illinois Libraries.

that it has surpassed all other periodicals in "hunting up men and women unknown as writers, and making them known in tens of thousands of farm houses through the value of their writings" ("King's English—Once More" 130). An 1893 article, "A Few Facts," advertises the number of farmers writing for the journal; it claims to have the largest list of paid contributors of any farm periodical and states, "Our books show 157 names of writers with whom we keep a regular book account, paying them for contributions, most of whom we have 'discovered' and many of whom are now widely known" (142). *Ohio* makes certain that the identity of the farmer writer is "widely known" and actually publishes articles introducing its contributors through biographies and photographs.

In one article, "Some of Our Contributors," the images of ten men appear at the top of the page, with a number accompanying each face and corresponding to the biographies offered below. A contributor's profile often touches on his education but focuses more specifically on his "style of farming" and professional participation—"He is master of his local grange, and a great worker in farmers' organizations"—and, at times, mentions something about his writing: "He began writing for agricultural papers when requested to describe the methods by which he realized so much money out of celery. His writings are practical and interesting" (373). Although profiles offer praise—"he is a clear and attractive writer" or "he always writes from practical experience"—editors are more concerned with ensuring readers are "made acquainted" with a diverse group of farmers specializing in different crops and regions, but who are alike in their identity as writers and agricultural professionals (374).[4]

Articles such as those I examine in chapter 4, which provide readers with advice on composition, grammar, and appealing to the agricultural press, also provide prospective writers with an identity as *Farmer* contributors. Features that emphasize the responsibility farmers have to contribute to their communities and profession by writing for the press, such as "A Neglected Tool," offer illustrations of the kind of farmer—and reluctant writer—editors wish to cultivate. Here the editor explains that "these old, veteran farmers who have never written a word for agriculture, have accumulated from many years' experience and observation, a fund of practical knowledge and information," and then describes one such "old, veteran farmer": "not long since we were conversing with a practical fruit grower. . . . Now, his *talk* was practical, useful, interesting, and his writing would have been equally so" (369). At the same time, articles focused on grammar, brevity, and clarity, such as "The Editor's Pencil," overtly illustrate the kind of thought processes a successful writer needs to adopt to write effectively for the agricultural community:

> We long to make every writer for our columns feel this: "what I am now writing will be seen by nearly a quarter of a million pairs of eyes. If because I do not write clearly, condense properly . . . if I thus waste one minute of the time of each reader, then I have caused a total loss of 150 days." (24)

More often, however, articles such as "Editor's Pencil" and "Neglected Tool" simply point to the knowledgeable farmer and Grange participant who represents their ideal writer, and they reinforce this illustration by negative example—spending more time outlining the identity and attitudes of the "class" of farmer who would not assume the role of contributor to his profession. In "Farmers Should Write for the Agricultural Press," for instance, G. P. Lewis catalogs resistant responses to the growth of agricultural papers—what detractors refer to as "book farming" or "paper farming." He outlines three "classes" of farmers who object to the idea that journal contributors should come from actual farming communities, claiming that the first class is "averse to innovation" and does not like "new fangled notions," the second class was from a young age taught the art of farming and did not place value in books, and the third class has a mistaken belief about the identity of the agricultural writer—"on the ground that the contributors are mainly scientific or theoretical men," a prejudice the editor uses the rest of the article to dispel (1).

Reader-contributors support editorial depictions of the kind of farmer who would refuse to contribute to the press and, by extension, his profession. "Writing for the Public" offers a comparison of the habits and attitudes of older farmers and young, "book farming" farmers. The writer, Red Oak, a "book farmer" himself, characterizes "young farmers full of vigor and enthusiasm" who feel called to write out of a desire to share knowledge and explore innovative techniques, whether or not they will guarantee success (1). Oak goes on to offer an illustration of the farmer who will not write, characterizing him as one who is not invested in the professionalization of farming: "Behold another class. There are men who call themselves farmers, who not only deride the agricultural press . . . but actually hold the profession or business in contempt" (1). Oak further explains that "the great residue of intelligent, experienced class of farmers" do not write "because in most cases *they can't*; that is, they are generally men of but little education and not practiced in the art of giving ready expression to their ideas" (1).

The tension visible here between two different conceptions of farming reflects the kind of class and myth rhetoric Chambers finds in Illinois Granger rhetoric, where "the movement's use of class as a rhetorical strategy played a role in constituting the farmers as a powerful collective" (188). At times, as Chambers finds in his analysis of the Granger movement and as is visible in Oak's article and in the journals I investigate, this collective was defined against the much critiqued "another class" of farmers. In chapter 4, I trace in greater detail the relationship these periodicals create among identity, agency, and literacy practices and examine the implications for broader cultural depictions of rural life. Here in Oak's outline of the new farmer, however, it is obvious that the book farmer identity promoted by the journal is significant, according to Oak and editors, because it reflects an active contributor.

Defining Literacy

In subsequent chapters, I trace connections among the literacy practices deployed by editors, the social contexts within which the periodicals existed, and the formulations of identity built within the magazines. First, however, it is important to consider what the *Bazar*, the *Journal*, and the agricultural journals understood as "literacy" for their readers. It is clear that all of these periodicals were engaged in defining both identity and literacy, and that the editors realized that the construction of the former demanded that the definition of the latter move beyond the ability to read or write one's name. Interestingly, it is in the treatment of illiteracy that these periodicals provide readers with an explanation of what they do *not* count as part of literacy and, correspondingly, why identity is linked to what they *do* count.

Although *Harper's Bazar* and *Ladies' Home Journal* approach the topic of illiteracy differently—the *Bazar* connects the issue to its discussion of club work and training domestic staff, and the *Journal* ignores the matter almost entirely—it is clear that both magazines' treatment of illiteracy is, as with the farm journals, a product of their construction of a literacy identity for readers. For the *Journal*, prolonged considerations of basic illiteracy in others simply do not fit into the magazine's construction of a literary marketplace—either in the correspondence columns or in its illustrations of the publishing business. The literacy efforts of the *Journal* are focused on helping women see themselves as savvy consumers and marketers in their reading and writing experiences, and the magazine does not portray illiterate persons as having a place in such interactions. Indeed, I would contend that it is this ability and desire to participate in the literary marketplace—

as a consumer or writer—that the *Journal* marks as the standard of literacy. Bok and his department editors do not expect readers to acquire better jobs or any measurable income by adopting their prescribed consuming, reading, and writing habits. What the magazine offered readers instead was social capital and some degree of authority in navigating the literary market.

Although for the most part equally unconcerned with questions of illiteracy, race, and immigration, the *Bazar* prompts its readers to imagine themselves as clubwomen, mentoring one another in intellectual endeavors and collaborating on local social issues. Thus in the *Bazar*, in one of a handful of articles discussing illiteracy, immigration, and domestic help, the writer outlines the work of New York women's clubs in generally promoting the local history of the city and, more specifically, in educating the children of immigrants and initiating them in forming clubs of their own ("Women's Work for Their Cities" 766). Here and in a few articles such as "A Social Need," the *Bazar* does take notice of the connection between immigration and illiteracy, but it also acknowledges that this is important because "women, . . . more than men, are held responsible for the morals of a people" and carefully frames its audience as capable of becoming mentors, not just to other women but also to others' children ("Immigration's Effect upon Women" 1347). The *Bazar* devotes the greatest amount of space to outlining the identity of the American clubwoman but, in places such as these, does also demonstrate how this identity can be positioned against others—in this case, immigrant and lower-income populations.

Similarly, almost all other considerations of immigration in the *Bazar* are relegated to the many discussions of servants. Quite obviously propagating racial and cultural stereotypes, articles such as "A California Housekeeper on Chinese Servants" argue that hardworking and intelligent immigrants often make up the domestic help workforce employed by the *Bazar* audience. Here and in ongoing columns such as "Mistress and Maid," middle-class women in general and *Bazar* readers in particular are positioned as possible mentors to uneducated or, more specifically, untrained laborers. Importantly, while immigrants and other low-income workers may be classed in contrast to the intellectual clubwomen of the *Bazar*, the magazine does at times suggest that illiteracy on its own cannot be used to define morality or "value," as in "Women and Men: The Alphabet as a Barrier." Here the *Bazar* traces the history of women and literacy before turning to recent discussions of immigration, asserting that "all this may not prove much, but it is enough to indicate that the value of a citizen or of an immigrant is not easily measured by the alphabet" (438). *Bazar* women assert their identities as clubwomen and mentors not through literacy as it is defined in census records or immigration tests, but by the adoption of contextually situated practices that allowed them to participate in their communities as club members.

The farming periodicals go even further in addressing what they see as national or "generally believed" arguments about literacy and criminality, working to make clear that their journals do not recognize a connection between illiteracy and immorality. In "Does Education Tend to Promote Morality?" S. H. Ewell, anticipating the arguments of contemporary literacy scholars such as Harvey Graff, offers the premise that "it is generally believed, without reason or argument, that all education tended to make people more moral," and then provides a statistical analysis of why illiteracy has no influence on crime rates (411). Citing national population and crime statistics, Ewell ultimately centers his argument on the local context, noting that "so far from education [and a ten-year educational campaign] in Detroit lessening crime, it has increased more than four-fold" and ultimately asserting that "a person may have unlimited education . . . but if he is not born with the elements of honesty in him, he is not to be trusted" (411). Other articles do address concerns over the regulation of education but also acknowledge, as in the 1888 "The Educational Bill," that "we do not underestimate the evils of illiteracy, but there are moral evils which no education can eradicate" (2), and in the 1884 "Will Education Do All?" that "illiteracy is not at the bottom of all our woes[; s]ome of the most cultured people that ever lived upon the face of the earth have been the most wicked" (2). Through such articles, the farm journals acknowledge that illiteracy or a lack of schooling can prevent men from participating responsibly in their local governments and professions but remind readers that education does not define morality. Instead, editors place the greatest emphasis on further supporting education so that farmers can assume their roles as active contributors to journals and thereby as mentors to young farmers.

Similarly, articles that discuss the educational benefits of farm journals and organizations, and the importance of writing for them, not only frequently assure the reader that he should not be afraid to make grammatical mistakes or "hesitate to write because he has not been educated at college" ("Farm Experience" 293), but also make clear that they do not deride the success and intellect of illiterate farmers. In "Agricultural Education Not a Success," Henry Voorhees questions the methods of education in agricultural colleges and critiques state funding of universities, but in doing so, he also expresses the idea mirrored in other articles that morality and agricultural expertise are not always dependent on literacy and higher education, for "who has not often seen the best paying farms, and finest improved, managed by very illiterate men?" He concludes, "I wish sometimes the College would send a professor to learn something from them" (80). It is obvious, in these places, that what editors mean by illiterate may or may not be the ability to read or write a name; rather, these men lack enough education to make them confident enough to write for agricultural publications and thereby act as mentors to other farmers. In Red Oak's article and throughout the farm periodicals, it is clear that not being "practiced in the art of giving reading expression" to ideas does not mean that farmers are not "intelligent, experienced" (1). Because their definition of literacy values content and contribution over mechanics, editors of farm periodicals are able to demonstrate that no anxiety or stigma should be attached to poor writing skills. In fact, editors are careful to ensure readers understand that they should not be ashamed of a lack of schooling, poor grammar, or difficulties in reading and writing; readers are reminded that the *Farmer* contributor excels in content rather than style.

Importantly, in arguments like that of Red Oak, which addresses those farmers resistant to "book farming," writers for and editors of farm journals suggest that the problem is not basic illiteracy itself, but rather not being concerned for the success of other farmers or being too critical of mistakes made by writers. The resolution, then, always centers on the recalcitrant farmers' willingness to join a discussion—not on their need to acquire better writing skills. Especially for *Ohio* and *Maine*, the ability of a farmer to read or write is not the issue as much as is their ability to contribute to professional conversations—an ability farming periodicals attempt to argue is dependent entirely on willingness to adopt the role of mentor in a community of professionals. Literacy is defined not by the ability to read and write, but rather by the ability to contribute and enact change in rural life and the professional community. Like the *Bazar*, the farm publications concern themselves with how their readers will assume a position within a community of contributors, not with any individual reading and writing skills.

In this way, the literacy identities offered by these journals contribute to a broader illustration of the complexity and diversity of literacy constructions operating at the turn of the century. Despite their occasional acknowledgment of other depictions of literacy and morality, these magazines do not rely on what Brian Street has described as autonomous interpretations of literacy but instead formulate their own definitions, convincing readers at the same time that the practices, ideologies, and identities promoted by the editor more accurately reflected their lifestyle. Although the *Bazar*, the *Journal*, and the farm periodicals present unique constructions, ultimately they all recognize what more recent scholars examine: that being literate demands different skills and goals in different contexts. That this belief appears in such a diverse group of magazines and is accepted by all the readers who ultimately participated in their periodicals only further demonstrates that our more current social theories of literacy have a long history. Certain writers, at least, were prepared to deconstruct the "literacy myth" well before Graff and other literacy scholars investigated the topic. In the next three chapters, I consider how magazine editors and contributors formulated constructions of literacy that moved beyond the definitions of census records and the practices of academic institutions, outlining literacy communities and identities where readers could practice meaningful habits of reading and writing connected to a sense of identity or multiple identities.

While these editors invoke three different classes of audience—middle-everyone, upper-middle-class women, and rural farmers—it is perhaps only the *Journal*, in its claim to be a "magazine for the millions," that articulates the truth. For one could simultaneously assert that each magazine had multiple audiences, rather than a single audience, and at the same time that it was one audience reading all three magazines. The *Farmer*s were never purely rural; they were formed by the ideals and work of urban editors and were read by men and women in different professions. Bok intentionally aimed *Ladies' Home Journal* at the family and specifically added material he thought men would like. The *Bazar*, too, recognized that not all of its readers were wealthy or were fashionable young women, and many readers no doubt skipped the club sections and focused on the fashion. Likewise, adults, teenagers, and children clearly read and participated in correspondence columns in all these magazines. However specific the identity of the audience overtly invoked by the editors, the actual readers of this collection of periodicals was incredibly diverse, as editors well knew and even counted on. To be truly successful, magazines needed to invite the interest of everyone even as they nurtured a niche group. Bok's advertisement that one in six Americans read the *Journal* is testament to this desire for a large market.

In addition, given the popularity of each periodical in this collection and what the magazines themselves tell us about how people circulated the texts beyond the subscribers, it is not difficult to argue that the readers of such texts were many and diverse, and that the audiences of the different journals overlapped. Certainly, any number of women would have subscribed to both the *Journal* and the *Bazar*, or exchanged them with one another, and it is likely that many *Ohio Farmer* readers also read the *Journal*. And in doing so, these men and women would not have subscribed to just one view of literacy and one kind of literacy identity, but several. In turn, such readers would have helped constitute a complex, multifaceted audience for each magazine. The fact that this collection of magazines was successful and lasted so long suggests that although they invoked a specific audience and literacy identity, they were indeed succeeding at speaking to audiences interested in acquiring literacy skills and identities in multiple and different domains.

2.
Buying and Selling Literacy: The *Ladies' Home Journal*

Edward Bok has always felt that but for his inability to secure an education, and his consequent desire for self-improvement, the realization of the need in others might not have been so strongly felt by him, and that his plan whereby thousands of others were benefitted might never have been realized.
—Edward Bok, *The Americanization of Edward Bok*

Created by the same editors who would also produce the *Saturday Evening Post*, the *Ladies' Home Journal* was one of the most widely read and influential magazines of the early twentieth century, in no small part due to the magazine's advertising success in marketing both itself and its sponsors. The scholarly history of the magazine has, for the most part, not ventured far from its gendered and consumer legacies. Two book-length critical histories of *Ladies' Home Journal*—*Inarticulate Longings: The Ladies' Home Journal, Gender, and the Promises of Consumer Culture*, by Jennifer Scanlon, and *Magazines for the Millions: Gender and Commerce in the* Ladies' Home Journal *and the* Saturday Evening Post, *1880–1910*, by Helen Damon-Moore—concentrate on how the popular magazine constructed a gendered commerce, establishing and promoting roles for women as (consumer) participants in the popular marketplace. Both Scanlon and Damon-Moore conclude that the *Ladies' Home Journal* urged women to be consumers rather than producers and that Bok in particular sought to portray conservative ideals of womanhood. Likewise, it is clear in his statements in the *Journal*; in his autobiography, *The Americanization of Edward Bok*; and in histories of the magazine that touch on him, such as *Reformer in the Marketplace: Edward W. Bok and* The Ladies' Home Journal, by Salme Harju Steinberg, that Edward Bok, the editor from 1890 to 1919, staunchly promoted conservative gender roles for women, encouraged the maintenance of "separate spheres," and wished to discourage, among others things, the increasing visibility of women's clubs.

The *Journal* was originally the creation of a husband-and-wife editorial and publishing team, Cyrus Curtis and Louisa Knapp Curtis, who began the column "Women and Home" in *Tribune and the Farmer*, of which Cyrus was the editor and Louisa the business manager. The column was so popular that in 1883, the Curtises began to publish a monthly supplement, *Ladies' Journal*, which soon eclipsed *Tribune and the Farmer* in popularity and became its own magazine. Under Knapp Curtis's editorship, the *Ladies' Home Journal* participated in defining a gendered commercialism, but it was also a magazine written primarily by women. As such, Damon-Moore makes clear that the magazine reflected a flexible perspective on the role of women, asserting:

> Knapp and her staff viewed their readers as peers and they spoke to them and heard from them in what they considered a two-way exchange. Images of women in Knapp's *Journal* were varied, and flexibility was the magazine's general orientation with regard to women's roles. (29)

However, when Edward Bok, the Curtises' son-in-law, took over editorship of the magazine in 1890, he reenvisioned the *Journal* as a "helping" magazine—a magazine capable of advising and informing women on all aspects of home and family life—and valued less "flexibility . . . with regard to women's roles."

Nevertheless, like all magazines, the *Journal* continued to feature multiple points of view, and certain elements of the magazine, perhaps especially the departments aimed at literacy education and the correspondence columns, combined Bok's consumer ideology with an argument for the critical and empowered role of female buyers in a literary marketplace. In the sections that follow, I examine the *Journal* under Bok's editorship. Particularly, I demonstrate how the magazine's emphasis on advertising and the capitalist market shaped its illustration of and engagement with women's advanced education before turning to the magazine's efforts to

April 1905 cover for the *Ladies' Home Journal*.
Ladies' Home Journal 22.5 (April 1905). Copy of image
made available by Oberlin College Library.

school readers in critical reading and writing practices. Through columns, or what the *Journal* termed "departments," such as "Mr. Mabie's Literary Talks" and "Just among Ourselves," as well as the series of articles aimed at educating prospective writers, the *Journal* situated its female audience as knowledgeable consumer-readers and as writers capable of appealing to a (mostly female) consumer audience. In doing so, the *Journal* negotiated competing visions of women's roles at the turn of the century, presenting readers with a literacy identity adaptable to multiple departments—and by extension, roles and purposes in readers' lives.

Serving a National Market

It is perhaps unsurprising that the *Journal*'s treatment of education and literacy should emerge connected with its own brand of consumerism and gender. That Edward Bok saw the *Ladies' Home Journal* as a magazine with a service mission is evident both in his own writing and in the histories that touch on his editorship. In his autobiography and in his frequent addresses to readers in "At Home with the Editor," Bok makes clear that his goal as editor is to ensure that the magazine not only remains profitable but also serves as an educational tool for middle-class American women, tutoring readers in domestic, social, literary, and consumer matters. In discussing his vision for the periodical when he first assumed the role of editor, Bok specifies that he wants to create

> a magazine that would be an authoritative clearing-house for all problems confronting women in the home, that brought itself closely into contact with those problems and tried to solve them in an entertaining and efficient way; and yet a magazine of uplift and inspiration: a magazine, in other words, that would give light and leading in the woman's world. (Bok, *Americanization* 162)

Wishing for the *Journal* to "become a vital need in the personal lives of its readers," Bok encouraged readers to write to the *Journal* for information and advice. He employed "an expert in each line of feminine endeavor," according to his description, to read, research, and respond to all letters—which ran from ten thousand to nearly one million in a single year (*Americanization* 174).[1] In taking over editorship of the *Journal*, Bok noted his reluctance, as a man, to assume responsibility for a magazine for women but argued that by employing female editors to work with him, he could be an expert on the home—the true sphere for which education should prepare women. His belief that women needed an education—the right kind of education—to be successful middle-class wives and mothers is evident in the stances toward education and literacy visible in the *Journal*, as I discuss later, and stems from his belief that "the middle-class woman was the hope of the nation and the 'steadying influence' in American life" (qtd. in Steinberg 66).

In *Reformer in the Marketplace*, Salme Harju Steinberg discusses Bok's educational history and his subsequent attitudes toward the public school system in the United States. After his family emigrated from the Netherlands in 1870, Bok, who did not speak English, attended a Brooklyn public school for several years before leaving to work at the age of thirteen. Both in his autobiography and in later editorials, as Steinberg notes as well, Bok claims that the public school system is ill equipped to prepare students for the actual challenges and careers ahead of them, a failing that self-education and work can mitigate. Steinberg maintains that Bok, having never attended college, "suspected that a college education harmed a man's chances for business success. Successful businessmen were characterized by traits like practicality, which he asserts no college could teach. The best school for success was poverty" (38). This perspective is also occasionally visible in *Journal* articles, such as "The Snobbery of Education" in April 1897. Through his writing, however, Bok sought to promote debate over reforms that were needed in public education. The *Ladies' Home Journal*, with its unprecedented circulation, offered Bok a national pulpit for his views. Despite his beliefs in the current weaknesses of the American educational system, Bok, and by extension the *Ladies' Home Journal* as a whole, promoted the understanding that literacy is dispensed by experts and schools, which he viewed as service institutions. That Bok saw his periodical as just such an institution is revealed in the tradition of expertise he sought to establish in the magazine's publication, in his rhetorical positioning of the periodical as a benefactor, and in the editorial persona he, and a number of the editors under him, adopted in *Journal* articles.

Bok's desire for his magazine "to be an authoritative clearing-house" of information and a figure of "light and leading in the woman's world" led to repeated moves on the part of the *Ladies' Home Journal* to portray itself as an authority figure in matters of the home, family life, and education. In his autobiography, Bok reflects on the connection between his lack of formal education and the creation of a popular magazine that could offer domestic and literary instruction for women, claiming that he

> always felt that but for his own inability to secure an education, and his consequent desire for self-improvement, the realization of the need in others might not have been so strongly felt by him, and that his plan whereby thousands of others were benefited might never have been realized. (176)

He is blunt about his belief that in upholding a service mission of instruction, the magazine had "become such a clearing-house as virtually to make it an institution" (180). Departments in the magazine that field letters from readers, such as "Just between Ourselves" and "Side Talks with Girls," often note that through these editorial departments, readers will have access to the knowledge of experts in the field. In previewing the creation of a regular column meant to answer questions on books and literature, to be called "The

Library Bureau," the *Journal* explains that it "has decided to add to its business an important department which will consist of a library bureau, fully equipped in all requisite features," and that "one of the best literary experts has been engaged to preside over the bureau; with two corps of assistants, one in Philadelphia and one in New York, and with special representatives in Boston, Chicago, and San Francisco" (Bok, "A New Departure" 33).[2]

It is true that the authoritative tone employed by Bok and other *Journal* editors highlight the power dynamics at play: between the presumably uninformed reader and the expert. In her consideration of the transition of the *Journal* between Louisa Knapp Curtis and Bok, Damon-Moore notes that under Bok's leadership, "readers were no longer being addressed by a peer as they had been under Knapp's tenure. Instead they were addressed by a condescending man who often patronized them" (68). Bok was a bit pompous toward everyone, as is apparent in his autobiography and letters, and as Damon-Moore and other historians likewise acknowledge. It is equally true that both male and female *Journal* editors are introduced as experts and subsequently maintain a position of authority in their writing.

The emphasis on readers having access to experts through *Journal* departments, for instance, is overt in the creation of a department aimed at young mothers. Fearing the "widespread unpreparedness of the average American girl for motherhood," Bok employed two female physicians not only to field questions to be published in the magazine but also to manage correspondence courses in taking care of infants (*Americanization* 176).[3] The educational credentials of both editors are very visibly displayed in the introductory columns, even in the title of "Pretty Girl Questions by Emma Walker, M.D." Bok later reflects on the success of this model, claiming that "promptness of response and thoroughness of diagnosis were, of course, keynotes of the service: where the cases were urgent, the special delivery post and, later, the night-letter telegraph service were used" (*Americanization* 178). Although medical instruction relayed through a popular magazine was a problematic and questionable practice, the mothers' column services were nonetheless used by thousands of women, according to Bok's own reporting, and the model was so popular that Bok attributed the ultimate success of the magazine to it, admonishing those who see magazines only as "an inanimate printed thing" rather than institutions of knowledge and service in the lives of readers (*Americanization* 179). The success of Bok's "service departments" and the unprecedented success of the magazine itself, with its authority-wielding editors, likewise suggest that readers may have perceived of the journal as Bok intended: as an educational institution.

The practice of concentrating magazine content on advice, education, and even self-help had been used by publishers before Bok and continues today. In the late nineteenth and early twentieth centuries in particular, American periodicals responded to and joined the increasing popularity of self-help literature that at times linked mental health, religion, and social and domestic happiness. In 1859, Samuel Smiles published *Self-Help*, a text that remained popular well into the twentieth century and correlated with the growth of the "mind cure" movement promoted by William James and frequent magazine contributor Horatio Dresser (Haller, Caplan). Popular magazines, including *Ladies' Home Journal*, would later join the emergence of a cultural emphasis on psychoanalysis in the 1920s, as Eva Illouz examines in *Saving the Modern Soul: Therapy, Emotions, and the Culture of Self-Help*, but the *Journal* at the turn of the century refrained from explicitly citing Smiles or using the terms "self-help" and "mind cure." Nonetheless, the approach taken by Bok and the editors of his service departments echoes this broader cultural trend: readers were encouraged to use the contents of the *Journal* to improve their social and domestic skills, health, attitude, and writing skills and, moreover, to view such efforts as self-directed and self-motivated growth.

The policy of constructing the magazine around a series of service-oriented departments headed by knowledgeable experts also fit within Bok's conviction of profitable altruism and is part of the magazine's portrayal of itself as a benevolent institution of service. Considering the policies of both Bok and the Curtises, Steinberg focuses on education as one of the topics these editors used to establish the *Journal* as a benefactor of readers' education, citing Bok's belief that "to insure successful philanthropy, . . . sound business methods had to support altruistic projects" (*Americanization* 42). While the printed magazine might offer education in the form of the service departments and informative articles, the *Ladies' Home Journal* further reinforced both its service mission and its role as benefactor through its popular, and heavily advertised, scholarship program. In the July 1892 edition, an article, "Girls of Whom We Are Proud," outlines the results of the third scholarship competition, in which young women sought to bring in large numbers of new magazine subscriptions to win a full scholarship to Vassar or Wellesley College.[4] The article praises the success of the women at their respective schools and advertises the continuation of the program, boasting that the *Journal*'s Educational Bureau "now places before the girls of America the most complete series of free educations in the fine arts ever attempted" (12). The program did, in fact, benefit quite a number of readers; in his autobiography, Bok comments that

> this plan was soon extended, so as to include all girls' colleges, and finally all the men's colleges, so that a free education might be possible at any educational institution. So comprehensive it became that to the close of 1919, one thousand four hundred and fifty-five free scholarships had been awarded. (*Americanization* 175)

It also, however, provided a continuous source of promotional material—and new subscribers—for the magazine, which regularly updated readers on selected scholarship students, including their stories and even photographs.

This is just one place where the *Journal*'s negotiation of a gendered consumer literacy identity is visible. Both Damon-Moore and Scanlon, in looking at the consumer culture of the magazine, assert that under Bok's leadership, the magazine moved away from the "multiple, fragmented images of roles" for women and toward a more cohesive, conservative construction that offered women only one way out of the domestic sphere: as a consumer (Damon-Moore 8). The structure of the magazine as a whole—even beyond the advertisements—certainly situated female readers as ideal American consumers. It is equally true, however, that in competing in the scholarship program, and, as I explore next, interacting with "Mr. Mabie's Literary Talks" and writing for editors like "Aunt Patience," *Journal* readers are depicted as active participants rather than passive recipients in the consumer market.

Moreover, it is through the assumption of this admittedly singular literacy identity that women are, conversely, illustrated as capable of pursuing multiple goals. The scholarship program focuses on the consumer aspect of how young women may secure educational opportunities (or books) but offers almost no commentary on the focus or purpose of study for those students. Indeed, while the *Journal* advertised the scholarships and subscription competition, another department, "Pretty Girl Questions," was presided over by "Emma Walker, M.D.," suggesting to readers one possible outcome of such study in spite of Bok's well-documented beliefs about women's ideal role in the home. The hybrid nature of a magazine with a diverse range of departments and a mass of advertisements meant that any kind of cohesion or unity of presentation was always tenuous.

In *Literate Zeal: Gender and the Making of a New Yorker Ethos*, Janet Carey Eldred examines the work, ethos, and narratives of mid-twentieth century female editors. In considering the previous representations of women's magazines in scholarship, Eldred notes that "academic analysis tended to characterize one dominant theme in a magazine, rather than to look for tensions among competing discourses" (115). The magazine is the product both of an overarching ideology and a patchwork of advertisements, departments, and articles designed to appeal to a wide audience that would have both recognized "separate spheres" for women and men and also looked forward to changing ideas about women's roles, as scholars such as Eldred, David Gold and Catherine Hobbs, Mary Kelley, and others explore. I would argue that in the subscription collection program, in the advice the magazine provided on writing for the public, and in the writing encouraged in correspondence columns, the *Journal* offered readers opportunities to participate in multiple ways in what they termed the literacy or literary market. In the sections that follow, I explore how the admittedly unified literacy identity the *Journal* constructed for readers—that of an informed participant in a literary market—was not static, but rather "departmentalizable."

Gender, Consumerism, and a Reading Identity

In *Reformer in the Marketplace*, *Magazines for the Millions*, and nearly every history touching on the *Journal* and Edward Bok, the editor and the writers under him are credited with establishing the trend in periodical writing of creating an editorial persona that was personal, emotionally engaging, and didactic. Whether or not such a claim is true, Bok sought to argue that it was so:

> The method of editorial expression in the magazines of 1889 was also distinctly vague and prohibitively impersonal. The public knew the name of scarcely a single editor of a magazine: there was no personality that stood out in the mind: the accepted editorial expression was the indefinite "we"; no one ventured to use the first-person singular and talk intimately to the reader. (*Americanization* 162)[5]

Bok was equally clear, however, that the intimate persona projected through the magazine also needed to have authority, because "the American public loved a personality: that it was always ready to recognize and follow a leader, provided, of course, that the qualities of leadership were demonstrated" (*Americanization* 176). In many ways, the *Ladies' Home Journal* sought to mimic a school presided over by benevolent teachers in the form of department editors. Bok establishes himself as a teacher in his column, "At Home with the Editor," where he addresses the letters he has received from readers, using the topics raised in their correspondence to offer lessons on a wide range of issues, such as domestic disputes, letter writing, and community involvement.[6] Equally important, however, other editors of the *Journal* departments, such as Hamilton Mabie in "Mr. Mabie's Literary Talks" and

Mrs. Lyman Abbott, known as "Aunt Patience," in "Just among Ourselves," adopt this practice as well.

Through these editor-teachers, *Journal* readers are offered both explicit and implicit advice in reading and writing. In particular, in his columns, Mabie addresses the questions and concerns of readers and provides lengthy discussions not simply of what to read but of how to read. Just as the *Journal* argued that literacy was a consumer commodity that had to be dispensed by an institution, such as the *Journal* itself, so too did Mabie demonstrate that participating in advanced literacy as a reader was analogous to entering the consumer market. Instruction in reading practices, then, was linked to readers becoming discriminating consumers so that they might also become discerning and knowledgeable readers.

Beginning in March 1902, Hamilton Wright Mabie headed "Mr. Mabie's Literary Talks," later "A Literary Talk with Mr. Mabie" and "Mr. Mabie Answers Some Literary Questions," in which he provides reviews of current publications, answers readers' questions about reading and courses of study, and offers lessons in reading practices. In all incarnations of the column, Mabie focuses his greatest energies on guiding the habits and choices of readers, rather than on advertising particular books. Like Bok, Mabie positions himself as both a teacher and literary critic with authority—an authority the *Journal* assumed its readers would already recognize because of his previous work as an essayist and lecturer;[7] Mabie is one of the only column editors whose name appears in the column title, and his column always concludes with an actual signature graphic, as though he has officially authorized the statement printed in the magazine, a practice not regularly adopted by other *Journal* writers. In fact, the first several issues in which Mabie appears explicitly assure readers that the editor's discussions are not influenced by the magazine's desire to advertise, with a note from Bok claiming that

> in connection with his work for this magazine, all the books written about are of Mr. Mabie's personal selection. In this choice, he is left absolutely free, and in no respect whatsoever is this selection influenced by the editor of the Ladies' Home Journal. Authors and publishers will, therefore, kindly refrain from sending any books, intended for review, to the office of this magazine. ("Literary Talks" 1902, 17)

In the discussions that follow, Mabie teaches readers "steps to profitable reading," littering his lessons with consumer-oriented terms and educating his readers on how to be critical book buyers, manage time effectively, and consume books properly.

The advice Mabie offers readers in his discussions is equally split between explaining reading habits they should emulate and outlining the kinds of material they should select. While Mabie's column does include book reviews and at times lists of selected books in a topical area—in October 1904, for instance, he focuses on reading about Japan—Mabie places greater importance on readers learning to select reading material for themselves. In these lessons, Mabie seeks to educate women as critical consumers of books, enlightening them on the deceptions of the publishing market and advising them in making knowledgeable choices. Mabie makes clear to readers throughout his columns that the current literary market, where newspapers, magazines, and books are produced more cheaply, challenges readers to be smart buyers. In the October 1903 issue, he discusses the "authority of the printed page," arguing that printed words, because of their appearance of permanence, are granted an authority that spoken words lack and advises readers not to trust something simply because it appears in print:

> If it is dull, prolix, uninteresting, or if we do not respect the talker's judgment we pay no attention to what he says; or if we listen we remain unaffected by what we hear. But if the same ideas and words were put into type for many people they have a certain weight. All definite expression exerts an influence, but the expression which is made in print seems to exert an influence which is often entirely out of proportion to its value. (15)

If readers should be likewise wary of the power of his and other *Journal* editors' words in print, his article betrays no sense of this paradox. Instead, Mabie attributes this "influence" at least partly to the consumer market, explaining that books were historically given high social and commercial value because they were more expensive and less readily available than they now are at the turn of the century. In this argument, he outlines the benefits and "evil" of cheaper books, claiming that readers now have greater access to textbooks and literature, but

> on the other hand, an immense constituency of uneducated readers, without critical judgment, ignorant of the standards of art and bent on entertainment simply, has come into existence and has made the trade of writing books, as contrasted with the art of writing books, extremely profitable.... the writing of books as merchandise, to be disposed of in the season in which they appear, and worn out, so to speak, in that season, is an honest trade, but it has no relation to the making of literature. (Oct. 1903, 15)

Thus one of Mabie's goals is to help readers navigate the literary market by arming them with the critical tools to distinguish between literature and "merchandise." This lesson in distinction fits in well with the *Journal*'s emphasis on its middle-class, female readers as the new primary consumer population intent on acquiring and displaying class markers such as the "right" library contents. In *Archives of Instruction*, Jean Ferguson Carr, Stephen L. Carr, and Lucille M. Schultz examine nineteenth-century readers, situating their significance within a culture that saw reading as "a crucial national project, one that will shape citizens, unite diffuse geographical space, and help negotiation differences in language, background and class" (84). Mabie and the *Journal* both responded to readers already invested in this "national project" and further contributed to cultural discussions about the value of reading by outlining how modern middle-class women could best participate in a reading culture: as discerning reader-consumers who would shape the family's reading habits. For Mabie's advice simultaneously places a great deal of faith in the audience's ability to be critical readers, as the "Literary Talks" column ultimately assures readers that they have the authority to make sound consumer (and literary) judgments for themselves and connects with cultural beliefs noted by Carr, Carr, and Schultz that saw reading and literary taste "as a way to demonstrate individual worth to the public" (84).

Throughout his columns, Mabie points out ways that the women in his audience might learn to discriminate in their buying habits and reading choices, the latter often being connected to the former. In the October 1904 issue, Mabie acknowledges that "every intelligent man and woman ought to be a newspaper reader; but every newspaper reader ought to be as discriminating in the choice of his journals as in the choice of his books" (19). He next outlines the characteristics by which readers might identify good and bad newspapers, claiming that

> there is no place in any intelligent home for the so-called "yellow journal." This variety of newspaper purports, as a rule, to be edited by those who work with their hands, and to espouse the interests of the masses who toil; but, in almost every case, this assumption of devotion to workers is a commercial device and is the cheap mask of the demagogue in journalism. (19)

The *Journal*'s sense of its audience is apparent here as Mabie makes clear that "the poor man," rather than the reader, "has no worse enemy than the 'yellow journal'" (19); *Journal* readers, on the other hand, are instructed to maintain their sense of class status with the suggestion that a good daily and, if possible, a good weekly journal ought to be in every home—a journal which may be of any shade of politics, but which ought to be clean, intelligent in its discussion of events, and fair in its presentation of news. (19)

That reading is thus a method of connecting with, and perhaps ultimately participating in, the American community outside the home is readily apparent in Mabie's discussions. Nonetheless, it is also here that the *Journal* outlines a more conservative literacy identity for women: they are empowered and educated to make literacy choices for the *home*. This stance directly connects with Bok's attitudes about women's roles in which women needed to be better educated not so that they could leave the home, but so that they could improve it. Damon-Moore, in considering Bok's editorials and departments, asserts that "Bok's answer to this threat [of the New Woman] was to emphasize the benefits of professional domesticity" (87). One component of this "professional domesticity," then, was the responsibility Mabie outlines: to navigate the literary market with discernment.

Significantly, however, for Mabie this consumer discernment is not a trivial skill and requires an educated buyer. Mabie ultimately leaves the choice of journals up to his readers, refraining from offering the titles of any "good weekly" journals, much as he does in the October 1903 issue, where "Literary Talks" focuses on breaking down the characteristics of "good" literature rather than providing lengthy lists of *Journal-* and Mabie-approved texts. In this issue, Mabie argues, much as he does with newspapers, that

> it is of prime importance, in view of the great number of books published, that readers should know how to distinguish the good from the bad, the book which is a work of art from a book that is a trade product. (15)

In this way, Mabie acknowledges how growing consumerism has changed the market economy and subsequently changed the skills and activities required of women. Warning readers that "it is not an easy matter to determine the rank of a book at the time of its first appearance," Mabie discusses ways the reader might learn to select worthy reading material, suggesting, for instance, that "one of the best ways of training the judgment and educating the taste" is to "store in one's memory" a number of passages from great books (15). Mabie is clear, however, that readers should be responsible for developing their own judgment—primarily through regular reading—of the books "which minister to our needs or will contribute to our self-education" (June 1902, 17).[8] He stresses that reading recommendations are best when the recommender knows the reader well and consults the reader's own interests and tastes. He warns his audience to be as critical of book reviews as of advertised books themselves, maintaining that "the reviews of new books are often partial, superficial, and untrustworthy, but one who reads them soon discovers whether the book under discussion is likely to be of value or interest to him" (17). Once again, Mabie reminds readers that to develop a "profitable" reading habit, they must become discerning consumers in their choice of material, in this case through becoming a critical reader of reviews.

Even as Mabie focuses on readers developing literary judgment, it is equally true that large parts of his advice are framed in terms of reader-buyers detecting inferior novels. He tells readers that while "educating the taste" may be a long-term endeavor,

> the inferior novel ought, however, to be easily detected by its exaggeration, its loose and awkward construction, its lack of sincerity, its vulgarity of standards and language. As a rule, novels of this kind, even if they secure a large sale, are not much talked about, and are soon forgotten. (Oct. 1903, 15)

In fact, Mabie offers "Five Marks of a Really Good Novel" for readers to use when they are selecting (or buying) books.[9] That Mabie is thinking of his readers as consumers is apparent in advice such as that given in the May 1902 issue, where, in instructing readers on "How to Form the Reading Habit," he laments that

> too many people read the books which come in their way instead of putting themselves in the way of getting the right books. They buy and borrow without thought or plan because they do not understand that reading ought to be a resource as well as a recreation. (17)

Here, as in many other places, Mabie not only positions his readers as consumers of books but also suggests how reading habits should be a part of "profitable reading," as he refers to it in the May 1902 issue. Once again, Mabie underscores how the reading practices he advocates align with a gendered identity for readers, an identity that is simultaneously actively exploring the market and constrained by maintenance of the domestic sphere, as becomes visible in the discussions of time management.

Throughout his discussions of the importance of acquiring the right kinds of books and journals, Mabie also impresses on his audience the importance of being equally critical of the amount of time spent reading. Following his exploration of recognizing good and "yellow" newspapers, for instance, Mabie also notes that the newspaper ought to be read just so far as is necessary to secure an adequate impression of current history, and no farther. . . . but under no circumstance can newspapers educate and stimulate men and women as the best books can educate and stimulate, and the habit of reading many newspapers, to the entire exclusion of the serious reading of books, is a great waste of time. (19)

Importantly, Mabie does not link his advice to just women: men, too, should not spend more time with newspapers than with books. However, given that Mabie has also suggested that women are the buyers of newspapers and other literary materials for the home, he is continuing his construction of the female "professional domestic"—responsible for guiding literacy in the home.

In later issues, Mabie also offers suggestions for when during the day women might find opportunities to read and hints that readers need to manage time as they would any other resource. In the May 1902 issue, he outlines a series of reading practices, including how audience members might schedule reading into their day, advising:

If you have ten minutes in the morning, ten minutes in the afternoon, and ten minutes in the evening, put them together by using them for one purpose and you have half an hour. . . . Three hours and a half a week, patiently utilized, are sufficient for making the acquaintance of a great group of books or learning a language. (17)

That Mabie believes his readers need to budget time for personal reading along with their other work in the home does not need to be spelled out. He goes further, however, in pointing out to readers precisely why it is important they be aware of the choices they make in regard to time spent reading; he asserts that "thrift of time is as necessary as thrift of money, and he who knows how to save time has learned the secret of accumulating educational opportunity" (17). Here and, as I explore in the next section, in other *Journal* articles, readers acquire advanced literacy "opportunities" by being savvy consumers—consumers who are, in this instance, thrifty with their time. The goals of literacy for women outlined here by Mabie blend competing ideas about modern womanhood: a desire for increased education and control over personal and family finances in connection with a modern, but very domestic, life. The literacy identity constructed in Mabie's column, then, does not offer readers radical changes, but rather incorporates modern desires into a revised vision of True Womanhood.

That at least some readers understood the connection among time, economy, and literacy education presented in Mabie's column is evident in some of the letters that appear in later issues, such as an additional editorial offered in the October 1905 issue, "Mr. Mabie on Self-Culture." Here Mabie opens his discussion with a reader's letter discussing a book that had been reviewed in the previous issue:

> I am confident that not one person in fifty of the class which this book is intended to assist can with any economy of time find his path to a class of books or course of study best adapted to his condition. It is not enough to tell us that we need something more than to rake together a mass of general information on various subjects: we need to be told where we can, without too great waste of time, find a supplement to a more or less limited education. We need to have pointed out to us just what books we should seek as indispensable amid the ocean of books which floods the libraries and stores. If we can read but few books comparatively then tell us which authors to select, and what one or two works of such authors are really essential to a fairly well-informed individual, asking them up in chronological order. (20)

This is, of course, just one response to Mabie's column and style of advice, but while some frustration is evident, that annoyance centers neither on Mabie's positioning of himself as the expert nor with his recommendations for the purpose of reading, but rather with the fact that he has not been instructive enough, suggesting that this reader at least is drawing a parallel between Mabie and his column and a teacher and reader textbook. While Mabie's column differs from school readers in very visible ways—the column does not include actual readings, the foundation of such textbooks—it seems clear that the column does mirror the instruction that students might have expected in readers. Carr, Carr, and Schultz demonstrate how school readers not only were diverse in pedagogical approach and content, but also shifted over the course of the nineteenth century in response to changing audiences and purposes for reading. In particular, there was a shift in emphasis from the elocutionary, which makes no appearance in Mabie's column at century's end, toward literary appreciation (115). The latter was certainly one of primary focuses of the *Journal*. In addition, the attention Mabie and the *Journal* give to discussions of authors, literary culture, and methods of reading might have borne a resemblance to the way late nineteenth-century primers and textbooks "move[d] toward literary culture" and included biographies that "focus[ed] on the authors as educated subjects, detailing their early schooling, their formative experiences, their setbacks and triumphs" (Carr, Carr, and Schultz 116). Mabie's obvious displays of authority, then, allow him to adopt the authority of these textbooks and, by extension, schools. For, as this letter makes clear, Mabie and his readers are not discussing just reading for pleasure—although Mabie is adamant that reading should be enjoyable too—but rather a thoughtful plan of study, "a supplement to a more or less limited education" (20). Mabie's reflection of other educational materials may have granted a legitimacy to readers' participation in the *Journal*-approved reading practices.

Mabie and some of his readers clearly saw his column as a valuable educational resource, and Mabie was careful to likewise highlight the economic value of time spent reading, yet another commonality between the *Journal* and readers. Here Mabie speaks of methods that will allow readers to make books "personal possession[s]" and to take full advantage of the educational resource that the books represent, just as readers take advantage of Mabie's column. Acknowledging that his *Journal* audience should read for pleasure, in the June 1903 issue, Mabie also recommends that they always read with a method, claiming that "there ought to be method in reading, and reading ought to be study in the truest sense: serious attention to thought, to structure, to style; such attention as makes a book, once read, a personal possession of the reader" (15). Mabie's suggestion that women wishing to use their reading as "study in the truest sense" pay attention to elements such as structure and style echoes approaches to literature used in school, but here these practices are part not only of critical reading but also of making the text a "possession." The idea of possessing texts appears in other issues as well, such as June 1902, where Mabie outlines different reading habits his audience might use, such as taking notes or writing summaries, but then assures readers that

> readers of all habits will do well to think over a book after it is finished, and make sure that they have it clearly in mind. Any device which serves to make knowledge or thought of the book ours is worth trying. (17)

The framing of books and knowledge as consumable possessions recurs in the places where Mabie considers how reading circles and clubs might help better distribute both. Advocating that men and women "of culture and some leisure" might benefit their communities and one another by taking part in reading clubs and book-lending circles, he argues that

> there is in this country a great unused educational capital in the possession of men and women of culture and some leisure, and there is a great need

and craving for education. Why should the demand not be met by the supply? (Sept. 1903, 15)

For Mabie and his *Journal* readers, adult literacy activities are treated as a matter of market forces and "unused capital." That reading is valuable as a form of self-education is emphasized throughout Mabie's columns, where he stresses the need for adults to continue sharpening their reading skills because

> the reading habit, intelligently formed and patiently adhered to, insures in time an education of the most vital sort. All men and women who are really educated are self-educated. Schools can do much, but the best thing the schools can do is to develop those habits of mind which enable a man to go on from the point at which the work of the school ends. (May 1902, 17)

The educational capital of books, moreover, depends, according to Mabie, on the practices of the reader: "when you have your book in your hand forget that there is any world outside its pages, *for the educational value of reading depends largely upon the habit of attention*" (17; italics added). As Mabie describes in later issues, even reading for pleasure can offer methods of tapping into the educational resource of books if readers are willing to give their whole attention to the author's words. In June 1903, for instance, he explains that

> it is a mistake to make reading a task, because much of the benefit which flows from coming in contact with another's thought or writing is received only when one's mood is so relaxed that the whole mind can be surrendered to another. (17)

Mabie's list of preferred practices—summarized in this same issue—is flexible, and he is quick to remind readers that they should adapt their reading habits to suit their situation and interests, advising loosely:

Six Rules for Those Who Read

I—Do not read at random; select your books in advance.

II—Read intelligently and with foresight; make a scheme for the season, not too large to be worked at.

III—Read books that interest you; follow the line of your taste unless your taste is wholly untrained; if it is, read good books by different fields until you find out what you care for most.

IV—Have a book always within reach and make the most of your spare minutes.

V—Read only good books and put your mind on them. To get the best out of books you must be able to remember them.

VI—Do not make a task of reading; read for enjoyment. (Jan. 1904, 17)

He remains adamant, nonetheless, that *Journal* readers who develop the ability to be critically aware of their book consumption—in terms of choice, time, and reading method—will derive the greatest advantage from the educational and social resources books (and journals) possess. Mabie thereby offers readers a sense of autonomy in their role as literary consumers and a purpose for their educational endeavors. He leaves unanswered, however, the larger purpose of one reader's larger quest for a "supplement to a more or less limited education," thus revealing the limitations of the consumer-based literacy identity in this department. Within Mabie's column and the *Journal*'s Library Bureau, female readers should pursue (and purchase) reading opportunities to add value to the domestic sphere.

Negotiating Market and Editorial Control

In this way, the *Journal* seeks to help its readers become expert consumers of the written word, a goal that also connects with the attitude toward women's writing practices that appears in the articles and columns alongside Mabie's "Literary Talks." Overall, the magazine assumes that most of the audience will remain readers and restrict their writing efforts to letters; articles like "Letter-Writing for Busy People," which acknowledges that "letter-writing may be the only literary work you ever do," attest to this fact (Hale 24). While the *Journal* does occasionally contain articles on letter writing, most of its writing-related articles are focused on the realities of the literary trade and how prospective writers may appeal to business-minded editors and publishers.[10]

At the same time, a correspondence-based column, "Just among Ourselves," was in fact nearly the only place in the magazine where readers' words were regularly reproduced, and although readers did create a textual community within this column, it is also in this space that *Journal* readers entered their work into the economy of the magazine. It is perhaps not a coincidence that nearly all the writers of these articles were male, and this at a magazine where Bok had made a point of hiring female editors to write the *Journal* columns. In fact, while the *Journal*'s gendered perspective on the literacy skills and needs of its audience was never explicitly articulated, Bok's editorial choices emphasized his belief that, for the most part, his female reading audience would be consumers rather than producers of public writing. Nonetheless, Bok advertised to his audience that the *Journal* was

THREE WRITERS OF THE SOUTH

THE CREATOR OF "OLD MAN GILBERT"

WHEN "Old Man Gilbert" appeared several years ago there was unusual curiosity as to the author's identity. Aside from its artistic literary merit Southern critics pronounced the book the most perfect reproduction of negro dialect yet attempted—not even excepting "Uncle Remus"; so it seemed a bit strange that a writer who was the recipient of such unqualified praise should be comparatively unknown to her fellow-craftsmen as well as to the general public. However, it was the signature only that was misleading, as Mrs. E. W. Bellamy, over the *nom de plume* " Kamba Thorpe," had long been a contributor to leading periodicals, and had also published two novels, " Four Oaks " and " The Little Joanna."

Mrs. Bellamy, whose maiden name was Elizabeth Whitfield Croom, is a native of Florida, where her father, a man of distinguished family and great wealth, owned handsome estates. There she passed her childhood and girlhood, until at the age of fifteen she matriculated at a collegiate school in New York, to remain until her graduation three years later. Shortly after she married a physician and planter of the Mississippi Valley, and upon the early loss of her husband and two children returned to her father's home, at that time in Eutaw, Alabama, but eventually removed to Mobile, Alabama, where she has a delightful home.

Mrs. Bellamy has a delightful personality that pervades equally the commonplace and æsthetic features of her life. In appearance she is slightly above medium height, very erect and slender in figure, great nervous energy of movement, and somewhat bearing the impress of frailty. She has a profusion of wavy, iron-gray hair, limpid hazel eyes, and a mobility of feature which makes her face a study in expression, and contributes incalculably to her irresistible charm as a story-teller and conversationalist. Her first book, " Four Oaks," composed partly to divert her own melancholy thoughts and partly to amuse her brother, appeared in 1867, and was, to borrow her own words, " wholly accidental." It was followed by " The Little Joanna." After this she wrote scarcely anything for a time, until her silence was broken by " Old Man Gilbert" and " Penny Lancaster," which were brought out within a year of each other, 1888 to 1889.

Two of Mrs. Bellamy's most pleasing short articles were " Tilly Bones " and " Vagaries of Childhood." Of her descriptive short pieces, perhaps the most graphic was published under the title of " Eyes and No Eyes: a New Version." Mrs. Bellamy's admirable work is familiar to all magazine readers; she has been a generous contributor to the leading periodicals. Her latest and one of her best serials, " The Luck of the Pendennings," was given to the public through THE LADIES' HOME JOURNAL, its conclusion being reached in November, 1895. ORLINE GATES.

THE ORIGINATOR OF "MONSIEUR MOTTE"

MISS GRACE KING'S line of ancestry—English and Irish on the paternal, French and Scotch on the maternal side—shows that interesting admixture of races which seems so often productive of talent. She was born and resides in New Orleans, there finding the material for her most delightful Creole stories. Her first story, " Monsieur Motte," was printed in a magazine about eleven years ago, and subsequently, with other stories, was issued in book form. In 1891 appeared another volume of stories, " Tales of a Time and Place," and in the same year Miss King wrote a novelette, " The Chevalier Alain de Triton," a story poetic in theme and treatment, one of those veritable chronicles of old Louisiana that are handed down from parent to child. Another of Miss King's works of fiction is " Earthlings," which was published in 1888; and about three years ago appeared another, " Balcony Stories," a charming book, wherein each little tale is a literary gem.

Miss King has the conscientiousness, patience and perseverance necessary for historical work. When preparing her " Life of Bienville " original researches were carried on at her instance in Paris, and upon visiting that city she made additional researches, which were incorporated in her sketch of " Iberville." Miss King is President of the Louisiana Historical Society. In collaboration with Professor Ficklen, of Tulane University, she wrote the " History of Louisiana," which has been adopted by the State Board of Education for use in the public schools, and a leading publishing house has recently brought out another historical work from her pen: " New Orleans; the Place and the People." She is rarely gifted as a linguist, reading and speaking French, German and Spanish, and is thus able to keep herself thoroughly posted on foreign literature. In return she has many foreign readers. Some time since Madame Blanc devoted an article in the " Revue des Deux Mondes " to Miss King's work. Some of her writings have been translated into French, and others have been published in German and Russian.

No one can know Miss King without realizing how high is her ideal of the author's vocation, yet at the same time she is guiltless of posing or affectation. Her dislike of publicity is almost marked trait; she would be known to the reading world rather as an intellect than as a personality. The vivacity of her mind shows itself in a face bright with expression, and her frank comments upon life and letters sparkle with humor and discernment.

JULIE K. WETHERILL.

MISS GRACE KING

THE AUTHOR OF "BUD ZUNT'S MAIL"

A DAUGHTER of a long line of aristocratic Southern ancestry, the Rouths on the one side, and the McEnerys on the other, distinguished in ante-bellum days, both socially and politically, Mrs. Ruth McEnery Stuart is possessed of all the inherent qualities which characterize a typical high-bred Southern woman. She was born in Marksville, Avoyelles Parish, Louisiana, but has lived the most of her life, and received her education and the childish impressions which always cling to one, in New Orleans. In 1879 she married Mr. Alfred O. Stuart, a well-known planter in Southwestern Arkansas, where she lived until her husband's death. During her brief married life—four years—and while living in Arkansas she came into close contact with the after-the-war negro of the Southern plantation, and these interesting types of inland country folk whose simple lives and quaint speech have become so familiar to us through the " Woman's Exchange," " Bud Zunt's Mail" and the delightful " Sonny " series. Mrs. Stuart's first printed story was " Uncle Mingo's Speculations," and immediately after, " Lamentations of Jeremiah Johnson" was given to the public; since then her fame has been steadily growing. She has lived in New York for five years, where she is established in pretty apartments, indicative of the dainty refinement of their presiding spirit.

Mrs. Stuart's sense of humor is so keen, her wit so ready, her memory so retentive, that she is as interesting a *raconteur* as she is a story writer. It has been said that it was as good as reading a novel to talk to her. She is overflowing with bright anecdotes, some of which she seems to consider her especial pets. Her immediate family consists of herself and her boy, a lad of fourteen years, who bears the name of Stirling McEnery Stuart. Mrs. Stuart, laughingly professing to apologize for writing dialect, says she does so only because the people she writes about talk just that way, and she does not see her way out of it. She has been asked why she did not write stories of New York life, which she promises to do in time, when she shall more thoroughly know her new ground. She has so far confined herself to Southern fields, because, having lived so long among Southern people, she is able to write with a full and sympathetic acquaintance with their lives as well as their vernacular. Mrs. Stuart realizes, in addition to her substantial earnings as a writer, a handsome income from giving public readings of her sketches.

" A Golden Wedding, and Other Tales," " Carlotta's Intended, and Other Tales," and " The Story of Babette " are thus far her only published volumes, though she promises another collection before very long. In these volumes are found, also, jolly patriotism verses, which Mrs. Stuart playfully refuses to call poems, but which in their rhythm and music prove her to be as graceful a versifier as she is a writer of most poetic prose. Mrs. Stuart may turn poet in all seriousness when she will.

CLARA R. JEMISON.

MRS. RUTH McENERY STUART

One of a number of profiles of notable authors, both men and women, that the *Ladies' Home Journal* provided. *Ladies' Home Journal* 13.10 (September 1896), 11. Copy of image made available by Oberlin College Library.

produced by an editorial board of women, and indeed, the lists of associate editors appearing on the title pages of the magazine attest to this policy. However, while nearly all articles concerning letter writing were written by women and the journal includes quite a number of features and biographies of both male and female literary figures written by women, Mabie's reading column and the articles discussing writing for publication were mostly written by men. These articles position their authors as authorities and gatekeepers in the literary business and their readers, correspondingly, as novice writers. What is significant is how closely these separate articles follow Mabie's example of directly linking writing practices with consumerism, in this case women writing for other consumer readers—a perspective that is ultimately visible in the correspondence columns.

Nonetheless, it would be a mistake to read either the correspondence column or the articles on writing as direct extensions of the literacy identity presented through Mabie's instruction. The activities outlined by Mabie were thoroughly entrenched in women's roles as consumers, while both forms of writing instruction I examine position women as producers and sellers in a literary market. Here a writer's expertise in matters of consumption is limited not to her own savvy consumerism, but rather to her rhetorical understanding and her ability to publish, and speak, in that market for herself. Importantly, while the articles on writing for the press and "Just among Ourselves" operate on a similar understanding of the need for a writer to appeal to a consumer audience, they differ greatly in the sense of purpose for writing. In this way, the magazine presented a limited range of options for literacy to a diverse range of *Journal* women.

If Mabie's "Literary Talks" column suggestively links literacy to consumerism in his discussions, the stand-alone articles featured in the *Journal* on writing manuscripts are able to discuss little else. In fact, articles such as "The Literary Beginner" and "Helps to Literary Success" spend an equal amount of time illuminating readers on the particulars of the book and magazine trade as offering advice on actually composing and sending manuscripts. In "Mr. Bok's Literary Leaves," readers are treated to a thorough outline of the earnings of popular authors—"Mr. Howells has undoubtedly a comfortable income, that is, comfortable for an author, but that income, I do not think, exceeds $15,000, of which two-thirds represent his work as editor of the 'Study' department in *Harper's Magazine*"—before the editor discusses the likely earnings for and costs to new authors in the subsection "Literature Not a Bed of Roses" (11). Beyond the discussions of the habits and material realities of known authors, what is striking throughout the collection of articles on writing featured in the magazine between 1889 and 1910 is how consistent they are in introducing readers to publishing as a trade and framing writing-related advice as a method of appealing to publishers and consumer audiences. Explaining for readers the process they will need to go through to submit a piece of writing to an editor or publisher is, of course, like most other aspects of the *Journal*, a matter of practical advice offered by an expert in the form of a *Journal* writer or editor.

Moreover, it is apparent that Bok and other *Journal* writers are assuming a high level of writing skill in their reading audience: the magazine does not use space to discuss grammar or organization but instead devotes time to explaining the conventions for addressing an editor or publisher. It is important to remember, as well, that each of the articles I examine begins on the premise that, while they may be ignorant of the business side of publishing, *Journal* readers do not lack the skills necessary to write publishable essays and manuscripts. In this sense, as tools of composition instruction, these articles are distinctly rhetorical, though they would have differed greatly from the composition texts Carr, Carr, and Schultz study from the same time period in that these articles are less concerned with how one learns to compose and more with how to prepare a manuscript or text for publication.

In an aptly titled 1891 article, "Writing for the Dollar," Bok addresses what he imagines are his readers' concerns about writing for income: "Is there a livelihood to be made in literature?" (18). He warns readers that "to write only for the dollar is folly," admonishing prospective authors not to make an income their sole object in writing; however, he devotes far more of his article space to ensuring that his readers do realize that they, in fact, are writing for a consumer market and that part of their strategy should be not to appear too interested in monetary concerns. He warns readers that

> the most irritating author is one who, in her letter, obtrusively shows that all she wants is to "get all she can." In a sense, this is right. What is worth printing is worth paying for. Get the best prices you can for your work. That is always legitimate. But don't make the price the whole object, the sum and substance of your letter to editor or publisher. (18)

Franklin B. Wiley also addresses the subject of letters to the editor in his series of articles, "The Literary Beginner." Wiley, like Bok, establishes himself as an insider in the literary trade by opening his article with a description of his experience: "Every year thousands of manuscripts pass through my hands, and among these are many hundred from literary beginners, who seize the occasion to write confidential letters to the editor"

(36). His goal throughout his series of articles is to educate readers on publishing, and he does so in his first issue by discussing strategies for writing to editors as businessmen. He recommends, for instance, that letters avoid "confidential details respecting your domestic or personal affairs, or with elaborate explanations as to why you have written the accompanying manuscript, and what your motives and objects are in submitting it" ("Literary Beginner 4" 38). In terms of style, readers are told not to "assume a jaunty, sarcastic or insistent tone with the editor" and are offered a list of phrases to avoid (38). Explaining that they should include the number of words in their manuscript and return postage, Wiley reminds his readers that they need to appeal to busy businessmen.

He further counsels writers to consider "the general appearance" of the letter and manuscript—that it is properly paged, folded, and neat—and cautions them that "occasionally old authors are guilty of this fault [submitting bad-looking manuscripts;] but they can better afford it" (36). That new writers—the kind who are reading the magazine—cannot afford to ignore appearances in their letters and submissions is a concept that recurs in both the articles offering actual writing advice and those merely describing the literary market. In "Helps to Literary Success," Bok explains that "something depends upon the mechanical preparation" of articles and stories, noting that "even the best dinner can be ruined by poor service; likewise are the chances of literary work lessened by the manner in which they are sent to market" (12). *Journal* readers are instructed to pay attention to handwriting and punctuation, as "it is irritating to an editor in reading a manuscript to be compelled to supply a comma here and a period there" (12). Overall, Bok and Wiley assure readers that writers need to consider mechanics, in particular, not simply to make a good impression or have their work be understandable, but because of the realities of the current market, where "manuscripts come by the thousands into the magazine offices" (12).

Like Mabie's column, Bok's and Wiley's articles are quite visibly framed as advice from publishing experts to newcomers unfamiliar with the publishing business. Nonetheless, what is significantly different about these features is the assumed purpose for women's literary endeavors. In a magazine obsessed with the home, these articles include no consideration of the hopeful writers' domestic situations; the purpose for this kind of literacy education is not to improve the home, but to allow the writer, or at the very least, her words, out of the home. In *Private Woman, Public Stage: Literary Domesticity in Nineteenth-Century America*, Mary Kelley surveys the experiences and identity tensions of women writers, whom she terms "literary domestics."

Similarly, Shirley Marchalonis in "Women Writers and the Assumption of Authority: The *Atlantic Monthly*, 1857–1898" and Laura Laffrado in "'I Thought from the Way You *Writ*, That You Were a Great Six-Footer of a Woman': Gender and the Public Voice in Fanny Fern's Newspaper Essays" also examine the role of gender identity and authority in women writing for nineteenth-century periodicals. Such scholarship speaks to the increasing opportunities for women at the end of the century to contribute to and participate in magazine culture, where even conservative editors like Bok would have welcomed, albeit perhaps in a limited sense, women writers as a way to appeal to a female audience, as Laffrado finds in newspapers where "women writers, who were not automatically denied access to a lower-status format like the newspaper and who were seen as potential magnets for female readers, found increased publication possibilities" (83).

It is likely, then, especially given Bok's careful warnings to readers that a great deal of money was not to be made in publishing, that the *Journal* imagined a limited career for its "students." Nonetheless, in contrast to Mabie's assertion that advanced literacy would allow women to improve their domestic lives, articles such as Bok's and Wiley's offered a more advanced literacy role for *Journal* readers. Kelley, in particular, discusses the tensions "literary domestics" felt in reconciling contradictory purposes for women's education and the preparation women did or did not have for entering publishing, asserting that

> regardless of the age at which a woman began her professional career, regardless of whether others had preceded her, for her and her society the act of national, commercial publication was steeped in significance. To enter the public realm was for the woman to enter a new realm of being. (83)

The response Bok, Wiley, and, as I address below, Wolstan Dixey imply they received from readers suggests that some *Journal* women were also both interested in pursuing publication and eager for the experience and expertise editors offered in their advice articles.

As they continue to school readers in the realities of the publishing business, Bok and Wiley are equally adamant that their *Journal* students need to learn to appeal to the mass market, to be sellers as well as consumers. In "Writing for the Dollar," Bok offers only general advice, telling readers to "write what the public wants; write in a plain popular style," arguing that "it is one thing to write well, but if the material produced is not in touch with the wants of the times, the work may go begging for a market" (18). The idea that writers, in developing their ideas and tailoring their composition style, need to consider not merely audience but also the tastes of the current literary market reappears in articles like Wolstan Dixey's "Poets and Editors," where Dixey first reminds writers that "poets, too, must live—at least they must exist, and the law of supply and demand will operate even among the loftiest spirits" (12). He then recommends that "it is always safe to be in the style" and tells hopeful poets that at present they should avoid overly sentimental wording, such as "'dewey violets' and 'babbling brooklets'; nor with the 'cutest' remarks of the cutest little children in the world" (12). Importantly, too, Dixey draws a direct connection between appealing to the public and appealing to a business-minded editor, asserting that editors function as representatives of market appeal: "It is an editor's business to taste for others; and even supposing him to insist on his personal preference, his taste has been formed mainly by contact with traditional standards" (12). Bok suggests that writers consider the tastes of the editor, or more precisely, the portion of the market he represents, in selecting a journal, directing them to "first and foremost spend a few days in carefully looking over the principal magazines and periodicals of the day, and notice the particular class of articles, poems and stories printed in each" ("Helps" 14).

Considering the "public appetite," *Journal* articles demonstrate, is also a concern for writers in terms of the time they spend composing, both for the amount of time they allow themselves for revision and reflection and for the appearance they create. In "Words for Young Authors," Bok reminds his readers that "literary success is like wealth: harder to keep than to make it," and then illustrates the dangers of rushing to publish a second book shortly following an initial success. His concerns ultimately center on market appeal: "The critic has used his words of encouragement of you and whetting the public appetite. Let the public wait a little while for your next" (13). According to Bok, writing too quickly will not produce "the best writing," and it will overwhelm the "appetite" of the market:

> Never get the foolish notion that the public is just pining for something else from your pen. It is not. It has never yet sat up nights for any author's work, and never will. Once you get the ear of the reading public: then the greatest caution is necessary. (13)

In terms of process as well, Bok cautions that writers spend more time considering their writing before committing it to paper, advising that they "sedulously avoid corrections, erasure and interlineations [in manuscripts]. Don't do on paper what you ought to do mentally" (12). He maintains that this is especially the case because writers want to make their work appealing to busy editors. Once again, Bok argues that *Journal*-reading writers must follow this rule because they do not have the monetary or literary capital to avoid it, citing that Victor Hugo was famous for submitting manuscripts full of mistakes, but that "Victor Hugo could afford to do a great many things you cannot" (12). Similarly, Wiley tells writers that they will need to copy several drafts, asking, "Have you ever written a really presentable first draft of a manuscript?" ("Literary Beginner 5" 26). He recommends instead that "the first draft needs to be copied after it has been revised" (26). Moreover, Wiley implies that because of the volume of works submitted for publication, all writers must take time in preparing the mechanical aspects of their manuscripts:

> [When] you send out a manuscript to win its way in the literary world, you enter into a competition with other writers which is every whit as keen as that in any other line of business. Consequently . . . you cannot afford to overlook or disregard even the slightest detail that may help you in disposing of your wares. ("Literary Beginner 3" 42)

Assertions such as these emphasize audience members' newcomer status, a reality Marchalonis asserts female writers for the *Atlantic Monthly* also experience. For although the writers she examines "were not afraid to assert the kind of authority more characteristic of men" in their writing, in broader cultural terms "the problem lay in acquiring the education that qualified them to do so and the courage to enter a traditionally masculine arena" (21). In a small way, Bok's, Wiley's, and Dixey's articles insert themselves into this void, providing a female audience with a rhetorical and discoursal knowledge of the publishing world and offering, at least in this part of the *Journal*, a new, nondomestic role for women's literacy. "Just among Ourselves" and other correspondence columns likewise provide avenues for readers to publish writing, but as I argue, they do so not by instructing writers on entering an outside business world, but by bringing the publishing market into the domestic sphere.

Although writers were not paid for their contributions to correspondence columns such as "Just among Ourselves," the editors of these departments do suggest that letter writers are entering into a *Journal* market and that their work needs to appeal to other reader-consumers. "Just among Ourselves" was one of the more popular correspondence columns and one of the few, more importantly, that actually published readers' letters rather than summarizing what a correspondent had said, a tactic that prevailed in most *Journal* departments. The column was presided over by "Aunt Patience," who ultimately identified herself and signed her columns as Mrs. Lyman Abbott.[11] Mrs. Abbott was a member of the Anti-Woman Suffrage Society, and her husband, a former Congregationalist minister, wrote for and edited *Harper's Magazine* before taking over the Christian magazine the *Outlook*. Like Bok, Abbott sought to foster domestic intimacy with readers in her column and promoted a conservative agenda in her writing. By printing her readers' words and conducting an ongoing dialogue among readers and herself, Abbott followed up on the advice offered by Bok, Dixey, and Wiley by guiding women into writing for other *Journal* consumers but tempered radicalness of this activity by situating her column—and by extension the magazine—as a domestic community.

The market value of readers' work is established early on in "Just among Ourselves," for the initial issue introduces the column by describing its purpose:

> What do you think, dear Journal sisters? I have persuaded Mr. Bok to let us have hereafter, in every number of our dear Journal, a page all to ourselves—a page which will be just for us, and through which the whole band of sisters can talk to each other on anything they like. Now, is not that nice? (24)

Although the title of the department suggests that its purpose is to promote "talk," the column editor, framing herself as an "Aunt," prints the concerns and ideas of readers and then offers advice, seeking to lead readers through her answers and through suggestions of further topics. Importantly, however, all of this is done within "the whole band of sisters." "Just among Ourselves" is a safe space for women to contribute to a national publication without fully entering the literary marketplace. Here, too, in addition to making readers understand that this column is meant to be an outlet for their thoughts and problems so that they can "talk to each other now just as if we were personal friends," the editor describes the creation of the column as though readers have managed to purchase the space by "persuading" Bok. More pointedly, she further notes that Bok promised "as few advertisements as possible on our page so that we might have plenty of room for our 'talks.'" The advertisements did, in fact, pay for space in the magazine, and although in the original issues the advertisements on the "Just among Ourselves" page are restricted to one or two, the space allotted to the advertisers grows over time as the space allowed for readers shrinks, visually suggesting the decreased value of this kind of writing compared with the literary works discussed by Mabie. The spatial economy of the column is therefore explicitly linked to the writing that women may publish there. Abbott explains to readers that they will need to curtail their letters to fit the space available, saying:

> I want you to write to me just as you would talk—only do not make your letters long. The page looks big, I know, but it is so quickly filled up, and I want as many of the sisters to talk as possible. So let us all think of each other, and rather write often than long, and then there will be room for all. (June 1890, 24)

Journal readers-consumers, apparently, cannot quite afford to write long letters for publication. The request for writers to be brief recurs in the column, as Abbott reminds readers in September 1890:

> We must be careful not to make our letters too long. Let us have space for many and we shall all be gainers. Do you know how much you can get into a telegraphic message of ten words? It is marvelous what an amount of information can be condensed into a telegram. I could talk longer about not talking so long, but will use example rather than precept. (12)

Journal readers appear to accept the editor's advice; in the initial issues of the column, letters range in length, and writers often open with "talk" not relating directly to the issue they wish to present or advice they wish to offer. In the months following Abbott's admonition, however, the letters generally remain short, and correspondents, although they do often acknowledge their enjoyment of the magazine or column, move more directly into their primary objective in writing. Of course, it is possible that the editor has edited the introductions of these letters to abbreviate them; nonetheless, the writing that appears in and is promoted by the "Just among Ourselves" column clearly values brevity, a writing practice that the editor links to the space that has been bought in the magazine.

If letters must be brief to be included in the column, it is also true that they must appeal to the tastes of the editor and other readers. Just as Bok, Wiley, and Dixey assert so often that writers need to consider the value and appeal their writing for the press will have for the consumer market, so too in the "Just among Ourselves" column must *Journal* correspondents seek to ensure that their letters will appeal to magazine consumers. In "What Would You Do? A Page of Girls' Questions," a short-lived attempt to offer younger readers a space to print their questions, the editor, Alice Preston, makes clear that a letter's potential to appeal to the consuming audience will determine whether or not it is published, explaining:

> I am glad to answer, personally, every letter sent me, but I want to select a few letters this month out of my mail and discuss them with you right here on this page of ours: letters which set forth questions that it will benefit us all to talk over because they involve some of the ideals of girlhood. (31)

"Just among Ourselves" does not outline this practice so explicitly, but it clearly operates on the same principle. As I explore below, Abbott takes a great deal of control in pointing potential writers to new topics, determining which topics are not appropriate for the community, and shutting down conversations she no longer wishes to see published. However, the writers also use precious space in their letters to point out why their topic is of interest to *Journal* readers and continue discussions that have proven popular by responding to previous letters.

Most often, writers simply cite previous correspondence or an issue that has appeared elsewhere in the *Journal*; however, in March 1891, readers begin what becomes an ongoing effort in the "Just among Ourselves" community to share and distribute magazines among themselves and less fortunate women. One writer describes her policy of saving old magazines and sending them out to others in her community; in the next few issues, readers respond to this idea, one reader noting:

> In my own house, I have for years gathered weekly newspapers and sent them to friends in isolated places, who, being deprived of society, long for the companionship which comes through reading, and yet by reason of the exigencies of life, cannot spend money to buy books or papers. (May 1891, 26)

Abbott commends the practice, and in this way, readers use the space of the column to assert some control over how the magazine can be redistributed outside the market. Indeed, it would be a mistake to characterize the entirety of the *Journal* and the exchanges in the "Just among Ourselves" column as linking with what was admittedly a rather overt consumer agenda. As Beth Dalia Snyder asserts in her article "Confidence Women: Constructing Female Culture and Community in 'Just among Ourselves' and the *Ladies' Home Journal*," the writers "combined within [the] column a rhetoric of commerce and sanctuary simultaneously" and were able to build a sense of community through their narratives (315). It was this sense of an intimate, domesticated community, in fact, that characterized the literacy identity performed in "Just among Ourselves" as both different from and connected to the literacy endeavors outlined in Mabie's column and in the publishing articles.

Likewise, the negotiation of power between reader-writers and editors in "Just among Ourselves" both mirrors the articles written by Bok, Wiley, and Dixey and, because sublimated in the guise of intimate female exchange, is framed as different from an actual writer-publisher relationship. Bok, Wiley, and Dixey overtly outline the difference in power and experience between an editor or publisher and a hopeful female writer, and the implicit focus of their advice is on how women might negotiate such disparity. Abbott, on the other hand, sought to conduct "Just among Ourselves" as a communal interchange presided over by a womanly peer. Nevertheless, it is equally true that Abbott retains a great deal of visible control over the words of her readers and even the overall content of the column; although the column is ostensibly created by readers' correspondence, it is obvious that readers have not purchased free space for their words, but that the column, like other departments, is controlled by the editor. In the September 1890 issue, for instance, Abbott, who offers commentary following every letter—with the length of her own contribution sometimes equaling or exceeding that of the correspondence—brings two separate topics to a close. Responding to a letter citing an ongoing conversation about left-handedness in children, the editor notes:

> To judge from the large package of letters received, I should think that the majority of people were born left-handed. Perhaps we have now accumulated all the advice which is necessary on this subject, and we will not give more space to it. (12)

At the same time, another writer's letter appears under the heading "Final Words about Cockroaches," with the editor's preface that "with this final suggestion we hope the last roaches may be destroyed, and we shall hear no more of them" (12).

Abbott does not simply take responsibility for concluding discussions; she claims authority for suggesting topics as well, as in one issue where she asks:

> What do you think, sisters, about the best way of managing a family library? Is it a good plan to put the books into a common stock, or is it better to have each member of the family own the little store to be kept in one's own room? The books are certainly an education and I think that would be one good topic for us to talk about together. (Oct. 1890, 14)

In this respect, the column's editor articulates the types of submissions she wishes to receive and those she does not, positioning letter writers less as readers entering an exchange, as the column's initial proposal insists, and framing them more as writers entering the intimate, but still consumer, *Journal* marketplace. That readers of the magazine, and therefore the column, had already been established as consumers in Mabie's column and as writers who needed to negotiate editorial demands in the advice of Bok and Wiley bolstered this construction. In the *Journal*, at least, however varied the goals for literacy or department-specific the identity for writers, women must learn to negotiate market and editorial economies.

Purchasing Subscriptions for Literacy

If, according to the *Journal*'s conception, literacy is dispensed through institutions and written texts are produced for and consumed by readers, then literacy is also something that has to be purchased in some way. Correspondingly, the periodical does not restrict its portrayal of consumption to the practice of reading nor of negotiation of market economies to writing; throughout the periodical's many considerations of the possible education of its readers, students of all kinds are consistently framed as buyers and earners in an educational market. Importantly, however, just as Mabie in his reading instruction and Bok, Dixey, and Wiley in their writing advice suggest that as consumer-readers and writer-salespersons, women have critical control over the choices they make in their literacy experiences, so too does the *Journal* suggest that the lens of consumerism can allow students to exert control over their educational choices, as is most visible in the magazine's scholarship program.

It is clear in the "Just among Ourselves" column that correspondents are negotiating commercial space in the magazine, with space budgeted for editors' comments, reader letters, and advertisements. But this is not the only place in the *Journal* where readers are framed as participants in a market economy, buying into the magazine's communal and educational opportunities. Bok's well-publicized "free scholarship" students have earned their opportunity to attend college, (and to have their story appear in the magazine, by selling subscriptions, a fact that, far from underplaying, Bok and the *Journal* repeatedly emphasize. Though the articles focusing on scholarship winners refer to the subscription competition as a "slight service,"[12] they nonetheless devote noticeable space to describing that service, as well as the success and initiative of the entrepreneurial student. In fact, in 1892, the *Journal* printed a supplemental booklet describing in detail how future readers could obtain a scholarship: "There will be found in this booklet a complete explanation of the offers, and just how they can be secured. Some twenty of the successful girls have been induced to tell the stories of their success in winning the offers" ("Girls of Whom" 12). The *Journal* notably emphasizes the story of how readers "purchased" their scholarship, rather than their ultimate experience as a student. However, in doing so, the magazine focuses on young readers' abilities as saleswomen, even pointing out that those who lost out on the scholarship still earned an income, as all competitors were compensated 25 cents for each subscription they solicited. Alternatively, a 1906 article advertises that any reader may enter a program through which she can earn books in exchange for the subscriptions she collects. In this way, like the scholarship winners, readers are both buyers of their own literacy experiences and sellers of literacy to others.

This tendency toward focusing readers and students as skillful buyers and sellers is equally visible in other places where the periodical discusses college life. While the *Ladies' Home Journal* addresses education frequently, it most often does so in terms of children—or at least, it frames the discussion in a way that situates the reader as the parent of the student, at whatever level. Throughout the term of Bok's editorship, the magazine published voluminously on the topic of educating children in the home and overseeing their progress in school. However, the *Journal* also published articles about young women attending colleges, directing these discussions at readers who either were entering their first year as college students or hoped to attend college in the future, possibly by earning a *Journal* scholarship. These articles do often emphasize how higher education may help or hinder a young woman's (inevitable) move toward middle-class motherhood, a pet dilemma of Bok's, but just as frequently devote themselves to educating readers on how a college education may be funded.

A series of four articles that ran in 1893, "The Girl Who Goes to College" by Anna Robertson Brown, outline a number of important issues for readers about to enter college; each one discusses cost. The first article, subtitled "Before She Goes," briefly describes what to expect in terms of costs and, in greater detail, lists the personal possessions a college student will need to purchase and bring with her (14). The second, subtitled "After She Gets There," discusses "Self-Support at College" and the "several ways in which a girl may provide for part of her expenses" (22). In 1904, a more overtly titled two-part series of *Journal* articles, "How Six Girls Worked Their Way through College" and "How Six More Girls Worked Their Way through College," are success stories not of attending college, but of endeavoring to pay for it. In these articles, young women attending various colleges describe in detail the jobs they held, the amount of money they earned, and the exact costs of their tuition and living expenses. Similar stories occasionally appear in the reader-supplied "Side Talks with Girls" column and in articles such as "How We Saved" (Jan. 1903) and "How a Girl Can Work Her Way through College" (Aug. 1900), which foreground students' roles as consumers of education but also, importantly, cast young women as being responsible in some way for earning that education. Not connected quite as directly to education, a column titled "The Girls' Club: With One Idea: To Make Money" focuses, as its title states, on ways young women could earn money, primarily through selling subscriptions and learning from other *Journal* readers, for "why shouldn't girls have some of the money that men make by the hundreds of dollars, yes, by the hundreds of dollars, from a magazine that wholly belongs to the American girl and the American woman?" (40). The column does not ascribe a purpose to the money earned, at times referring to it as pin money but at others mentioning education and the ability to buy more books.

What is striking about this collection of articles is how deftly they avoid the fraught question of the purpose or outcome of women's advanced education. Elsewhere in the *Journal*, readers were presented with Bok's views about the purpose of education—namely, that women learn the skills necessary to professionalize their domestic endeavors, which for Bok would also have included at least partial management of family finances. However, as Damon-Moore notes as well in her consideration of the magazine under Bok's tenure, this message was not always consistent across departments. These articles concerned with how women might obtain further education, then, leave room for a range of goals and values for women's place at college and in culture.

In *Educating the New Southern Woman*, David Gold and Catherine L. Hobbs trace the shifting, and at times contradictory, attitudes toward women in higher education, noting that women's colleges, particularly the southern public institutions they study, often faced and negotiated the competing goals and values for education held by students, parents, and funders. Likewise, Kelley observes that the educational experiences of "literary domestic" writers of the nineteenth century were thwarted by clear signals about the limitations of and roles for women's intellectual pursuits, signals that were in conflict with female students' developing sense of self-identity. The *Journal*, taken as a whole, certainly responded and contributed to the wider circulation of both conservative and more liberal beliefs about the purpose of learning and intellectual pursuits for women. Still, in articles on the scholarship program and earning money for college, the *Journal* provides no response to or acknowledgement of this conflict, perhaps allowing for the diverse audience Bok so doggedly sought to read in their own answers.

It is in this way that the *Journal* supports a multifaceted literacy identity that simultaneously varies by department and yet never fully contradicts itself. I would argue that this departmentalized identity allowed the *Journal* to speak to a diverse audience and a turn-of-the-century culture grappling with conflicting possibilities for women. The *Journal*'s marketing genius perhaps is that it reconciled such differing ideals not by presenting a single solution, but by allowing a limited range of values to coexist under a consumer umbrella, implying for readers that they might see their own literacy identities as departmentalized; that they might pursue different literacy goals and practices in different areas of their own lives. The glue for these multiple roles, for the *Journal*, was a decidedly consumer-oriented package. Yet in portraying its audience as enacting various participatory roles in a consumer market, the magazine also encouraged readers to exert control over the choices they made as consumers and as sellers in the literacy market. More pointedly, throughout the various literacy experiences Bok and the *Journal* imagined for its audience, readers are credited with both having and desiring a high level of literacy. Thus while the *Journal*'s goal was certainly to educate readers on literacy in a consumer era, it was also to provide women with the knowledge they would need to determine how they would participate.

3.

Joining the Club: Clubwomen, Magazine Readers, and Scholars

> *There is no educational factor in this country to-day of greater significance or which gives to women, and therefore to the race, a broader education than does the woman's club. Coming, as it does, in her maturer years after she has finished her school and college course; when she is in the midst of every-day practical life, it gives her the possibility of keeping up her intellectual life.*
> —Nettie Bailey, *Harper's Bazar*, 1905

In her autobiography, Margaret Sangster, editor of *Harper's Bazar* from 1889 to 1899, notes that even in its early years the fashion magazine "had a pervasive literary flavour from the first to the last page" (207). Although *Harper's Bazar*, founded in 1867, was predominantly a fashion magazine aimed at upper-middle-class readers interested in European fashion, the periodical always had literary roots. The original publishers, Harper and Brothers, also founded the popular *Harper's Magazine* and Harper Collins Publishing. Nonetheless, Sangster, according to her own account, was reluctant to become the editor of a fashion magazine because her skills and interests focused on "the other departments."

Both an echo and foil of Edward Bok, Sangster was committed to educational and social concerns in culture and in her magazine but was equally interested in expanding women's roles outside the home. In her autobiography as well as in her advice book for women, *Winsome Womanhood*, she demonstrates her commitment to the women's club movement, home study and reading, and women's increasing participation in community and workplace affairs. In fact, Sangster focuses the greater part of her chapter on "The Life of an Editor" not on her own experiences, but on acquainting readers with publishing houses and the value of female editors. Making note of an address she gave to a women's club at Smith College, Sangster claims that "no vocation alluring to women possessed wider opportunities and richer rewards than [journalism]" (279). In the pages that follow, she makes an argument for how satisfying the job can be, ultimately suggesting that women need to take a more active role in the publication of magazines. Hinting at the trend established by magazines such as the *Ladies' Home Journal*, she observes, "It is noteworthy that the magazines intended for home reading, and presumably read by women to a greater extent than by men, are at present edited and engineered by men" (282). In her autobiography and other articles, too, Sangster makes clear her conviction that women of all ages should seek out intellectual pursuits. The goals of such endeavors, according to Sangster, are not only personal improvement and pleasure but also social betterment. A strong advocate of the women's clubs Bok so deplored, Sangster makes clear in her writing that women need to form connections with one another to educate themselves and to influence not just their homes but also their communities.

Her beliefs, not surprisingly, echoed the agenda visible in *Harper's Bazar* at the turn of the century, an agenda that was every bit as pedagogical as the *Journal*'s and equally reliant on a belief in inherent differences between men and women, yet was more attuned to the value of women inhabiting a sphere outside the home. The "Home Study Club" feature Sangster put into place in the last decade of the nineteenth century was continued into the twentieth century by the next editor, Elizabeth Jordan, a writer and suffragist. The pedagogical agenda forwarded by the magazine under both Sangster and Jordan drew on models used by women's clubs, specifically women's study clubs, promoting a gendered understanding of literacy that was acquired and enacted socially; for the *Bazar*, as for women's clubs, advanced reading and writing skills were best learned and practiced in a community of women. In fact, in addition to numerous articles supporting women's clubs and a regular column, "Club Women and Club Work," that reported on the activities of clubs across the country, nearly all discussions of the literacy skills readers should acquire centered on the reading and writing practices used in women's clubs.

Image titled "Nobody is really so superior as to be too good to marry," which accompanies an illustrated article describing the experiences of college-educated women. *Harper's Bazar* 37.12 (December 1903), 1139. Copy of image made available by Oberlin College Library.

Although individual articles concerning education and letter writing were by no means uniform, together with the "Home Study Club," "Club Women and Club Work," and "Our Girls' Exchange," they imagined a distinct place for advanced literacy in the lives of their readers. Specifically, they asserted that readers needed to take part in advanced literacy practices to enter into a community of women and exert a positive influence on their families and communities. In the "Home Study Club" and the various articles on letter writing, in particular, *Harper's Bazar* promoted a pedagogy centered on collaboration, critical reflection, and awareness of an audience-community—strategies the "Home Study Club" identified as being inherent in club work. In the sections that follow, I first explore the

Advocating an Intellectual Life for Women

Although the period between 1890 and 1910 incorporates two separate editors for *Harper's Bazar*, and any critical consideration of the magazine as a whole must take into account not only the articles and features centered on literacy but also the advertisements, fashion notices, and myriad other columns, nonetheless the stance *Harper's Bazar* takes on literacy and women's education during this period is remarkably homogenous and appears surprisingly frequently.[1] Even the fashion plates regularly offer lengthy discussions of the current designs for schoolgirls, college students, and clubwomen. Repeatedly, articles and columns stress the fact that all (female) readers can and should embrace advanced learning; that readers need to further their writing skills, experience discussing literature, and knowledge of history, culture, and current events beyond what was provided in school. These articles suggest that this out-of-school learning is necessary because, for women especially, education needs to be suited to their specific situation in life.

While Sangster and Jordan advocated women's suffrage, frequently illustrated women with careers, and supported women's social work in their communities, embracing the "new woman" in a way the *Journal* did not, the *Bazar* did not wholly dispense with the idea of separate spheres for men and women; instead, the periodical expanded that sphere beyond the merely domestic. Examining how educators at southern women's colleges reconciled traditional views of southern womanhood with the increasing reality of women working outside the home, Gold and Hobbs assert that they "look[ed] at once backward toward a protectionist ideology regarding young white 'girls' and forward toward an increasing consensus that new educational and economic opportunities were required for the coming 'new woman' of the South" (16). Like the *Journal*, the *Bazar* had to appeal to an audience with a range of beliefs about education for women and did so by looking both backward and forward. According to the *Bazar*, this means that their female readers need to embrace literacy practices that are inherently social (and hence inherently female) and place value in shared intellectual endeavors. In all discussions of education and literacy, it is equally obvious that the *Bazar* imagines an audience composed of middle- and upper-middle-class women who have been well educated, though they may not have had the opportunity to pursue education beyond the secondary level. *Bazar* writers assume, then, as will be obvious in the sections that follow, that their readers have the leisure time and financial resources to pursue the study practices the magazine advocates—ideally with other women like themselves.

Although the *Bazar* certainly contains articles advocating and discussing formal education for children and young women, the magazine is equally clear that women of all ages should to take pleasure in educational pursuits and should see themselves as social intellectuals. This belief is in line with what Sangster advocates in *Winsome Womanhood*, where she urges young women to read beyond what is required for school and, more pointedly, encourages older women to join club activities and pursue further learning with other women. Sangster's perspective is echoed in articles such as "The Busy Woman's Reading," by Mary R. Baldwin, which appears in the February 1898 issue and offers advice to readers on self-cultivated reading habits on the belief that "the well-filled shelves of the public libraries, the multiplicity of magazines, the enlarged field of the newspapers—all these offer the woman of today the mean for mental cultivation unknown past ages" (164). Baldwin, in agreement with other *Bazar* articles such as "Reading for Pleasure," implies throughout the article that her readers will agree that the possibility of continued learning outside school, or beyond school years, is something all women desire and in which they can take pleasure.

Published in the March 1890 edition, "Reading for Pleasure" vaguely argues for the value of reading literature but, more overtly, offers a romanticized description of the social and home lives of book lovers. Importantly, while describing the pleasures of books—"delicious bits of word-painting, in stories that beguile the tedium of today and obliterate yesterday's pain, the wide world teems with wealth for the genuine lover of books" (230)—the article frames much of the value of sustained reading in the social value it has in the family and among the community. As Bok did in the *Journal*, a number of *Bazar* articles frame women's intellectual lives as domestic. For families that read often, for instance, "the vocabulary of such a household derives constant reinforcements of the picturesque from allusions which are the coin current in the family talk, and the very children in the nursery grow familiar with people who never walked the earth" (230). Here, the value of reading and study lies not simply in improving home life but also in fostering relationships, allowing the *Bazar* to forge a connection between intellectual and social pursuits. The article makes equally clear, however, that advanced reading can and should inform women's social lives outside the home as well. Acknowledging that reading is usually thought of as a solitary activity,

"Reading for Pleasure" illustrates women "gathered in cheerful groups the land over" sharing their reading, "all receiving much more from the frank interchange of opinions and the free discussion awakened than any one of the group could gain were the reading carried on alone" (230). Here and elsewhere, the magazine suggests both that continuing education and reading will improve women's social relationships and that women's social inclinations will inspire their intellectual pursuits.

Although the magazine's general discussions of education often touch on men and women, and different classes, the articles that focus on reading, letter writing, and other advanced literacy practices, such as "Reading for Pleasure," tend to concentrate on a construction of middle-class women as social intellectuals, as women whose enjoyment in reading and educational endeavors is rooted in their social interactions in the family and community. This is visible again in Baldwin's reflection on reading, "The Busy Woman's Reading." Here Baldwin acknowledges that "the busy woman has her limitations, and this fact makes it necessary for her to use wise discrimination in her plan for self-improvement," but further notes that trying to read and study on her own is not a wise time-saver (164). Baldwin argues instead that

> if she really gets filled with the subject, and if she has a generous make-up and a proper diffusiveness of temperament, she must give out of what she has received [from reading], and must find it impossible to conceal the impressions made upon her by getting into the atmosphere of great minds; and if she makes no mistake in choosing one to share her enjoyment of a writer, she must receive in return something that will help her in one way or another to read to a greater advantage in the future. (164–65)

Baldwin is quick to point out that reading the "proper" texts—those recognized by "a leader of thought"—is important (164). It is also true here, though, that in addition to the pleasure derived from shared reading, women can and should also share their reading experiences with others and thereby help one another improve their literacy development. More important, Baldwin frames this as a natural part of her reader's identity; indeed, she "must find it impossible" to do otherwise.

Elsewhere in the *Bazar*, editors link their depiction of women as social intellectuals to their construction of the clubwoman, but the belief that their readers, who possess a "generous make-up and a proper diffusiveness of temperament," will find it natural to combine reading with relationship building and will not want to pursue study alone but in friendly groups also informs the advice the magazine offers on letter writing. Although the "Home Study

Club" column, as I explore later, assumes that readers will regularly be writing papers for club work or reflections for their own benefit, *Harper's Bazar* as a whole offers advice on only one form of composition: letters. A variety of articles present readers with advice on formatting and paper styles, as well as general discussions of appropriate content for business, social, and personal letters. In addition to being distinctly classist, however, the *Bazar*'s treatment of letter writing emphasizes how letters enter into women's social lives; thus a diverse range of articles recommend that writers spend more time reflecting on the content of their letters and that they consider the relationships they are building with others in their writing. Even more than they offer *Bazar* readers advice on actually writing letters, numerous articles insist that readers understand that the ability to write appropriate and eloquent letters is a social imperative. An article simply titled "Letters," for instance, claims "friendship implies courtesy as well, and demands the visible signs of fondness and faithfulness. As a mere matter of good breeding, the writing of letters should be made an essential part of our various codes of behavior" (354). At the same time, in "The Laws of Letter Writing," Priscilla Leonard simply asserts that "every woman needs to know how to express herself suitably in social correspondence" (1126). Leonard, throughout her article, attributes this need largely to impression management, assuring readers:

> We can more safely neglect the laws of conversation, for here voice and eyes and gesture supply the deficiencies of our language, and express things without much need of words. But when we must commit our fortunes to a written page, to be read, perhaps at an unpropitious moment, hundreds of miles away, it behooves us to know how to make that written page say what we would, and make the exact impression we desire. (1125)

The rhetorical connection between letter writing and ethos building, according to Nan Johnson in *Gender and Rhetorical Space in American Life, 1866–1910*, and Lucille M. Schultz in "Letter-Writing Instruction in 19th Century Schools in the United States," is equally visible in composition textbooks and letter-writing manuals at the end of the nineteenth century. Both Johnson and Schultz note the popularity of letter-writing instruction in the second half of the century, especially among middle-class audiences, asserting that advice in composing letters was often combined with the advancement of traditional class-based identities for women and children, respectively. As should already be clear, the *Bazar* quite overtly invoked middle-class, upwardly mobile tropes throughout the publication and likewise cast letter writing as a "matter of good breeding" ("Letters"

354). In this way, the advice offered in the *Bazar* connects with the values visible in the textbooks examined by Schultz, where she argues that "19th century letter-writing instruction not only excluded groups of people, it also perpetuated that exclusion and at the same time worked to preserve the culture of the upper middle class" (123). This kind of class-based exclusion existed throughout the *Bazar*, which drew narrower and clearer class lines than the *Journal*. Just as significantly, moreover, Johnson makes clear that letter-writing manuals drew equally clear lines around women's identities, contending that while manuals toward the end of the century sometimes acknowledged the necessity of advice on business correspondence, these texts still "generally reinforced conservative definitions of female roles rather than expanded the rhetorical territory of women" (79).

Despite Sangster's and Jordan's, and their journal's, modestly liberal stance on women's roles, the *Bazar*'s treatment of letters falls back on conservative depictions of women's sphere, offering advice in the "various codes of behavior" for purely social letter writing ("Letters" 354). Whether doing so was a conscious echo of the advice manuals editors knew were popular among their readers or was merely an example of the hybrid nature of a text composed by many writers, editors, and commercial products, it is nonetheless true that the social intellectual portrayed in the *Bazar*'s advice on letter writing is a not a "new woman," but a traditional nineteenth-century lady.

Numerous letter-writing articles in the *Bazar* assume that readers both need and want additional advice because of some deficiency in previous schooling, suggesting either that they have not received formal schooling in the genre or that they now face different rhetorical demands as adults. For instance, "Fashionable Letter-Writing," which offers practical advice on the current styles in business and social letters, begins with the belief that

> there are many points to be considered in the art of letter-writing, as it enters largely into the everyday life of most people, and yet after young ladies have left the school-room, and young gentlemen have left school or college, they are supposed to be above and beyond requiring instruction on this head, while in reality few have mastered little more than the rudiments. (389)

The article proceeds to make two concepts clear: that school could not have prepared young writers for the new writing situations they will face as young adults, and that overcoming this deficiency requires conscious guidance and practice, such as that offered by the magazine. Accustomed with writing letters only to their parents, the writer imagines that it is when girls merging into womanhood and boys into manhood, even more than if after-years, that want of fluency in letter-writing is acutely felt by them . . . [and] to commence a letter to a comparative stranger, or to a person with whom the writer is but slightly acquainted, on any matter of interest, is the first difficulty to be got over. (389)

Because many "are conscious of their deficiencies" (389) but are also inclined to avoid the skills needed for writing letters, "Fashionable Letter-Writing," like other advice-driven articles such as "The Business Letter" and "The Endings of Letters," offers to fill the gap.

Numerous articles lament that women have become too hasty in their writing practices. Although each in the collection of articles I examine was written by a different writer, all were women who suggested the same method of improvement: that writers spend more time reflecting on what they are saying. Here, as elsewhere in the *Bazar*, readers are encouraged to embrace educational pursuits that will improve their social lives, and using the magazine to foster a concerted effort to improve letter-writing skills is one way for a reader to expand her identity as a social intellectual. Likewise, the advice offered to alleviate anxiety over writing skills center not on form, but rather on the thought a letter writer puts into her interaction with her correspondent. For instance, in an early issue of "Our Girls," Margaret Hamilton Welch broadly recommends to readers, "Think a moment of the things you want to say, tell them as briefly as possible in a way that you think will interest your friend, and presto! Before you know it composition day will have lost its horrors!" (A80). Welch tailors this advice more specifically to improving the content of letters, offering an example of an overlong letter written in an "exaggerated style" and advising readers:

> One of the best ways to improve letter writing for a girl of this age is to cultivate her powers of observation and pass on to her friend the impressions she has received. . . . Try to tell her of the things that are happening to you, even the simple matters, in a pleasant lively way that shall yet skip such exaggerated expressions as "what on earth," "under the sun," "hopping mad," and the like. (A80–81)

In advising readers to "cultivate her powers of observation" and share these with friends, Welch echoes the values visible in the articles on social reading, illustrating a purpose for letter writing that goes beyond the superficial and centers both on building relationships and on shared intellectual endeavors.

Similarly, articles such as Leonard's "The Laws of Letter Writing," Isobel M. Taylor's "Letters—Written and Received," and "On Letter Writing" give even more specific examples of the types of information and content that should be included in letters of invitation, condolence, and congratulations, but likewise continue to urge readers to spend time considering the practical and even intellectual value of the content of their letters. "Letter-Writing" makes clear that critical reflection is important not only for formal social letters but for more personal letters as well, arguing that "ordinary letter-writers are too apt to trust exclusively to the epistle they have received from the correspondent whom they are addressing for suggestions of what to write about," and with both women writing letters that merely respond to the previous letter, "a long correspondence thus often becomes a perpetual circle of wearisome repetition, where the writers lose their separate individuality and become one" (282).

Here, working to incorporate thoughtful, meaningful discussion into correspondence is not just a way to make the text stimulating; it also enables women to maintain a distinct discoursal identity. To this end, perhaps, the *Bazar* sets up social letter writing as different from, and more important than, business writing. While social letter writing is linked to enjoyment and thoughtful reflection, the advice surrounding business writing, by contrast, emphasizes content only insofar as it pertains to matters of clarity and concision. Leonard, for example, offers an example of a "young woman wishes to write a business letter, and has no experience[:] the laws she must apply are three—clearness, promptness, and brevity." She recommends that readers achieve brevity and clearness by writing an initial draft, and then condensing it, before recopying the whole (1125). As Johnson also finds in letter-writing manuals, the *Bazar* devotes less time to business letters and continues to concentrate on the socially oriented correspondence editors imply more closely suits the reader's situation and sense of self.

In keeping with the magazine's emphasis on writing as an important component of building a woman's social self, the *Bazar* urges women to spend time not only giving critical thought to the "observations" they wish to share but also considering the audience. For these articles, considerations of audience were defined by a writer's understanding of the personality of and her relationship to a letter's recipient. In "Points in Letter-Writing," the author claims that

> one of the fine arts in letter-writing ... is to conform your style of writing perfectly to the person whom you address. Many things must be

considered. The age, the degree of intelligence, the social position, and the amount of familiarity you have with your correspondent are only a few of the points. (646)

Taylor, in "Letters—Written and Received," similarly maintains that "in addressing a letter the character of the correspondent should be studied so that each will receive what he will most enjoy" (810). Taylor further articulates, however, how audience consideration may influence both the content and style, as well as choices in material issues such as paper type and penmanship, stating that "the golden rule of 'doing to others as you would that they should do to you' would revolutionize the penmanship of many, and the patience would make perfect work in some, if all letters were easily read" (810). In this way, Taylor returns to the values demonstrated in articles more focused on content, such as "Letters," which assert that letter writing demands a certain conformity to established "codes of behavior" (354). That Taylor invokes the golden rule reveals how closely she, and other *Bazar* writers, connected letter writing not simply to maintaining social conventions but also to fostering relationships. As with the discussions of reading, the way *Bazar* writers such as Taylor frame their letter-writing instruction merges into the belief expressed elsewhere in the magazine that literacy practices are an important way for a woman to develop both her intellectual and social sense of self.

Creating a Community of Women

Ultimately, however, the goal of the editors of *Harper's Bazar* was not simply to urge women to consider the importance of reading and letter writing as social-educational pursuits, but to advance an educated, engaged community of women. Thus the *Bazar* counsels women to form communities around their literacy practices, particularly advocating women's clubs. If the *Bazar* argues that its socially minded readers should pursue literacy and intellectual work beyond school, it is equally adamant that the best method of doing so is to adopt the practices of women's clubs. To this end, the magazine not only features numerous articles discussing and advocating the club movement but also contains columns dedicated to club work: "Club Women and Club Work," which reports on club news and the activities and syllabi of individual clubs; "The Home Study Club," which introduces women into the pedagogies of club study; and "Our Girls' Exchange," which encourages young readers to construct a textual community based on the values of women's clubs. Through these features, the *Bazar* is not simply acting as a spokeswoman for the club movement, but rather is introducing a national audience to women's clubs and their literacy practices, shaping the way women, perhaps not already involved in clubs, perceive the movement and its pedagogies, and ultimately, I would argue, influencing the club movement by modeling strategies readers will take with them.

In the section that follows, I outline the *Bazar*'s portrayal of the values and goals of women's clubs, which centered on the fulfillment women could find in the educational and social endeavors of women's organizations. Then, I turn to the magazine's efforts to teach readers how to adopt the reading and writing habits of women's clubs, demonstrating how the *Bazar* illustrated the value, and even potential authority, of being a clubwoman.

The women's club movement began roughly in the mid-nineteenth century and continued into the first decades of the twentieth century, encompassing a vast range of people, practices, and organizations. Anne Ruggles Gere in *Intimate Practices*, Theodora Penny Martin in *The Sound of Our Own Voices: Women's Study Clubs, 1860–1910*, Mary Kelley in *Private Woman, Public Stage*, and Kristin Kate White in "Training a Nation: The General Federation of Women's Clubs' Rhetorical Education and American Citizenship, 1890–1930" describe how predominant and influential clubs were in the lives of late nineteenth-century women and American culture at large, but also demonstrate that the content and aims of these organizations cannot be fairly represented by a single group. As Margaret Hamilton Welch reflects frequently in her regular column in *Harper's Bazar*, "Club Women and Club Work," a club may consist of a few rural women coming together to read literature or have a large urban membership with women participating in multiple separate departments, each focused on different interests, studies, and social causes.

Gere's history, which addresses the club work of a diverse range of participants including African American and working-class women, focuses on the literacy practices that formed the foundation for interaction within any club, but it is equally true that not all clubs claimed study as their primary purpose. Indeed, the women's organizations Kelley examines defined themselves according to their community work, whether as abolitionist groups or benevolent societies. Nonetheless, for many women's clubs, some degree of study—whether of literature, history, or items of cultural and communal interest—was both a reason for formation and a serious endeavor in forwarding social agendas. Martin designates these as "study clubs" and contends that in these clubs, "which filled the gaps between society's formal institutions and the informal needs of individual women, members developed—along

CLUB WOMEN AND CLUB WORK

THE NEW YORK COLLEGE WOMEN'S CLUB.

The object of the College Women's Club of New York is threefold. First and prominently, to aid talented poor girls to gain a college education in order to become self-supporting. The second, to bring about more helpful relations among all college-bred women, for the general advancement of higher education. And the third, the furtherance of social intercourse among its members. From a moderate beginning, two years ago,

MRS. WILLIAM KING,
President of the Georgia Press Club.

the club has become a strong and influential organization. It counts about forty regular members and a list of over a hundred associate members, per its last annual report, both lists constantly increasing. It had, last year, two beneficiaries—one a student in the collegiate department of Indiana, the other in the collegiate department of the old Moravian Academy at Salem, North Carolina. A desire of the club from the first has been to found scholarships, and it now acknowledges with grateful satisfaction the gift of its first from Mrs. George E. Dodge.

The lines upon which the club is founded are broad, and the standards high, and it already occupies a prominent place socially and educationally in New York. By an amendment of the constitution, which went into effect last May, no woman may now be admitted to associate membership, it being the purpose of the club to keep this list open for college men only. This step has been taken because the club recognizes the importance of having a common meeting-place for college men and college women. They are now being educated together in coeducational and affiliated colleges, and the men are even beginning to open their Greek-letter fraternity to students of women's colleges. There are men's university clubs and women's university clubs, but no centre for them to come together in club life, and this opportunity the New York College Women's Club offers.

The club has recently become much interested in the attempt to reinstate Evelyn College, the affiliated college to Princeton University, which recently closed the doors from lack of endowment. It will make a definite and determined effort to throw open once more this institution to the educational world. It has, too, some interesting plans in regard to the erection of a club-house that will undoubtedly soon be realized. It is hoped to make this the headquarters for a number of the best women's clubs in the city, enabling the association to pay running expenses until it is rich enough to hold the house successfully for its own purposes. There will be an assembly-hall where entertainments can be held, a restaurant, and all the necessary adjuncts and accessories of such a centre.

The social life of the club is a large factor in its progress. The four afternoon meetings of the society—in November, January, March, and April—provide always rich intellectual and musical treats for the company. At least two evening meetings are held, which are brilliant festivities.

Miss Irwin-Martin, the capable president of the society, is a Colonial Dame, and was for some time recording secretary of the New York City Chapter of the Daughters of the American Revolution. With a distinct charm of manner and high intelligence she unites a special ability as a presiding officer, having a distinguished and elegant bearing, and speaking with great ease and aplomb. Another side of her life is her untiring philanthropy, Miss Irwin-Martin being an active worker in East Side mission meetings for men and boys. Other officers of the club are—vice-presidents, Mrs. O. D. M. Baker, Mrs. S. N. Penfield; recording secretary, Miss Penfield; corresponding secretary, Mrs. Herman Meyer; treasurer, Mrs. Edmund C. Stout; auditor, Mrs. F. J. Swift; directors, Mrs. N. C. Rogers, Mrs. J. W. Hutchinson, Jr.

THE GEORGIA PRESS CLUB AND ITS PRESIDENT.

One of the most active and devoted club workers in Georgia is Mrs. William King, of Atlanta, now president of the Georgia Woman's Press Club. This organization, which has membership throughout the State, is made up of a company of strong, intelligent women, all engaged in newspaper work, and all deeply interested in it. The club has united with the International League of Press Clubs, the General Federation of Women's Clubs, and the State Federation of Georgia.

Mrs. King inherits from her father, Judge A. S. Clayton, of Athens, Georgia, a strong love of literary work. Judge Clayton was the author of several books, and a constant contributor to magazines and papers. This in addition to serious public work both in the Legislature and in the national Congress, and on the bench of the Supreme Court of Georgia. It was not, however, until after Mrs. King became the mother in law of the brilliant and too early lamented Henry W. Grady, of Athens, that she applied her literary talents to newspaper work. "Mr. Grady," she says, gratefully, "was my teacher and my inspiration, putting me, with scant experience, at the head of a department on the Atlanta *Constitution*." This auspicious novitiate was the beginning of a newspaper career that has successfully and brilliantly extended over a period of eighteen years. Mrs. King was an early member of the Woman's Press Club of Georgia, and was a delegate to the Woman's National Press Association congress in Washington in February, 1898, where she was made vice-president for Georgia of the International Press Union. After a two years' service as vice-president of the Press Club, Mrs. King last June became its president. Still another honorable office now held by Mrs. King is that of vice-president for Georgia of the National Congress of Mothers. Her strong and magnetic personality and high literary qualities fit her admirably for her place as leader, and the Press Club, under her guidance, must materially advance.

A TRAINED NURSES' CLUB.

The Metropolitan Trained Nurses' Club of New York is unique because it is the first and probably the only incorporated club for trained nurses in the country. Many training-schools and hospitals have their special clubs, but this is different, because it represents all the best schools. Its conservatism is shown by the article relating to membership in its constitution. Only a trained nurse in good standing, having a diploma from a training-school of a large hospital containing one hundred beds or more, and who can give nine names, as references, of three physicians and two patients, may become a regular registered member. She has, too, to reside in New York one year before she is eligible. This conservatism has given the club high standing, and has made membership in it a certificate of excellence in itself. The club-house unites two city residences, at 104 and 106 West Forty-first Street. Here are pleasant parlors and reading-rooms for the use of the members, with living accommodations for a considerable number. Twenty-seven members

MISS JEANNE C. IRWIN-MARTIN,
President of the College Women's Club.

now live there, and with the chastity that is an attribute of a nurses' home, there is usually room for one or two more. The establishment is most attractive. It is cosily and artistically fitted, as the accompanying picture shows, the bedrooms presenting a dainty and attractive appearance that must be particularly welcome and restful to a tired nurse. The artistic taste of Mrs. M. H. Willard, the president, who is emphatically the presiding genius of the club, is shown in every detail. Mrs. Willard, who is a New York woman of social position, has contrived to impart that indefinable touch of refined elegance to simple belongings which is possible only to those "to the manner born." A motherly housekeeper is in charge of the club-house, to receive intelligently telephone calls and to look after the comfort and interests of the nurses in many ways.

The club has been in flourishing existence since 1893. The regular meetings are held the first Monday afternoon of every month from November to May, at three o'clock. A social meeting takes place the second Thursday evening of every month, and, in addition, an annual reception is held in December, invitations to which are always eagerly welcomed by the members' friends. The management of the affairs of the club are in the hands of three competent and very efficient directors, one of whom is the president.

The club is valuable to nurses both as a working and as a social club. Its conduct is in direct accord with the furtherance of their interests, and physicians have come to rely upon its list for competent service. When it is realized that in round numbers there are 10,000 trained nurses in Greater New York, it is no surprise that the membership of the Metropolitan Trained Nurses' Club is a large and rapidly growing one. The list has representatives from New Jersey, Connecticut, Long Island, Pennsylvania, Washington, Massachusetts, and Maryland hospitals, and also from those of England and Canada. This demonstrates at once the publicity and its conservatism, both prominent factors in its pronounced success.

The present officers of the club are—president and treasurer, Mrs. M. H. Willard; vice-president, Miss Isabella K. M. Elliott; second vice-president, Miss Louise Bower; secretary, Miss Annie Miller.

MARGARET HAMILTON WELCH.

PARLORS OF THE METROPOLITAN TRAINED NURSES' CLUB.

"Club Women and Club Work" column, by Margaret Hamilton Welch, which regularly featured images of clubwomen, club activities, and club meeting spaces. *Harper's Bazar* 31.53 (December 1898), 1133. Copy of image made available by Oberlin College Library.

with the stirrings of intellectual independence—an awareness of and confidence in themselves," allowing them to expand cultural understandings of women's sphere (3). As White likewise uncovers in her consideration of the rhetorical and political work of the General Federation of Women's Clubs, women's clubs increasingly stressed mass educational endeavors and tied such work to an "ideology of citizenship" for clubwomen (21).

While Kelley, Gere, Martin, and White offer extensive histories of the club movement based on their investigation of myriad club-related documents such as syllabi and club papers, they do not give much attention to the club movement in popular magazines or turn to the treatment of club work in *Harper's Bazar*. In particular, the *Bazar* sought to address and refute popular arguments against the growth of women's clubs and to convince readers of the value of joining clubwomen by illustrating the primary practices and goals of clubs.

Reactions against women's clubs, which were summarized in the *Bazar*, centered on the belief that they promoted liberal political and social agendas and were a platform for women's rights—a perspective to which the editor of the *Ladies' Home Journal*, Edward Bok, firmly adhered.[2] Many clubs featured in the *Bazar* articulated distinct social agendas and a commitment to being involved in the community, but these goals were certainly not always liberal or suffragist. Looking to clubs more focused on literary and academic pursuits, Martin likewise asserts that they often held conservative goals and sought to reassure the opposition by avoiding controversial and political topics (34). Gere and White, opposingly, find more liberal and political practices even among the study and literature clubs, noting how women expanded the boundaries of what counted as literature and how it was to be studied, using club work at times to inspire activism in the community. In the previous chapter, I argued that the *Journal* makes use of departmentalized variations of values for women's roles and literacy practices. Similarly, it would be a mistake to suggest that the *Bazar*'s overwhelming support of and emphasis on women's clubs and social literacy meant that the magazine deployed a singular value system. Indeed, throughout "Club Women and Club Work" and "Home Study Club," editors publish the work of contributors describing very different clubs and communities with a range of goals, some transgressive and others conservative.

What these illustrations have in common with one another and with the articles of the editors and writers of the *Bazar* is an emphasis on the fulfillment women find in clubs, the desire to be useful in some kind of local community (even if just the club itself), and a tendency to frame club work and social work as still a part of woman's natural sphere, if not a domestic sphere. Kelley finds a similar style of framing in women's political and social organizations throughout the nineteenth and into the early twentieth century, claiming that

> to support their work in abolitionist and benevolent associations, women developed careful arguments to bolster their ethos, often relying on popular beliefs about women's domestic natures.... The practice of justifying political activism by linking it to protection of the home was a common rhetorical tactic for women's political groups. (17)

Strategic rhetorical framing was also deployed by writers and speakers of another major women's organization, the Women's Christian Temperance Union, as Carol Mattingly examines in *Well-Tempered Women: Nineteenth-Century Temperance Rhetoric*, where she contends that "the great strength of temperance leaders was their ability to meld a progressive message with a rhetorical presentation and image comfortable to a large number of women and men" (2). While for the temperance movement such rhetorical pragmatism represented thoughtful, motivated choices on the part of women, for magazines such as the *Journal* and the *Bazar* it can probably be best described as marketing savvy. Just as the *Journal* couches informed consumerism as a matter of domestic importance, so too does the *Bazar* depict the literacy and communal work of women's clubs as a natural extension of women's work.

In one of many *Bazar* articles advocating women's clubs, "The Significance of the Woman's Club Movement," Nettie Bailey outlines how common women's clubs have become, "a permanent factor in our civilization," and addresses the positive influence women's clubs have had on women personally and on their communities (204). Bailey traces the origination of women's clubs to the turn civilization took when "the race began to understand that there was a more just and satisfactory way of settling differences than by fighting; when ... the idea of arbitration took root in the race mind," arguing that at this point women were able to be useful outside the home, "and all unconsciously the woman's college and the woman's club came to give them the necessary training to take their part in the work of the world" (204). Although Bailey is clear that women's sphere is still separate from men's, and makes no mention of women's involvement in political matters, she puts forth a lengthy argument for the necessity of the education women undertake in clubs, claiming that women, the new "leisure class," have the time to do education work "along ethical lines" so that they might take part in solving social problems; in fact, "women must do the studying, the investigating, the detail work [in these matters] for which men have not the time, and leave them to do the executing" (204). Here and in Welch's writing, club advocates simultaneously push at the boundaries of what may be considered women's work and reinforce a conservative gender divide. This tactic would no doubt have helped the *Bazar* market women's clubs to a broader range of readers, just as the organizations Kelley examines used a similar tactic build ethos among their audiences.

At the same time, Bailey echoes the overall perspective of *Harper's Bazar* in attesting to the blended educational and social purpose of women's clubs. For Bailey, Welch, and the *Bazar*, the goal for women's clubs or communities is both to allow women an engaged space for reading and intellectual pursuits and to provide women with a platform for influencing a community, goals that editors depict as intrinsically connected. Bailey asserts that "the woman's club of each town or city should be the centre from which should radiate such an influence as would stimulate the community to higher thinking and living" (207). Her illustration is at once radical in its sense of scale of influence and conservative in the style of influence implied: "stimulate ... higher thinking and living." Such a description, moreover, clearly relies on nineteenth-century tropes of womanhood that emphasized women's moral influence, and yet Bailey leaves room for any number of social and even political agendas that might fit into this definition.

To enact social "influence," the *Bazar* makes clear to its readers that they must engage in serious reading and educational programs. "Club Women's Seriousness," for instance, responds to criticism of women's clubs, noting that "a protest is coming from various quarters that club women are taking themselves too seriously" (1112). In fact, opponents like Edward Bok did fear that club work and study would distract women from needs of the family at home. In their scholarly interrogation of the movement, Martin and Gere also similarly note the condescending manner in which academics viewed the efforts of clubwomen.

The clubs advertised in the *Bazar*, however, continued to attest to the seriousness of their educational agenda, arguing that the subjects club members studied would interest and benefit their families and local communities. In fact, in "Club Women and Club Work," Welch devotes as much time to clubs' educational pursuits and reading as she does to their community work. In each issue, Welch offers an overview of at least one club from somewhere in the country; in praising what is admirable in the featured club, Welch draws attention to what is or should be valued in club work, and among these values is rigorous intellectual activity. Praising the Phalo Club of New York, for instance, Welch makes clear that the "membership is made up of deep students and serious scholarly thinkers. Every topic is considered from a philosophic point of view and with full conception of its widest use" (Oct. 1897, 820).[3] Although the specific educational and writing-oriented activities of individual clubs varied as greatly as the organizations themselves, the programs reproduced and club discussions included in *Harper's Bazar* argue for a collection of widespread tendencies. Namely, Welch and other article writers in the magazine suggested that women's study clubs should tailor their study topics to accommodate local culture, issues, and resources.

The purpose of doing so was, of course, to allow clubs, and by extension *Bazar* readers, to better incorporate their commitment to community—both the community of the club and the community around them. Gere makes clear that women's clubs operated with a definition of literacy that differed from those most commonly circulating at the time, maintaining that the practices promoted by clubs "encouraged a symmetry and synergy of active reading and ongoing writing development, [so that] clubwomen developed an ideology of literacy that emphasized participation rather than passive reception" (25). This concept of participation within a community of women is repeated often in the *Bazar*, both in articles such as Bailey's discussion of the social significance of clubs and in Welch's reviews of different clubs' activities, where they continually stress the strength of members' connections with one another and the responsibility of each member to the others. Bailey asserts, too, the need for education to be based not simply in reading but also in acting:

> We begin to feel that *real* education consists in doing as well as absorbing . . . and have begun to understand that only by actually *doing* can we weave into our own mental structure that which we read and study, and so make our own the knowledge and experience of all times and people. (205; italics in the original)

To this end, clubs tailored the topics, reading materials, and meeting practices to suit the circumstances of individual club members. While the literature "approved" by the academy was common on club syllabi, the *Bazar* assures readers that clubs can also choose topics based on the offerings of the local library and important issues currently being covered in local newspapers. And while clubs would have produced a great deal of written material in the way of programs, meeting minutes, and even published papers, the articles and columns of the *Bazar* emphasized the primacy of reading journals and papers at club discussions.[4] Moreover, it was in the preparation of these papers and the arrangement of these discussions and reading schedules that *Harper's Bazar* intervened with the "Home Study Club" column; borrowing the values and practices ascribed to women's clubs in other parts of the magazine, the "Home Study Club," edited by E. B. Cutting, promoted continued out-of-school study and advanced literacy for readers by describing ideal reading and writing practices. Teaching women to conduct club work and advanced reading programs on their own, "Home Study Club" forwarded a pedagogy of collaboration and reflection, urging readers to develop advanced reading and writing skills in a community of other readers.

A Club of Magazine Readers

In the February 1908 edition of the magazine, in a brief note at the front of the issue entitled "With the Editor," Elizabeth Jordan previews the new and continuing features of *Harper's Bazar*. Pointing toward goals of self-improvement rather than fashion, she assures readers:

> That there will be good literature in the Bazar goes without saying; that the practical domestic departments will be far-reaching in their helpfulness is equally assured. *The greatest strength of the Bazar, however, lies in its power to aid in the development and culture of its readers.* Therefore, its famous and effective crusade the past year in behalf of improved speech among American women will be followed by the upbuilding of our Home Study Club, plans for which are outlined in this number. (192; italics added)

The stated goal of "aid[ing] in the development and culture of its readers" was already established in the numerous columns offering advice and information on books, language, cultural events, and manners. However, in the "Home Study Club," the *Bazar* went beyond simply recommending titles and authors worth readers' attention and outlined for readers specific courses of study and methods of reading. The plans Jordan speaks of in vague terms are articulated more specifically by E. B. Cutting, the editor of the column, who sets herself up as an expert on the pedagogies of women's clubs and a teacher for her readers.[5] In the article "Women and Home Reading," which serves as the first incarnation of the monthly "Home Study Club" column, Cutting explains that "Home Study" will function as a space where readers' letters and requests for advice on study club plans and personal reading programs are published and answered.

The magazine, which had long published a reading recommendation column, "Books and Readers," had also, according to Cutting, been regularly inundated with letters requesting suggestions on books to read and advice on studying. Identifying clubwomen, mothers "who were beginning to read aloud to their children," and "the girl who is going to college [and] the girl who wants to go but is unable to do so" as her audience, Cutting indicates that the "Home Study Department" will

> give advice in the matter of books to read, courses of study to follow, and [will] assist in every possible way those readers of the Bazar who are organizing home-study clubs, and are seeking direction in the way to maintain them. (154)

Cutting, in the discussion that follows, makes clear that the *Bazar* will be a resource for "busy women and girls who wished to study, but were too occupied to do so systematically," outlining for readers how best to go about a self-study program and how to establish and manage a serious women's club or reading circle, making obvious that the latter is the preferred method of extra-institutional education for women. The department that develops out of this outline follows up on the goals Cutting identifies, setting itself up as an authority capable of instructing women on how to be scholars "at home." In particular, as I examine through the discussion and syllabi offered throughout several years of the column, Cutting emphasizes, and offers advice in, two distinct qualities of advanced readers: collaboration with other readers and critical reflection and discussion. For Cutting and the women who contributed to her column, the reward for engaging in these literacy practices was that it would allow women to build an engaged, active community.

While Cutting's proposal that the *Bazar* "act as a clearing-house for book and study information" and the format of the department as a space where readers can seek advice firmly establishes the magazine as an authority figure on pedagogy and literacy practices, it is equally true that this authority is even more overtly named by the readers in their published letters. In this way, Cutting's editorial control is less overt than that of Bok, Mabie, or Abbott in the *Journal*, as her authority in "Home Study" appears as that of a mentor or club leader; she shapes the content of the column but does so as an experienced clubwoman speaking to and offering advice to other clubwomen. To this end, Cutting often establishes what will be valued in the column not by generic requests or statements of purpose, but through her engagement with individual contributors where she praises or warns against specific practices. Although multiple letters are addressed in each column, Cutting unfailingly praises methods that she finds laudable and explains the value of subsequently recommended practices: "I think your agreement to read for a half hour a day is admirable, and you will find it adds greatly to meetings if you report on the volumes that have absorbed you during the week" (Sept. 1908, 913). Moreover, she at times admonishes writers for failing to include necessary information, such as a return address or the date when the club would like to start studying the mentioned topic, and also suggests where the writer may be unwise in choice of topic. For instance, in the December 1908 issue, a club explains that it wants to study the history of literature, and Cutting replies:

> Your club is certainly ambitious and has undertaken a great deal of work, and I make the suggestion that you limit your study either to certain phases of literature in the countries of the world, or else that you take given periods in different countries, and study the various forms of literature as found in them at these times. (1272)

In May 1910, Cutting is even more skeptical of a club's study plan: "you will not, I hope, mind when I say that I am sorry to see your club is planning to take up miscellaneous work, rather than to select a given subject and make a thorough study of it" (362). Both moments of criticism are clear, but friendly, and serve the additional purpose of signaling to other readers practices they might want to avoid as well.

Moreover, in addition to these places where Cutting signals her expertise, the letters of contributors openly call on the column to stand in as an authority, giving Cutting the role of a club leader. One reader begins by admitting:

> You will think our club rather sentimental, I fear, but we thought it would be interesting to have a biographical winter, and study the lives of various great men, and the influence their love affairs had upon them. But where and with whom shall we begin? (Sept. 1908, 913)[6]

In the very next issue, another writer begins by expressing her belief that "the outlines for club work you have given have seemed so helpful, I would like to know if you would give me a few ideas." Later in the same column, another correspondent notes, "Having read with interest the suggestions given to literary clubs for study, I take the liberty of asking help for our programme committee" (Oct. 1908, 1034). The strategy used here reappears throughout numerous issues: contributors begin by making note of how helpful Cutting has been to readers in the past, even hinting at the quality of the texts selected by her, before making requests for advice.

Cutting's perceived role as an expert clubwoman suits both the content and structure of the column. For although its title remains "Home Study," everything about the practices the column promotes is communal and socially oriented. Indeed, most letters sent in to the "Home Study Club" are written by women working in clubs and wanting advice for the course of reading, paper writing, and discussion they will pursue. The skills Cutting proposes her readers acquire, then, are rooted in the sense of communal discussion and work that defined women's clubs in general; specifically, she demonstrates to readers how they should adopt reading habits that emphasize collaboration with other readers and foster critical reflection and discussion with other learners. Indeed, Cutting makes clear that the column was established in part to help home readers maintain a systematic approach to reading and study, readers who "did not know how to best make use of" a library, were "too occupied to [study] systematically," or "felt the limitations of the small places in which they lived, and knew no way in which to overcome these limitations" ("Women and Home Reading" 154). More pointedly, however, she notes that establishing outcomes is important, once again referring to groups rather than individual readers:

> There are a number of good habits to form in the matter of reading in an appreciative way, which it might be well to make as a condition of membership in your clubs. You could agree among yourselves to devote so much time each day to good reading. (156)

Readers take this advice to heart, often noting in their letters that they, in clubs or informal groups, want to begin "systematic study of American literature" (Jan. 1909, 102). In turn, throughout all issues of "Home Study," Cutting uses the space to teach readers how best to create a community of reading and writing women.

For Cutting, the most significant component of creating such a community was adopting collaborative reading practices dependent on the strategic division of materials and tasks among club members. Therefore, the "Home Study Club" frequently advises women to divide, or even appoint a leader to divide, a broad subject area into smaller parts, represented by individual texts, among all members of the club. The purpose of such division is both to allow the community as a whole to cover more material and to allow all members to make a contribution to a larger project. At times, Cutting offers lengthy lists not only of primary texts but of reviews and secondary sources as well, noting how each member might select different texts and report to the group.

Beyond simply recommending that clubs divide material among their members, Cutting explains how this practice can shape the content of meetings and allow club members to take responsibility for sharing knowledge with others. At one point, Cutting offers a reader advice on book selection and an introductory meeting on a historical study, then states:

> I would continue the plan of having four members give an informal talk at each meeting, and assign to each certain phases or people of the reign you are studying. For example, under Henry VII, have one member report on the establishment of the Court of the Star Chamber. (1035)

Cutting repeats similar advice throughout her responses, as she does in December 1908, when she again suggests that a group "have the members choose which of the romances each will take, and, in turn, report on the impressions each received of the book she read. In this way you will gain some knowledge of the different writings of an author" (1272). Similarly, she recommends that another group "might assign different chapters to the members of [the] club, or different sections of one chapter to several members, and in this way have instructive and interesting meetings" (1272). Here and elsewhere, Cutting emphasizes the value of working collaboratively in reading: splitting material up allows club women to expand the number of texts the group as a whole can become familiar with and, equally important, provides multiple points of inquiry for club discussions. It is also clear that the division of materials or tasks requires that individual club members have the chance to "report" back to the group on an area in which they now have some knowledge. Like Cutting, *Bazar*-inspired clubwomen should become teachers and mentors of one another.

Moreover, to successfully participate in such a collaborative study project, Cutting asserts that both communal and individual reading needs to be followed by reflection, in the form of either writing or discussion. Cutting moves beyond simply suggesting that readers take time to reflect on what they have read, usually in preparation for a club discussion; she also commonly explains to readers the reflective strategies they should use, usually advising them to review their knowledge of the text's content, and then to discuss their perceptions of the text with other club members and compare the views presented in scholarly articles. In the initial proposal for *Harper's* study club, Cutting specifies that if they are reading in a group, women should "consider how the plot is developing, the way the different characters are meeting situations, and get the opinion of each member as to what she would have done under similar conditions" (155). Late incarnations of the "Home Study Club" outline more rigorous interpretation and critique of novels, but throughout, Cutting places an emphasis on readers reflecting on their own experiences and observations to connect with the reading.

At times, Cutting helps readers by suggesting the types of themes and ideas on which they might choose to reflect. In the December 1908 issue, for instance, she recommends that a club tailor its reflections to a familiar issue and one, significantly, that might prompt an "interesting" discussion of classical depictions of gender, noting, "You would find it would be interesting to make note of the various household utensils mentioned in Homer, the ornaments for women, and the weapons for the men" (Dec. 1908, 1271). Likewise, in the October 1908 issue, she advises that each club member complete her reading by "draw[ing] a comparison of the evidences of the artistic temperament in the three types of artist—poet, musician, and painter—and make your own conclusions as to whether or not it is at variance with the moral qualities" (1035).

In this way, Cutting recommends her readers use reflection as a way to formulate their own ideas and observations; this reflective practice, moreover, forms an important part of the collaborative reading and discussions she is outlining. At times, Cutting advises that readers turn to scholarly critiques of writing techniques to further inform their reflections: "You will find it a great help to you, in all your study relating to the novel, to read and study with much care the admirable volume of Charles Horne, *The Technique of the Novel*" (1034).[7] Nonetheless, in many issues of "Home Study," Cutting makes clear that readers will derive the most benefit from their study if they take time to reflect on their own reading of a text before turning to reviews or scholarly critiques. Again, *Bazar* readers are encouraged to compare their own observations with those of others. Proposals for these kinds of reflections regularly accompany the texts Cutting recommends but are also often joined with the suggestion that readers should extend this practice by writing down their reflections and observations to prepare for club discussions.

The discussion, according to "Home Study," that readers engage in with other club women or family members is aimed at both reporting on and sharing the reading and writing the women have done on their own. Doing so, the *Bazar* makes clear, fosters better ideas to inspire critical discussion in an engaged community. Once again, Cutting not only outlines the process women should pursue but also points to its pedagogical value; discussing how women are to share their study experiences with one another, she tells readers:

> The asking of questions should be encouraged, for it will almost surely lead to further study, as when, for instance, the member who is reporting on the week's politics says Congress is assembled. Another member asks how the members of Congress are elected. If no one is able to give the information, the presiding member should require a report on it at the next meeting. It is in this way that the benefit of these clubs is so far-reaching. ("Home Reading" 155)

The "far-reaching" benefits of the club go unnamed by Cutting, though Kelley notes that socially or politically oriented women's organizations often used club work as a way "to increase their familiarity with the literate practices of legislative activity" (22). Whatever the agenda of the club discussed here, however, it is clear both that establishing this kind of discussion is intrinsically linked to forming the community and that, once again, division of work and reflection form the foundation for thoughtful, useful discussion.

Just as she gives women advice on improving their reading habits, Cutting often outlines for clubs the reflective questions they can ask individually and as a community. At one point, she recommends, "I would ask four of your members to describe the following pictures, tell the story of the lives of the artists, the circumstances under which the pictures were painted, and where they are now to be found" (Dec. 1908, 1272). For another club, she demonstrates how the group discussion can be connected to their strategic division of material, telling them:

> Agree among yourself which of the writings you will all read—The Marble Faun, for example—and devote one meeting to a discussion of the book. Contrast the characters of Miriam and Hilda. Have you any solutions for the mysteries of the story? I predict that the discussion will last above one meeting. (Dec. 1908, 1272)

Cutting's prediction that the discussion "will last above one meeting" attests to how much she and the women she is advising value their club discussions. To this end, Cutting does sometimes outline for readers how a discussion might progress, as she does in the September 1910 issue, where she explains:

> It is a good plan to assign different characters to members of your circle, and ask them to join in an informal talk at the meetings upon the characters they have studied. . . . She will be at liberty to call upon the different members for their opinions and in this way an interesting discussion will be started. (566)

It is equally clear in the advice she offers that Cutting does not simply wish to help *Bazar* readers create questions for their current study material, but that she is using "Home Study" to teach women how to conduct group study themselves. In June 1911, a reader requests help with a study topic but also indicates that her club has had difficulty generating discussions out of the papers they read. Cutting answers:

> I suggest that for your other meetings, in order to promote this [group discussion], you have one or two members prepared to ask questions which would promote a discussion. These members should be told by the writer of the paper what her subject is, and something of the manner in which she means to treat it. One member should be prepared to take the opposite position, the other to concur with the author, and you will find that if they state their points of view immediately upon the close of the paper other members will be glad of an opportunity to either agree or disagree with them. (302)

Here Cutting is not only illustrating how women should respond to the writing of fellow club members but also offering readers a model for conducting an informal class.

Most of Cutting's responses to readers involve discussions of what they would read, but she also consistently points to the reports that club members would give or the written reflections individual students should compose after reading. While papers were an important part of many women's study club, for the most part these texts were meant to be informative and preparation for speeches made at meetings (Martin); in the "Home Study Club," writing fulfilled this purpose but also represented a way for students to process and reflect on the reading they had done. All readers of the magazine are advised to keep a study journal:

> Not . . . the diary of sentiment, but rather the note-book of ideas, a place where you jot down the impressions of the day, for it clarifies one's thoughts to put them in writing. Write down also any question which occurs to you in connection with your daily reading, or some point which was not clear to you at the last club meeting, and which you wish to bring up at the next. It is in such ways that you will be of help to one another as well as to yourselves. ("Home Reading" 156)

Here and elsewhere, writing is useful for "clarifying one's thoughts" and preparing for further study and discussions with other students. The September 1908 issue of the magazine demonstrates how composition connects with women's ability to share and distribute knowledge among one another. Responding to a group studying the biographies and marriages of "great men," Cutting advises them:

> At each meeting, before commencing to read, ask one member to be prepared to give briefly a sketch of the writer. Have another member give a list of his works. . . . Then, as all these volumes are well illustrated, so enabling you to have a clear idea of the appearance of your heroes and heroines, you will be ready to hear the love stories. (913)

In this way, the reading and short reports that students prepare ahead of time contribute to the discussion and allow members to expand the material they are able to cover.

It is not uncommon, moreover, for Cutting to direct readers to compose their reflections on specific topics, as she does later in this issue, assuring another reader that "it would be helpful to have a notebook at hand and write in it your impressions of them. Make a comparison, for example, between the faithfulness of Ruth and Esther" (1154). Cutting is even more pointed about the benefits of reflection in her advice to a reader wanting to "do some systematic reading in American literature . . . to make the most of my reading so as to be able to discuss what I have read" (Jan. 1909, 102). Cutting advises:

> Think over carefully what you have read, and try and analyze what the author meant and what effect his writing has had upon you, and why. Then I would write down in a notebook the impressions I had received. This will do two things: it will help you remember what you have read and it will teach you to form judgments of literary styles. (102)

At times, readers are advised to compare their own written reflections with more scholarly critiques of a subject or author. In the April 1909 issue, for example, Cutting recommends:

> Write down from day to day . . . your own estimate of the author you have read that day. Upon reading the critical reviews of this same author note and compare your estimate and that of the reviewer, and then add that to the notes you have already made in your book. In this way you will develop your own critical faculty. (426)

Here Cutting suggests that this reflective writing practice will allow the reader to construct her own resource on literature by keeping a thorough catalog of her reading: It "will simplify your work because when you wish to refer to any one of the authors you can do so more quickly" (426).

Underlying all the advice Cutting offers readers on reflective writing and composing reports is the belief that the work they do in writing about what they have read will be a benefit to other members of their clubs; they are writing to instruct and share ideas with a community and to inspire further discussion. More important, it is by adopting these practices that readers can become active clubwomen. It is also clear that for Cutting, in undertaking responsibility to report to the club and in participating in the sharing of knowledge, clubwomen are able to exert agency and authority, if only among themselves.

If the contributors to "Home Study" granted Cutting the authority of a club leader, it is equally true that Cutting worked to negotiate and borrow from the academy a legitimizing authority for the club work she was promoting. Both Martin and Kelley explore the extent to which clubs copied and appropriated the words and structure of political and academic institutions, in part as a way to legitimize their own educational and social endeavors. In fact, Kelley found that some clubs' desire to copy parliamentary procedure—procedure, in other words, that was "official" for a powerful institution—meant that "some women actually earned a living by providing instruction in parliamentary procedure to clubwomen" (22).

It was equally common, however, for clubs to organize around academic procedures. For instance, clubs commonly referred to their study and meeting schedules as "syllabi," and although schedules varied, the *Bazar* consistently refers to a commonly recognized beginning and end to the "club year," which loosely coincided with the school year. Similarly, Welch makes note in her column of the fact that "the days of 'first meetings' are just upon the world of club women—the reassembling after the summer separation" (Oct. 1897, 819). Cataloguing the documents of clubs around the country, Martin likewise notes that the club year generally ran from September through May, like college semesters, and that moreover, "in addition to the academic discipline of regularly scheduled class meetings, required attendance, and assignments to be completed at home, clubs adopted many of the trappings of women's colleges" (68). Agreeing with the work seen in the *Bazar*, both Martin and Gere assert that club syllabi, though addressing a broad range of topics often centered on literature, also relied on the authority of college book lists and, later, the bibliographies from university extension courses (Martin 101).

Just as many clubs borrowed practices from the political or academic realm to authorize their social and educational endeavors, so too does Cutting connect the literacy practices she advocates with higher educational institutions, thereby granting these practices an "official" status. In the

April 1909 issue, for instance, Cutting advises a reader intending to study French literature:

> It is just possible that you might be able to obtain old examination papers from some of the colleges, but I rather doubt it. There is no reason, however, why you should not apply to the heads of the French department of any of the colleges and make your request. I should begin with Harvard. (426)

Similarly, Cutting occasionally suggests readers look to the reading lists put out by colleges and at times prompts readers to test their knowledge, as is the case of the woman pursuing French literature, by creating a card catalog of bibliographic information for future quick reference. She advises, "Keep a card catalogue of the books you read, the publishers, authors, and editions being noted on each card. In this way you make a bibliography for yourself" (426).

Even more frequently, however, rather than suggest readers rely on the content or reading lists of colleges, Cutting simply adopts the practices of a classroom. She recommends a self-designed syllabus, for instance, for a group wishing to read Shakespeare:

> The following outline will serve for your programme, and you will be able to assign to different members single topics which they will read papers upon at the meeting of the club. England in Shakespeare's Time: (a) The historical setting; (b) The literary setting. 2. Stratford and Shakespeare's surroundings: (a) Early life and school-days; (b) Marriage and London life; (c) Retirement and Stratford. 3. The Elizabethan Theatre: Read. *William Shakespeare*, George Brandes, Chapter XV. 4. "The Merchant of Venice": (a) Sources of the Place; (b) Outline of the play—the main theme. 5. Study of the characters—Antonio, Bassanio, Shylock, Portia. Mark the scenes and lines which describe these characters. What impression do you get of Portia's personal appearance? What are her chief characteristics? Give the scenes and lines. I have given the outline for one play, but this may be applied to any that you may read. (Dec. 1908, 1271)

What is significant here is that, as Martin, Gere, and White note in their histories, part of what defined the literacy practices of women's clubs (or any other extracurricular group) is that they were pursuing an education without a formal instructor or the kind of authority figure or figures that would be part of any institutional setting. The lack of such an institutional authority is what often delegitimized the scholarly work of clubwomen. For this reason, according to Gere and Martin, clubwomen often "borrowed" the authority of schools by making use of their book lists and strategies. Kelley and White, at the same time, document how clubwomen also studied and adopted legislative practices, likewise drawing on the legitimacy of the state to organize their own club work.

Here, however, Cutting sets *Harper's Bazar* up as having a similar legitimizing power, albeit one that exists in the popular rather than academic realm. More important, readers are encouraged to work collaboratively and become authorities for one another. Even as Cutting, rather like a teacher, marks out plans of study for interested readers, she then urges women, in their future study endeavors, to draw inspiration from their own discussions, the proposed programs of other clubs, and their own reading when deciding meeting agendas and strategies. At the same time, however, Cutting reminds readers in nearly every issue, often more than once, that the "Home Study Club" is itself a scholarly resource for book references and study plans; over and over, Cutting tells recipients, "I shall be very glad to hear from time to time how your work progresses and also if there will be any way in which the Home Study Club can help you." More pointedly, she notes:

> The following outline of work which I send you I hope will be helpful, but if any questions arise which seem difficult, or if there is anything confusing about the outline, I shall be glad to give you explanations of it. (426; Mar. 1909, 312)

In this way, Cutting portrays herself not only as an informational source but also, through statements like those above and assurances such as "I have outlined a sufficient amount work to keep your members busy for the meetings the rest of the year" (312), as both a teacher and fellow club member, a role to which her readers can and should also aspire.

Harper's Bazar was certainly not the only magazine or newspaper to include departments advising subscribers to read certain books or study certain subjects; as Cutting's note in the original issue suggests, readers were—without the prompting of a designated "study" column—accustomed to seeking this kind of advice from popular magazines, and probably the *Journal* in particular. What is different about the *Bazar* is the inclusion of a space for lengthy and specific plans for reading, study, and composing in a collaborative community of women. *Harper's Bazar*, like other magazines, blended institutional beliefs on pedagogy and literature from the academy with the philosophies and goals of the women's club movement, as well as texts and issues of interest circulating in popular culture, and for many

Americans, this hybrid source was important for shaping the literacy events and self-improvement plans practiced at home. However, for "Home Study," the authoritative role Cutting assumed was one that *Bazar* readers could also assume as clubwomen.

Community and Agency in the *Bazar*

Just as the "Home Study Club" makes clear to readers that part of taking the study they do seriously involves connecting that reading with a community, so too do other columns throughout *Harper's Bazar* support the idea that engaging with the magazine, as a reader or a contributor, means connecting with a community. Cutting makes this necessity apparent from the beginning of "Home Study" by claiming that "the main purpose of the department will always be kept in view—the establishing among Bazar readers of a fellowship in the realm of books" ("Home Reading" 154). For Cutting, the textual community in the "Home Study Club" is analogous to the physical communities the magazine is urging readers to create in their educational endeavors. Thus the tone and structure of her department are established so that

> all matters pertaining to books or study we will discuss through the pages of the Bazar in that familiar friendly spirit which would prevail were we gathered around the library table with its shaded lamp and the answering glow from the fire. (156)

The image Cutting creates is both domestic and intimate, but it also articulates a guideline for readers that is and has been supported throughout discussions of literacy and education in the magazine: that the literacy practices "Home Study Club" readers take up will be part of a social exchange in the pages of the *Bazar* and among their families and neighbors. This perspective is visible not just in the "Home Study" department in the editor's responses to correspondents; it is equally visible in the written contributions of young women in "Our Girls' Exchange." The social literacy values that form the foundation for the reading practices Cutting advocates also appear in the reader-submitted writing published by the magazine. Significantly, as well, the framing of "Our Girls' Exchange" situates its contributors as clubwomen, appearing, at least, to give them the agency and autonomy Cutting hopes her readers will assume in their club discussions.

"Our Girls' Exchange" was a reader-sustained advice column for young women that began running in December 1909 under the title "Our Girls." In December 1910, the "Our Girls" column shifted from being an advice column headed by Anna Ogden with periodic editor commentary to a column exclusively calling for the contributions of readers. In 1911, the column shifted its title to "Our Girls' Exchange" and began printing contributors' names beneath their letters. The column covered a variety of subjects including fashion, school and reading, advice on boyfriends and engagements, and health. Although each contribution appeared under a title supplied by the editor, after 1911 the column ceased naming the editor; each writer, on the other hand, was identified by her initials and her city and state. Although this column did not outline a purpose and method, as the editor of the "Home Study Club" had done, "Our Girls" did suggest the value of young readers contributing their writing and knowledge to others in a textual club within the *Bazar* community. The description of the column that heads each issue indicates:

> Our girl readers are invited to fill this department every other month. Their contributions will be paid for at the usual space rates. Each contribution should cover, in not more than 200 words, some special interest or discovery of the writer which she believes will appeal strongly to other girls.

Whatever the motives of the magazine, the fact that "girl readers" would be paid the "usual space rates" for their contributions suggests that, within the column at least, their writing is valued. In contrast to the correspondence department in the *Journal*, "Just among Ourselves," where readers have had to "purchase" space from Bok, *Bazar*'s "Our Girls" appears to operate with a considerably different view of its readers contributions to the magazine community. Spatially, both columns coexisted on pages filled with advertisements, though this was true of many other magazine departments as well. However, I would argue that it is the *Bazar*'s clublike atmosphere that shapes the treatment of its young contributors' work, as "Our Girls" is clearly modeled on the ideals that shape the "Home Study Club" Cutting identifies for assumedly older readers. As they would in a club, the words and thoughts of clubwomen have value within the magazine.

In the column, writers acknowledge their sense of purpose for contributing to the clublike community of "Our Girls" by outlining a purpose for their advice or knowledge and suggesting and responding to the topical concerns of the column. Although the young women whose writing appears in "Our Girls" are not working collaboratively to read and examine a subject, they do work collaboratively to define and populate the advice column. In doing so, writers overtly acknowledge their understanding of an audience community and the purpose their writing holds for that audience. The description of the column notes that interested readers should compose on topics of "some special interest or discovery of the writer which she believes will appeal strongly to other girls." It is obvious, in most of the compositions printed in the column, not only that writers have made use of this advice but that they have often felt the need to articulate this appeal in their writing, demonstrating both their conception of the needs to the other "girls" in the column and the value of their own written contribution. In the July 1910 issue, L.B.W. of Brooklyn begins her discussion of finding a job in bookbinding by making clear, "I think that many girls who read the Bazar may find the experience of a friend of mine interesting and perhaps helpful" (456). Other writers are even more specific than L.B.W. in that they name particular audience populations that will most appreciate their advice; in the March 1911 issue, for instance, one L.G. states that "the business girl, who is obliged to stick close to the store or office all day[,] . . . is likely to appreciate this suggestion," while V.M.H. notes, "I believe that this will interest high school girls" (149).

The contributions are obviously focused on relating specific advice or, at times, explaining a topic, such as bookbinding, about which the writer feels she possesses some expertise. It is equally true, however, that the writers in "Our Girls" are relatively consistent about making clear the value of their topic, even if only to point out, "Here is a suggestion for the girl who has but little to spend for the pleasure of gift-giving" (May 1911, 251). In the place of an editor doling out advice to readers, "Our Girls' Exchange" has writers who openly call on the knowledge of contributors, shaping the content of the column by making requests for information and responding to other writers. "One of Four," for example, asks in the March 1911 issue, "Will some girls who live together tell me, through the Exchange, how they manage the matter of visitors?" (149). At the same time, A.B.S. in May 1911 addresses an issue raised in a previous column, stating, "Apropos of the question suggested in the Girls' Exchange some time ago: I agree with the girl's mother" (215). Even when they do not respond directly to the requests, topics, and questions posed in previous issues of the magazine, contributors to "Our Girls" still respond to the techniques and style of other contributors, clearly building on the success of previous readers who have gotten their writing published.

As the column progresses over time, the scope of the contributions becomes more systematic, so that the most common form of contribution addresses a practical difficulty and offers advice—on such matters as how to fix a dress, handle gentlemen callers or a long engagement, or pay for schooling. Moreover, the issues on which advice is given move in trends.

Over time, clothing and questions on social situations, such as how to remember new faces at a party, become the most popular topics. In this way, while the official description of the department leaves the content largely open, and in the first issues the compositions cover a broader range of topics, over time readers establish a loose agenda, noting often how these topics suit the needs of the readers in their community.

Editors and Clubwomen

It is not surprising, perhaps, that the writing by young women published in "Our Girls' Exchange" so closely resembles in tone and style the rest of the material in the *Bazar*—editors naturally chose contributions suited to the agenda of the magazine, and the young women no doubt modeled their writing not just on one another's contributions but also on what they read in other parts of the magazine, encouraged by advice on social letter writing offered by Cutting and others. It is equally true, however, that by not only inviting young readers to publish their work in a nationally circulating magazine but also offering to pay for their contributions, the *Bazar* was strongly encouraging young women to participate with the magazine and guiding them toward the kind of activity Cutting and Welch endorse for older readers in their respective columns. "Our Girls" thus joined "Home Study Club" and "Club Women and Club Work" in initiating readers into the values and practices of women's clubs. In fact, in many respects, the *Bazar* acts as a means of promoting the kinds of practices and ideals already espoused by many, for the illustration of club work in Welch's column and the instruction featured in Cutting's column fall closely in line with the critical understanding of women's clubs visible in scholarly histories. The contribution offered by the *Bazar* is that it moves the literacy work of women's clubs from the intimate realm of the clubs and brings it to a nationally circulating outlet. Further, in introducing and instructing new audiences in the reading and writing practices of clubs, the *Bazar* ultimately influences those very practices.

This is not to assert that what is called the "women's club movement" was not already highly publicized and organized, as is evident in organizations such as the General Federation of Women's Clubs, or that clubs did not already have the means to circulate texts beyond their own circles of members. Women's clubs already had their own publications, which, in addition to publishing the papers club women had presented to one another, also offered similar advice to that seen in "Home Study Club," as Gere, Kelley, and Joan Marie Johnson in "'Drill into Us . . . the Rebel Tradition': The Contest over Southern Identity in Black and White Women's Clubs,

South Carolina, 1898–1930," all discuss. Nonetheless, the *Bazar*, unlike club journals, even ones that circulated broadly, was aimed at a much larger audience, and one, more importantly, that was not already composed of club women. The *Bazar* thereby took responsibility for soliciting new participants in club work and demonstrating how they should interact.

By outlining and explaining women's club practices to new audiences, the *Bazar* brings a club-inspired definition of advanced literacy and a clubwoman literacy identity to a national readership. Even more pointedly, in adapting its club-oriented conception of literacy to letter-writing advice and interactions in the correspondence columns, the *Bazar* taught readers to embrace the identity of a clubwoman in literacy events outside club work. In this, too, the *Bazar* may have mirrored the tendencies of actual women's organizations. In her consideration of southern women's clubs at the turn of the century, Johnson finds that these organizations played an important role not only in the identification of individual members but also in the formation of regional and racial identity, shaping "understanding of what it meant to be black or white in the post-bellum South" (526).

For the South Carolina clubwomen Johnson studied, the creation of new postbellum identity constructions for women was connected to clubs' sense of purpose (reform work, in most cases) and, for white clubwomen especially, entailed the blending of old ideals with an emerging sense of identity. Likewise, although the *Bazar* does not present a singular social agenda for women's clubs in general, the magazine does connect to its illustration of the *Bazar* clubwoman a general sense of purpose for club-based literacy that allows editors to appeal to and blend with a range of ideals about modern American womanhood. In this respect, the *Bazar*, like the *Journal*, succeeds because of its flexibility. In *The American New Woman Revisited: A Reader, 1894–1930*, Martha H. Patterson surveys a diverse collection of turn-of-the-century periodical articles, including one by Bok, discussing the New Woman and contends that the emergence of the concept of the New Woman was complex, in part because writers "agreed that women were changing, but they contested the direction that change should take as its meaning" (2). In articulating the purpose for and value of women's club literacy in broad terms—in particular, forming stronger relationships among women, creating a fulfilling space for intellectual endeavors, and fostering a woman's ability to be useful within a community—the *Bazar* situates itself as both progressive and moderate.

Still, according to the *Bazar*'s definition, the reading and writing practices promoted by and modeled in "Our Girls," "Home Study," and "Club

Women and Club Work" give women a great deal of agency, urging readers to believe they are responsible for deciding on and executing their own study programs and, more important, that they must act not simply as students but as teachers as well. Within the club model the magazine illustrates, women learn to construct agendas to teach themselves and one another. Like the *Journal*, then, the *Bazar* offers its readers the promise of some degree of agency and even authority in their literate lives.

Where the *Bazar* moves beyond the *Journal*, however, is in demonstrating how certain literacy practices can allow women to form and act from communities. Even so, although the *Bazar* is unusual in designing so much of its content around the values and practices of clubs, it is not the only site empowering readers to pursue advanced literacy in collaboration with others. As I discuss in the next chapter, farming journals also encourage readers to see themselves as valuable participants in a literate community advancing agriculture as a profession. *Michigan Farmer*, especially, was invested in promoting and reporting the club activity of reading circles, farmers' clubs, and Grange groups. While *Michigan Farmer* does not do the kind of work the *Bazar* undertakes in educating readers into club practices, it does introduce readers to the values of the reading and discussion habits of different kinds of clubs. For example, in a column called "Home Chats with Farmer's Wives," the editor observes:

> Our readers have been prompt to give suggestions concerning clubs and reading circles, (two very interesting ones being described in this number), and these cannot fail to be encouraging to those who have no such advantages, that is it will help to stimulate them to start one in their own community. (Feb. 1898, 112)

It is common, too, for *Michigan Farmer* to offer reports on various clubs and reading groups, continually suggesting that readers need to be interested in these kinds of activities. In "Neighborhood Literary Societies," for instance, the editors explains that

> the practicality and advantages of a "Young People's Reading Society" in every neighborhood, have already been presented in these columns. Now that we are about going into winter quarters, it is time to organize. The interest in literary matters awakened by such societies is usually very great, study and thought are induced, the attrition of mind upon mind sharpens the intellect, while the social benefits are not to be ignored. (7)

Farming journals depended on their own constructions of a community within the text and within the profession to assert a more powerful role for farmers and rural communities in a new economy. In this way, *Harper's Bazar*, in conjunction with other widely circulating magazines, disseminated an outline of advanced literacy work that required readers to connect with other readers, but it moved beyond this to coach women in putting this outline into practice as clubwomen.

4.

Special Invitation to Write: Magazine Readers as Contributors

No agricultural paper in the land has begun to do as much as The Ohio Farmer has in the way of hunting up men and women unknown as writers, and making them known in tens of thousands of farm houses through the value of their writings. We seem to ourselves almost as eager to discover writers of that kind as Columbus was to discover America, or Grant to find a way to Richmond. Of all things we would not discourage any writer who has valuable facts or experience to communicate.

—*Ohio Farmer*, August 15, 1895

In an article simply titled "Farm Experience" in the November 1880 issue of the *Ohio Farmer*, the editor reminds readers of his "standing invitation" for them to contribute to any and all departments in the magazine. He recognizes, however, that his audience now consists of thousands of readers "who have never had a special invitation to write" (293). The *Ohio Farmer* sets out to amend this omission by ensuring that farmers and their families, "the learned and the illiterate," understand their responsibility to contribute to and participate in publications such as the *Ohio Farmer*. In hopes that readers recognize the knowledge and authority farmers possess about what the magazine sees as the developing scientific industry of agriculture, its editors ensure that the *Ohio Farmer* consists in large part of reader contributions, imploring the audience, "Let no one hesitate to write because he has not been educated at college" (293).

The call expressed here is not unique to the *Ohio Farmer*. A wide range of farming publications at this time urge farmers to contribute to the agricultural press, visibly connecting involvement in an agricultural community with improved literacy. For these farming publications, therefore, the readers' interaction with the magazine was both a part of their literacy education and an important component of their development as participants in an advancing agricultural community. To this end, the editors of (and contributors to) these magazines took responsibility for advocating the particular ways the magazine was to be read and constructed by its audience. This engagement with the magazine was illustrated as being a part of readers' lifelong education in agriculture and participation in the welfare of their community—the two primary goals for literacy education reinforced by these publications. These values formed the foundation for how farming journals justified the purpose of advanced literacy for their readers and underscored the discourse values outlined by the magazines.

Ultimately, in placing so much importance on the contributions of their reading audience, two particular farming magazines, the *Maine Farmer* and the *Ohio Farmer*, went further in soliciting compositions by intervening in the literacy education of readers, insisting that magazine readers needed to be taught how to become writers for the agricultural press. In this mission, these two journals provided readers with a journal-specific definition of good writing that valued content over style, brevity over length, and above all fact-based discourse designed to inform readers. Moreover, these journals intervened in what they saw as an imperative moment in American agriculture and rural life, crafting a new professional identity for farmers that required them to become literate participants in a scientific profession. In the sections that follow, I consider the numerous articles contained in *Maine* and *Ohio* that sought to both encourage and teach prospective writers, focusing on the writing practices they fostered and the farm-writer identity they insisted was vital for the advancement of rural communities.

Two recent collections by Kim Donehower, Charlotte Hogg, and Eileen E. Schell, *Rural Literacies* and *Reclaiming the Rural: Essays on Literacy, Rhetoric, and Pedagogy*, examine sites, practices, and sponsors of literacy in rural communities. In doing so, they articulate a definition for "rural literacies" that highlights "the particular kinds of literate skills needed to achieve the goals of sustaining life in rural areas" (*Rural Literacies* 4). Donehower, Hogg, and Schell are especially interested in analyzing and advocating critical pedagogies that are sustainable: that consider how rural literacies adapt to new needs in rural communities (*Rural Literacies* 155). As I consider, before the end of the nineteenth century, readers and editors of farm publications were already concerned with definitions of literacy that valued the efforts of farm writers. That these publications were so critical of the pedagogies and literacy identities that did not empower rural voices or support the values of the agricultural profession—and were simultaneously so intent on sponsoring new rural writers—demonstrates that our more current concern with rural literacy and extracurricular practices has a long history.

Turn-of-the-Century Farming Publications

My understanding of farm journals is informed by an investigation of six publications in print at the turn of the century: the *Ohio Farmer*, the *Maine Farmer*, the *Michigan Farmer*, *Farmer's Home Journal*, *New England Farmer*, and the *Southern Planter*. These publications vary widely in longevity, geography, and readership: the *Southern Planter* and *New England Farmer* circulated regionally, whereas the others are state-specific, and though most have disappeared, *Ohio Farmer* and *Michigan Farmer* are still in publication through Farm Progress, a company that grew out of the *American Farmer* magazine. As a result, I concentrate on *Ohio* (1852 to present) and *Maine* (1833 to 1924), in part because of their longevity and availability. Although they reveal differences in terms of tone and content that I point to later, the *Maine Farmer* and the *Ohio Farmer* are alike in their perceptions of their rural audiences, their emphasis on a specific state community, and their relation to other, similar agricultural journals popular in the mid to late nineteenth century. These two journals also stand out, moreover, for the *amount* of attention they give to writing. It is likely that other journals either not preserved or not available digitally give equal attention to writing. That farm journals in general sought reader contributions and two journals of a collection of six devoted closer concern to writing suggest that this kind of pedagogical work in agricultural publications was neither ubiquitous nor obsolete.

The growth of agricultural journals coincides with the growth of farm Granges and other agricultural societies, the appearance of agricultural colleges and extension programs, and the birth of the Progressivist-inspired Country Life movement. In addition to Granges, local farm clubs and state and national agricultural societies also increased in size in the late nineteenth century. Participation in farmers' clubs and agricultural societies necessitated literacy skills that the journals I studied are quick to argue mirror the skills editors wish to promote. Like the journals, these associations were composed not only of those living in rural areas but also of urban-based participants, and they included dentists, businessmen, and professors in addition to farmers, as Gerald Prescott finds in his study of Wisconsin agricultural organizations. Members would have read and drafted constitutions and bylaws, and prepared reports and newsletters. In fact, many farm journals originally grew out of the more local publications of farm and rural societies. Thus the publications I investigated were not the only platform for discussions of farming and rural life, nor the only outlets for the writing of rural people. They were, however, among the most persistent and widely circulating. John J. Fry estimates that the circulation of agricultural journals increased from 1 million in 1880 to 5.5 million in 1895 to 17 million in 1920 (36–37). He cites a 1914 Department of Agriculture survey that

> revealed that many more farmers received farm newspapers than received government agricultural bulletins, attended farmers' institutes, or made use of a government demonstration agent. When surveyed as to which source of information was most helpful for their work, farmers reported farm newspapers twice as often as all other sources combined. (35)

In short, agricultural journals were popular and influential texts at the turn of the century.

At this time, farming publications saw it as their purpose to educate and inform their rural readers not only on farming matters but also on issues surrounding the household and, especially, important matters of state government. In terms of content, farming journals and newspapers obviously included a great deal of material on livestock, crops, agricultural machinery, and Grange meetings, but they also included sections devoted to children, household matters, and local social issues. Like the *Journal* and the *Bazar*, farming journals were complex texts divided into very different departments with a range of editors, readers, and contributors.

In particular, *Maine* and *Ohio* employed a large number of "department" editors responsible for the various sections within the journal. A few of these editors are named in individual issues; however, as not all articles are signed, it is not possible to trace many editors individually. It is clear, however, from Fry's history and from the Ohio State Grange's *Centennial History of the Junior Grange in Ohio*, that department editors no longer worked as farmers but were often associated with agricultural associations and institutions. For instance, while Harriet Mason was the editor of the Women's Department of *Ohio* (1896–1900), she was also leading the first Junior Grange in Ohio.

Mortimer Lawrence, *Ohio*'s owner and publisher from 1873 to 1921, worked only briefly as a farmer and instead pursued agricultural publishing as a career, also establishing *Michigan Farmer* and *Pennsylvania Farmer*. From 1878 to 1900, *Maine* had George Twitchell for its managing editor, a dentist who, after briefly owning a farm, began studying and promoting the science of agriculture. The agricultural editor, on the other hand, was Z. A. Gilbert, who held positions on the Maine State Board of Agriculture and in a number of other societies and characterized himself as "a farmer and a laborer," saying, "I have left my flocks and herds to other hands while I meet with you" (220). Like Lawrence in *Ohio*, Gilbert espoused Progressive views of agriculture, contending, "We must, then, educate the coming farmer.... Though farming be our vocation, reading and study should be our recreation" (228).

While contributors to farming journals debated education continually, they did so in a manner far different from what is visible in the nationally circulating women's magazines. The women's magazines I consider occasionally offer examples of specific schooling experiences, but they deal more frequently with larger ideals and educational issues. In contrast, state- or community-specific farming journals do not separate debates over education from the specific circumstances of their more local audiences. As with everything else in these journals, debates over schooling center on particular contextual subjects. Contributors to *Michigan, Southern Planter, New England Farmer, Farmer's Home Journal, Maine,* and *Ohio* are as concerned with the practical matters of what happens in their schools as they are with the very real question of how parents and taxpayers are paying for that education—in both money and time—listing actual tax rates and book prices where necessary.

While *Harper's Bazar* and the *Ladies' Home Journal* envisioned a middle-class, urban, female audience, farming publications needed to cater to the entire family. Even if, as in the case of the *Ohio Farmer*, the majority of the publication emphasizes farming matters and Youth and Household sections are separated into spaces overtly assigned to the women and children of the family, farming magazines nonetheless assumed that the audience for each issue of the magazine was a family, rather than an individual. In *Maine Farmer*, this is even more apparent, with the journal striking a balance between pointed discussions of crops and livestock and items devoted to family and community matters. *Harper's Bazaar* may address a relatively consistent "she," but the *Farmer*s speak to "boys and girls," "sisters," and fellow farmers or Grange members in every issue. In general, this audience make-up was typical for other farming publications, both those specific to other states and the larger national magazines.

Moreover, agricultural magazines imagined an audience that did not have the leisure time or disposable income that their *Journal* and *Bazaar* counterparts were assumed to possess. This is not to say that *Farmer* readers were not also subscribers to the *Bazaar* or *Journal*; in fact, given the circulation figures for the *Journal*, some of them certainly were. However, while both *Harper's Bazaar* and *Ladies' Home Journal* made obviously class-based assumptions about their female readers—that they were the wives and daughters of professional men, that higher education for men was a given and higher education for women a not impossible ideal, and that women did not need to work outside the home—this group of farming journals made very different assumptions about their audiences. In short, articles in farming publications demonstrated that editors imagined their readers did not have much leisure time, that all male and female members of the family needed to contribute to farm labor, and that education, while important, was a luxury beyond the primary years—"as only six out of every one hundred children have the advantage of what we call higher education, the important question arises, what is the duty of the State to the ninety-four percent?" ("Rural School Problem" 402).

Paired with the genuine concern journals regularly expressed for the basic educational opportunities offered within the state—whether in common schools, libraries, or Grange organizations—were the two somewhat divergent beliefs that a classical higher education was suspect in its ability to adequately prepare young men for lives in farming communities and that farmers and their families needed to embrace more advanced education to keep pace with the rest of the nation. Both beliefs, as I explore later, overtly shaped the kind of literacy work the magazines sponsored for the benefit of their readers. In 1884, for instance, *Michigan Farmer* outlines many of the fears also expressed in other agricultural journals about the compatibility of a classical college education for farmers' sons and the corresponding desirability of an education at an agricultural college. S.N.B. of Lansing, a contributor,[1] asserts:

> As soon as we farmers can get rid of the foolish notion, that there is no thorough education without a knowledge of the classics, the sooner will we feel able to give a greater number of our sons a thoroughly practical training that will be helpful to them on the farm, or in the office or factory. ("Education of Our Boys" 1)

For S.N.B., "a college course arranged and a college equipped especially for their benefit" is more practical not only financially but also academically, as he believes that it is at universities, unlike technical or agricultural colleges, "where scientific courses are esteemed inferior to the classical" (1). Part of the value of a scientific and experience-based education, according to farming journals, is that it should not preclude literary and rhetorical advancement. S.N.B., remarking on the orations given at a recent graduation from an agricultural college, claims:

> We have proof that the accuracy of thought and expression, which must be exercised in every day's work, in the laboratory and class-room and work on the farm, lead to as elegant and forcible use of language as can be acquired by the old classical courses, which have long been claimed as essentials to good writing and forcible oratory. (1)

While these journals addressed the entire family, their primary target was adult (male) farmers,[2] an audience they presumed had been educated at the primary level but may not have been adequately prepared to enter the new scholastic community of agriculture that the journals so adamantly wanted readers to embrace. S.N.B. argues:

> It must be admitted that if the educated farmer is to make his influence most felt, and if he is to hold his place alongside that of the men in other professions, he must become a forcible speaker as well as writer. (1)

At the same time, in *Michigan Farmer*, the editor makes clear that "it is a question of whether the farmer is to 'keep up with the procession.' If he is to do so, his children must be better educated than he was" ("Editor's Table" 422). Just as the editors at the *Journal* and the *Bazar* saw themselves as reaching out to an audience of readers experiencing great change in their culture and economy, as well as in the roles they assume, so too did the editors at agricultural journals address a community of readers that, they believed, needed to adapt to a new climate. In his history of rural life, *Born in the Country*, David B. Danbom observes that the type of concern expressed in *Michigan* and *Ohio* was part of a wider trend that would have reflected the feelings of many readers in rural areas:

> While they [farmers] enjoyed lives of greater material abundance than their parents or grandparents had, they felt themselves at the mercy of an economic system whose rules they could not influence. . . . To live in the countryside in 1900 was to have the sense that the nation was passing you by, leaving you behind, ignoring you at best and derogating you at worst. (134)

All of the farming journals I investigated emphasize approaching agriculture as a science and promoted educational and intellectual efforts on the part of farmers as a means of improving the profession and rural life. This community purpose—of adopting a professional, scientific approach to farming to elevate agriculture—shaped the journals, the literacy practices they promoted, and the identities they wanted readers to assume as writers. The journals connected with the general beliefs of the Country Life movement that became visible after 1900. Danbom, in "Rural Education Reform and the Country Life Movement," advises against viewing the Country Life movement, which encompassed a wide range of focuses and efforts, as a singular philosophy; generally speaking, however, proponents of the movement aimed to improve the quality and efficiency of life in rural areas (462–65). Liberty Hyde Bailey, the chair of the Commission on Country Life in America, defines the movement as "a world-motive to even up society as between country and city; for it is generally understood that country life has not reached as high development within its sphere as city life has reached within its sphere" (1). Bailey and other Country Lifers, as both I. Moriah McCracken in "'I Pledge My Head to Clearer Thinking': The Hybrid Literacy of 4-H Record Books" and Danbom attest, made educational efforts a primary concern and equally emphasized "extracurricular" learning through extension work and 4-H clubs.

It is apparent, however, that in their desire for rural areas to reach the same "sphere as city life" and "keep pace" with the rest of the nation, Bailey and the journals partially reinscribe the very devaluation of rural life they seek to eliminate. In *Born in the Country*, Danbom notes that even as country life advocates "sought to professionalize farming[, they] unconsciously conceded the correctness of the urban standard of value" (151). The journals promote the development of agriculture science to the extent that farmers who refuse to adopt scientific practices are denigrated, making clear the extent to which they carry the "ideological freight" Deborah Brandt describes in her theory of "literacy sponsors" (20). Editors, and even contributors, overtly link the literacy practices and identity they are promoting with their agenda for agricultural and rural life. While *Maine* and *Ohio* published articles articulating opposing views on farm matters, on issues of writing and literacy all appear in agreement. Because editors selected which contributions to print, it is uncertain how fully readers agreed with the perspectives on literacy visible in *Maine* and *Ohio*. Brandt asserts that "although the interests of the sponsor and the sponsored do not have to converge (and, in fact, may conflict), sponsors nevertheless set the terms for access to literacy and wield powerful incentives for compliance and loyalty" (19); the fact that both publications found willing contributors suggests journal subscribers either agreed or were willing to work within the publications' terms. Fry, speaking of readers' adoption of the farm practices advocated in journals, argues that "farmers' correspondence with farm newspapers and their actions show that they selectively adopted and adapted any advice" (36). It seems likely that readers would adopt a similar approach in their reaction to articles containing advice on writing.

At the very least, contributors are especially vocal in their belief that advanced writing skills did not necessarily grow out of formal education, but rather out of domestic reading habits, participation in the intellectual work of clubs and Granges, and active interaction with and contribution to the farming journals. In this respect, as I explore in greater detail later, farm journals argued for pedagogies and writing styles that valued the experiences and habits of rural readers. For the editors of and contributors to the agricultural press, writing instruction needed to be connected to rural contexts and practices. Agricultural journals such as *Maine* and *Ohio* certainly sought to encourage participation, but they also maintained a very specific vision of *how* contributors would write and participate and thereby limited the options available to writers.

It is equally true, however, that in outlining discourse values specific to rural audiences, editors sought to empower writers and practices they believed were distinctly rural or agricultural. *Ohio* and *Maine* in particular frame their calls for readers to become writers as a more literate form of the intellectual interaction in which any "good farmer" already engages. In *Maine Farmer*'s "Book Farming," a contributor, W, situates the discussion of farming practices as a naturally occurring learning experience, claiming that "a good farmer leans over the fence to rest and talk with his neighbor, and they tell each other the what and how of their crops. It's a cheery talk, and they learn mutually" (1). He adds that "when it is in print it is only that talk over the fence dressed up a little for a larger audience, and a good many learn by it instead of one" (1). For W and other contributors and editors, reading and contributing to the journal are merely responsible extensions of the educational "talk over the fence." In this way, the relationship between the journals and contributors was reciprocal: the journals offered a platform for farmers' voices and the promise of professionalization, while they were paid in readership, cheap articles, and a reinforcement of their vision of agriculture and literacy. Considering the literacy practices sponsored by 4-H clubs in the late twentieth century, McCracken asserts that historians of rural literacies need to consider how even bureaucratic practices that visibly restrict literacy experiences can still be meaningful and prepare writers for more complex writing tasks later (139–40). It is clear that the agricultural journals' singular purpose for farm writers did not leave visible, printable room for alternative possibilities. Nonetheless, journals supported readers in exploring one kind of writing, and it is possible that readers may have connected this to other practices they encountered in academic and social settings or may have tailored the publications' agenda to their own.

Imploring readers to "let no one hesitate to write because he has not been educated at college," editors and contributors in *Maine* and *Ohio* ultimately encourage readers to extend their "talk over the fence" and in doing so point to a set of discursive values specific to the agricultural press: that content should be educational and derived from experience, and the language accessible to all. Articles between 1875 and 1905 forward an identity and set of writing practices for farmers that simultaneously reinforce certain limitations, even as they offer readers a strategy for entering the conversation ("Farm Experience" 293).

Defining the Farmer Farmer

For both *Ohio* and *Maine*, the call for farmers and members of their families to write for the journal is important to their most foundational publication objectives: to provide an educational resource for those involved in agricultural work, to promote the field of agriculture as a science, and to encourage readers to adopt the literacy identity of a professional "book" farmer. To accomplish such goals, *Ohio* continuously publishes "invitations" for readers to write, reminding the audience that the quality of the journal is determined by its readers' interaction with it and with one another. To this end, *Maine* and *Ohio* spend a great deal of time defining what they saw as the new professional farmer, emphasizing that this farmer was one who embraced and contributed to the goals and values of the agricultural press. Arguing that the *Farmer* farmer was an experienced practitioner concerned about his community, these journals encourage readers to adopt the role of the farm writer.

The role agricultural organizations and networks played in creating, or re-creating, a communal identity for rural communities is explored by Chambers in his dissertation on the Granger movement in Illinois. Chambers, like Danbom and the contributors to *Ohio* and *Michigan*, cites the rise of the Granger movement and rhetorical identity constructions as, in part, a product of a changing economic and technological landscape, asserting

One of the features that illustrated the work of farmers embracing the scientific or experimental approach to farming advocated by the journals. *Ohio Farmer* 98.11 (September 13, 1900), 1; copyright © 2016, Penton Media, 121033:0116SH. Copy of image made available by the History, Philosophy, and Newspaper Library of the University of Illinois Libraries.

that "the Granger movement united individual farmers as a collective entity, allowing them to effectively address the economic, industrial, commercial, and political issues that threatened their status" (21). Chambers examines how Illinois Granger rhetoric negotiated and combined traditional agrarian myths with an emerging rhetoric of class to construct a "yeoman class" composed of two "complementary personae, the farmers as revolutionaries and the farmers as stewards of the people" (210). These personae provided the "yeoman class" with a place in contemporary American landscape by allowing "farmers to constitute themselves as the agricultural class, an organized, collective identity with the political and economic power to overthrow organized capital's system of oppression" (201–2). For the Illinois Granger movement, as for the farm journals I examine, the construction of a collective identity for farmers was a vital part of advancing and professionalizing the agricultural community. For the agricultural periodicals, as textual communities within the larger agricultural community, promoting the scientific, or "book," farmer meant constructing it as a literacy identity. It was imperative, then, for journals such as *Michigan*, *Maine*, and *Ohio* to both encourage readers to adopt this identity and teach them how to do so.

For *Ohio*, in fact, the policy of "discovering" (or creating) farm writers was a point of pride. In an 1895 issue, the editor boasts:

> No agricultural paper in the land has begun to do as much as The Ohio Farmer has in the way of hunting up men and women unknown as writers, and making them known in tens of thousands of farm houses through the value of their writings. We seem to ourselves almost as eager to discover writers of that kind as Columbus was to discover America, or Grant to find a way to Richmond. ("King's English—Once More" 130)

Ohio Farmer "hunts" these unknown writers repeatedly, showing readers the service they can undertake for the agricultural community. The "value of their writings" is stressed again and again as being educational for both reader and writer. In "The King's English—Once More," the editor makes this clear, citing the inherent value of the experience and expertise readers may convey to fellow farmers through their compositions, adding that "of all things we would not discourage any writer who has valuable facts or experience to communicate" (130).

Although lengthy invitations to write are not common in *Maine Farmer*, the journal nonetheless makes clear that members of its audience are encouraged, and even expected, to want to contribute, as is visible in editorials and frequent articles giving advice to contributors. Like *Ohio*, *Maine Farmer* articulates the purpose of readers' contributions in terms of the value they may hold for other readers and the community at large. In an 1877 article, "Writing for the Public," one reader-contributor, Quercus Alba, offers his understanding of the journal's perspectives on the value of compositions by explaining that

> what young farmers want is practical advice from practical men, men whose opinions they are bound to respect. There are farmers who with their pens, can, in an hour, impart to the young farmer as much on a certain subject as they can learn in a lifetime of study and experience. And what a great benefit to the beginner to commence with the advantage of the experience of a lifetime gained in this manner. (1)

Alba echoes the editor of *Ohio* in suggesting that the writers, and farm professionals, the journal is seeking already exist among readers, further implying that what defines this person is practical experience and the desire to be of service to younger members of the profession. Over and over, besides providing suggestions for writing and advice on writing well, these publications stress the responsibility prospective writers should feel for imparting knowledge to others and for adding to a growing published account on the science of agriculture.

In order to solicit submissions from these kinds of writers—those who are interested in being an active participant in their field and are knowledgeable about it—the editors of both *Ohio* and *Maine* offer a great deal of practical advice to readers on their contributions, outlining the goals for publication, articulating strategies for invention, and giving advice on grammar and language, as I consider in the next section. At the same time, many of these articles are visibly preoccupied with the reluctance they imagine readers feel about writing something for publication. In "A Neglected Tool" in *Ohio Farmer*, the editor acknowledges that the

> majority of farmers, even those who read and are intelligent, use the pen too little in behalf of their own profession. They can *talk* well enough, but ask them to *write* out the same thing they have told you, and they will excuse themselves. (369; italics in the original)

The article, which continues to offer advice to reluctant writers, offers an anecdote about a particularly successful farmer who "lost no time in telling us that he 'never wrote a line for a paper—couldn't write,' etc. Now his *talk* was practical, useful, interesting, and his writing would have been equally so—but the idea, to him, was preposterous" (369). Believing that one "couldn't write" is not an excuse, for *Ohio*, for not attempting to draft articles for the journal. Once again, moreover, editors argue that their readers, whom they repeatedly describe as practical, experienced farmers, already possess the qualities necessary to join a professional farming community. A later article, "Farm Experience," clearly expounds on this belief, explaining:

> I like to read those articles on farm topics whose burden of information is expressed in the plain and simple language of the practical farmer, who understands his business and aims to make himself understood to the illiterate as well as the learned. (293)

Here, as in other articles encouraging readers to write, the editor defines for readers what good writing means for the publication: it uses "plain and simple language," imparts professional wisdom to other farmers, and is accessible to all readers. At the same time, the editor continues to define the kind of writer he desires: one "who understands his business and aims to make himself understood" (293). Appealing to a majority of readers who no doubt could have accepted such descriptors as "practical," "experienced," and "understands his business," editors for *Maine* and *Ohio* work to aid readers in identifying with the professional farm writer the journals created and promoted.

Nonetheless, that not all members of rural communities agreed with the vision of agriculture and of the professional farmer-writer constructed by journals and agricultural organizations is visible in these encouragements as well. In "Farm Experience," an editor or contributor connects his encouragement for farmers to contribute with the observation that "thousands of them [farmers] can hardly be induced to put pen to paper for this purpose, and many more refuse to aid in the work of disseminating knowledge thro public organizations such as farmers clubs" (293). It is not just reluctance to publish writing, but a "refus[al] to aid in the work of disseminating knowledge" that editors deplore, clearly arguing that by not participating in the kind of community created by journals and organizations, farmers are impeding the advancement of the profession and rural life. In places, the criticism of this "kind" of farmer is pointed; in "Neglected Tool," the editor censures farmers for withholding knowledge. He argues that

> these old, veteran farmers who have never written a word for agriculture, have accumulated from many years' experience and observation, a fund of practical knowledge and information that would be eminently useful, could they be persuaded to impart it to the world. (369)

In this and other articles, editors and contributors contrast their illustration of the "old, veteran farmer" with the new writer-farmer or Grange farmer. Chambers traces a similar tension in the identity constructions of the Illinois Granger movement and its associated publications, demonstrating how speakers and writers rhetorically supported the myths and personae they wished to promote in part by denigrating illustrations of farmers and rural life that they saw as outmoded or detrimental to their cause. It is certainly true that in defining two contrasting figures—the "old, veteran farmer" who refuses to write and the experienced farmer eager to advance his profession—the agricultural editors seek to force readers to identify with one or the other.

Editors, and contributors too, assert that farmers who refuse to assume the new role called for by farm organizations and publications are hurting the agricultural community. In "Writing for the Paper" in the *New England Farmer*, Geo. H. Brown reasons that

> if we learn a good thing, not lock it up in a safe nor get it patented and try to live by the sale of the article, but send an account to our paper, and thereby make it common property, and then agricultural knowledge will increase. (1)

For Brown and others, the knowledge generated within the agricultural community belongs to, and is desperately needed by, the agricultural community.

For the willing farmer but reluctant writer, editors are quick to make clear that inexperience with writing or lack of literacy education should not preclude readers from joining the ranks of the new professional farmer. Brown's article is, in fact, reprinted in *Southern Planter* with the editor's note that he feels the same, a concept he expands on in "Farmers as Writers and Executors," where he discusses farmers' social responsibility to write. He, too, addresses readers who may be reluctant to write for the press, claiming:

> The excuse we most often hear given by farmers when asked to communicate their views on any agricultural topic is, that they are not in the habit of writing for the papers, and that it is more agreeable to read what others have written than to attempt to write themselves. This is a grave error, for if all were to act on this principle there would be nothing valuable in agricultural journals, and they might as well cease to exist. The principle, too, will not bear the test of moral obligation, for he who receives ought to be willing to give. (413)

Here, as in other farm journals, the moral inflection given to literacy skills is not that they reflect on the moral constitution of the individual, but that they enable that person to enter into a responsible community of professionals. Agricultural publications such as *Maine* and *Ohio*, then, intervened by publishing articles aimed at teaching readers how to become farmer-writers, so that they could take up this communal responsibility. In the sections that follow, in which I explore the specific writing lessons offered by these publications, subtle distinctions among articles will be obvious, even as it is equally clear that they do lean toward a loose consensus: that valuable composition springs from experience and engaged reading habits, that readers could learn to write by writing, that content rather than style determines value, and that improved literacy skills held practical value for rural audiences.

Teaching Readers to Become Farmer-Writers

In hopes of encouraging the perhaps reluctant audience to begin writing, both *Maine* and *Ohio* offer readers advice on how to become a farmer-writer by outlining strategies for invention and composition.[3] Invention, in particular, was linked to readers' experience and reading habits. In "Hints to Correspondents," an editor admits that the journal is "often asked by correspondents for some suggestions respecting writing for the press and for subjects to write upon" and reminds readers:

> The articles of the most value to the readers of our paper are those written because the author has something important to tell. Then to find a subject, it is only necessary to recall the experiences of life in which discoveries have been made that have benefitted you. (408)

Similarly, in "Farm Experience," the editor of *Ohio* states:

> We endorse the sentiment expressed by one of our correspondents, recently. "A busy life of practical experience on a farm with a proper exercise of energy and observation, constitutes farmers the highest authority in matters relating to their peculiar branch of the industry." (293)

For both *Ohio* and *Maine*, the desired content of contributions is practical information on or points of inquiry into farming matters, a topic on which both magazines argue their readers are already experts. Just as articles aimed at encouraging contributions regularly suggested that their readers already represented the type of farmer necessary for the new agricultural profession, so too the articles intent on helping readers become writers asserted that farmers already possessed the expertise and knowledge necessary to inspire articles. In this way, advice for invention is deeply rooted in the publications' identity constructions. Importantly, too, in calling farmers "the highest authority" on agricultural matters, editors offer potential writers a degree of power in the textual community that exceeds what either the *Journal* or the *Bazar* could offer readers.

Michigan Farmer, as I touched on in the last chapter, urged readers to take advantage of the educational opportunities offered through participation in Grange meetings, libraries, and study groups and demonstrated to them both the different forms their participation might take and how these activities would be beneficial to improving knowledge, comfort with writing, and public-speaking skills. Likewise, *Maine* and *Ohio* encouraged audiences to read more often and outlined specific reading practices they should cultivate, especially for reading the farming journals themselves. Most frequently, and in agreement with the *Bazar* and the *Journal*, illustrations of ideal reading practices took place in a domestic setting—or, at the very least, on home property, with farm workers encouraged to read outside during breaks and discuss recent articles "over the fence" with their neighbors.

The setting was an important part of the conviction expressed in *Maine* and *Ohio* that literate and intellectual development could occur more successfully in real-life contexts than in classrooms. This, too, the editors of both *Farmers* had in common with Bok and Sangster. Students in school were assigned generic readers, which various articles in both *Farmer*s accused of being unable to hold readers' attention, while adults read newspapers, journals, and books connected with their life pursuits; students studied grammar, which a number of contributors to these journals doubted could help improve actual writing skills, while adults wrote letters, articles, and notes for Grange discussions. I address how this belief about writing pedagogy played into the writing practices advocated by the farming journals in the next section; in terms of reading practices, however, *Maine* and *Ohio* reinforced the idea that parents needed to support reading habits at home and should undertake their own development as readers in the same context. More significantly for this discussion, however, while numerous farming journals illustrated reading practices as an important step in self-education and participation in community-based groups like the Grange, *Maine* and *Ohio* further established reading as a part of invention; journal audiences were to use their reading experiences as a way to join the agricultural community and to prompt writing.

In keeping with *Maine*'s and *Ohio*'s trend of sympathetically recognizing impediments to writing for publication—including perceived lack of skill—discussions of reading also continuously returned to the journal's acknowledgment that audience members did not have a great deal of time to spend on lengthy reading. They repeatedly reminded readers, however, that the winter months offered more opportunities. These and other farming magazines made clear that during this time, conscientious farmers and their families should commit to a reading or study plan, and that farming periodicals could help them prepare. *Michigan Farmer*, especially, devoting the most space to clubs and study groups, reinforces the importance of viewing the winter months as a time of self-cultivation, ostensibly as yet another part of "elevating" rural communities and its members; articles such as "The Winter's Educational Campaign" in an October 1904 issue, "How Can We Profitably Spend Our Winter Evenings?" in a March 1905 issue, and "Farm Home Reading" in an April 1907 issue all suggest this. In "Reading for Farmers and How Some Farmers Read," I. N. Cowdry, in *Ohio*, likewise portrays winter evenings as the best time for farmers to read (and study), recalling how he "love[s] to sit down these long winter nights and read the experiences of different writers of The Farmer. . . . How much one can learn, how many little suggestions he can cull from the pens of many excellent contributors" (262). Here contributors join in asserting how valuable are the articles written by the "book farmer," while they show audiences how reading the journal might aid them in also becoming valuable and experienced members of the profession.

Similarly, another contributor, A. B. Lightner, in "A Farmer's Notions about Agricultural Journals" in *Southern Planter and Farmer*, laments that not enough farmers read the agricultural press carefully, and "if the hard-working farmer would read more and work less (I mean the hard-working man), he would succeed far better" (561). *Ohio* argues in "Mission of the Agricultural Paper" that the agricultural press exists for the purpose of providing farmers with a practical education that they can get through reading at home; that just as readers are called to write for the press, so too should they allow their reading of the journal to help them become more knowledgeable farmers who will have something valuable of their own to contribute later on. The editor here argues that

> no one can read such a paper as The Ohio Farmer without getting ten times its cost from it. . . . It is exactly the same as with drill and discipline of an educational course. One is not conscious, from day to day, of the broadening, elevating process, but the four or five year's [*sic*] course develops the powers within and makes the man. And so with the close reader of a reliable agricultural journal. (290)

In this way, "Mission," much like Lightner, demonstrates for readers one way they may go about cultivating the knowledge to assume the role of a farm writer: be a "close reader of a reliable agricultural journal" (290). G. E. Monroe, a reader of *Maine*, likewise asserts that reading farm journals is "one of the very best means of acquiring an education at home" (1).

As with other discussions of education and home reading in the agricultural press, the ability of higher academic institutions to provide educational development superior to what a motivated student may achieve on his or her own is questioned. Partly because so much of these publications are taken up by contributions from their audiences, this message is not consistent. While some articles criticize college education, others clearly seek to make college a more achievable goal for students from rural communities—usually with the idea that attending an agricultural or state college will help young people better adapt to and advance the new, "elevated" agricultural community. The idea, however, that close reading of the journal, in conjunction with participation in farm organizations, is a practical and successful way of gaining the knowledge necessary to become a professional farmer is present rather frequently in all journals.

Just as *Ohio* and *Maine* ultimately acknowledge that members of their audience might find the prospect of writing for publication daunting, so too do they recognize the difficulties that might prevent farmers from reading the journal carefully and learning from it. After relating the enjoyment he currently receives from reading the paper, I. N. Chowdry confesses that reading agricultural journals carefully requires effort and thought, as he discovered when he first subscribed:

> I shall have to admit that the reading was dry, and I had to force it down quite hard; but I kept reading; first I fell in love with Terry, then Brown, Chamberlain, Gould, Talcott, Powers, etc., and at last The Farmer itself. So you see that some persons must educate themselves to read such papers. (262)

The solution, for Chowdry and other editors and contributors, is for farmers to adapt their reading practices so that they gain the knowledge they need. Likewise, a contributor to *Maine* in "What and How Shall We Read?" worries that even those farmers who have "educated themselves to read such papers" do not read them with enough care, and instead journals are "hastily run over and cast one side to be forgotten" (2). He urges readers to alter their reading practices to include study of the farming papers, saying that unfortunately many farmers, claiming they lack the time, simply skim articles and thus do not take advantage of the full educational value of publications such as *Ohio* or *Maine*.

To correct such a tendency, *Ohio Farmer* in particular encourages its audience to read carefully, making sure to formulate and articulate the opinions inspired by the reading material in both family and Grange discussions and in responses to the journal itself. After listing possible topics for writing, the author of "Neglected Tool" suggests:

> If you can do nothing more, ask questions for other readers to answer. If you read anything in our columns that does or does not agree with your experience, let it be known. We want our readers to feel that The Ohio Farmer is *their* paper, to be used by them in every legitimate way. (369; italics in the original)

Contributing to the journal, for "Neglected Tool," is about interacting with other readers, both in responding to what they have published and in eliciting further discussion in the journal. Likewise, the editor in "Farm Experience" calls for readers' participation, stating:

> Let us have a hearty support from every reader during the coming season of long nights and comparative leisure on the farm. Read the articles in The Farmer carefully, and if anything in them does not meet your approval, criticize it. (293)

Again, readers are encouraged to read for points of contention or omission and to see periodical articles as a foundation for discussion points—points that they should use as inspiration for writing for magazine publication.

In addition to reading, both *Maine* and *Ohio* recommend that the best method of learning to write for the press is simply to get into the practice of doing so. Repeated practice in a community of peers is, according to a number of articles, the best way of improving as a farm writer. In "The Young Farmers' Corner," a reader of *Ohio* identified by the initials G.C.S. requests that the journal set aside a column where young farmers, new both to the profession and to writing for publication, could have their work published—"where the younger generation of farmers could have a corner all to themselves, and have it in charge of a young farmer. In this way they would feel that they were not entirely unnoticed" (93). Importantly, for G.C.S., "there is another advantage in a department of this kind. The young farm boys would be encouraged to write their experiences on the farm, and in this way would learn to write material for the paper in later years" (93).

The editor responds to this suggestion by agreeing with G.C.S. that young farmers especially need to practice writing for the papers but maintains that new writers may do so just as well by contributing to the main journal and do not need a separate column:

> The gentleman is also correct in his statement that the young man must be trained to write for the papers. We have brought out more new writers, perhaps, than any other farm paper now published. We believe, however, that the young writer feels a greater pride in having his articles appear alongside the writings of those of the old "war-horses." (93)

As elsewhere, editors insist that the professional agricultural community they envision is one that consists of experienced farmers not only eager to share knowledge with others but also receptive to the ideas of fellow members, no matter how "simple" the language or young the farmer. Here the editor cites pride as a motivator but also reiterates the idea that a writer will learn best by practicing in a real community.

Elsewhere in *Ohio*, too, the editors urge readers to "write often," a sentiment echoed by *Maine*. In "On Writing," reluctant *Maine* writers are assured that any attempts they make at composing will help them improve, for "indeed, one good successful effort will greatly diminish every succeeding effort, and make writing easy" (4). Readers are then taken through a description of what the composition process should entail, with an emphasis on revision. Writers are instructed to at first merely convey their thoughts and

> then carefully and repeatedly read it over and correct it: study ever sentence, weighing every expression, and making every possible improvement. Then lay it aside a while, and afterwards copy it with such improvements as occur at the time; then lay it aside and after some days revise it again and see what further improvements and corrections you can make, and copy it a second time. (4)

Following this strategy, "On Writing" asserts, will help writers become more skilled in future compositions:

> If you repeat this process half a dozen times it will be all the better, nor will the time you spend upon it be lost. One such composition will conquer the difficulties in the way of writing, and every time you repeat such an effort you will find your mind improving and thoughts multiplying. (4)

Even articles more intently focused on offering mechanical advice return to the idea that repeated practice will lead to improvement; in "Hints to

Writers" in *Ohio*, the editor concludes by encouraging, "If what you write at one time is not published, write again, and again" (94).

Moreover, editors believed not only that farmers could improve their writing skills, and ultimately their ability to speak to a community of professionals, by repeated practice in the periodical community, but also that repeated writing practice in a real community was the best way for children—future young farmers—to learn as well. Reflecting on a column in *Maine Farmer* that, for a number of years, was composed entirely of the letters and contributions of the younger members of the journal audience, D. Q. Cushman, himself a reader of the *Farmer*, asserts:

> Writing is a great benefit and pleasure to us all, and I am glad that the *Farmer* has in it what they call the "young folks' column," and I am glad that the young folks fill it so well as they do. And I could wish that other papers would do the same thing. It would be no damage, but in my judgment, be a benefit to all who are concerned therein. ("Original Occupation" 1)

While the "Young Folks' Column" originally published stories presumably written by the journal's staff, in 1881 *Maine* began soliciting the contributions of young readers, much as it continued to urge farmers to write. In "A Call," Annie urges readers to "respond to our Editor's kind invitation and write for the Children's Column," asking, "Has not Maine as good writers among the young folks as among the older ones?" (4). Although, within the column, writers are not offered further composition advice or grammar instruction in the way that older readers are in other parts of the journal, for the next several years young readers' contributions account for most of the material published in the "Young Folks' Column."

Young writers often talk about school or experiences at home, frequently commenting on what they like about the column and their desire to see their name in print. In a later article also reflecting on the "Young Folks' Column," Cushman again explains its importance, stating that he

> highly value[s] the "Young Folks' column," not because its contents are superior to the rest, but because the articles are written by young people—those who are just commencing a course of action and pursuits in life. The pen is the instrument of power, and those who learn to use it will have means in their hands that will educate and bless their fellowmen. The learning how to use the pen is one of the most important branches of education. ("A Few Thoughts" 2)

The column not only is helpful in aiding children in learning to compose but also, according to this contributor, is important in encouraging them to participate in the agricultural press in much the same way that the journal encourages their parents to contribute, and in this way it is an important part of schooling them in the kinds of literate activities they need to be prepared to engage in when they are older.

Cushman's sense that *Maine Farmer*'s inclusion of a space for young people to publish their writing was educationally beneficial is echoed in other comments made about the column, reiterating the idea that learning to write for publication is an important lesson for the "young folks." Elmer W. Ness, one of the "young folks," states simply, "I think it is a nice plan for the little folks to write for papers, as it teaches them to compose" (4). While Ness's comment sounds suspiciously like something a teacher or parent or editor prompted him to write—or wrote for him, given that he is supposedly eight years old—it does contribute to the overall belief in *Maine* that contributing to the journal could be a learning experience. Somewhat predictably, quite a number of the letters published in the column describe school experiences. More important, however, is that many of the letter writers note that they are currently on a break from school because they are ill, lack a teacher, or school is closed for lack of students able to attend, suggesting that perhaps parents, too, are using letters to the column as a home writing assignment—a practice encouraged by the journal's repeated prompting for readers to write and its simultaneous critique of the composition education offered in primary schooling.

In "Our Public Schools," the writer (it is unclear whether an editor or contributor) complains that a recent school committee found that students had been taught to "parse and construe sentences, and point out the various parts of speech," but that "when called upon to write an ordinary letter they were utterly unable to apply the rules and principles they had so painfully learned" (2). The article writer doubts that this system of education, which teaches the principles of writing apart from the contexts students will actually face—writing letters and articles for the Grange and journals—is useful, arguing instead that students learn by doing, being taught "to read and write and cipher just as they learned to swim or to skate" (2). Such critiques of the type of pedagogy present in public schools, and colleges especially, appear often in these farming publications, where writers focus on the problem of educating outside the intellectual contexts of their daily lives.

Editors' advice to writers corresponds to this overall belief that practical experience in everyday contexts is the best method of education in any subject. One such article, "On Writing," asserts that another fault in young beginners is viewing composition as a task imposed on them by their teacher, and making it their chief object to cover a certain quantity of paper with writing, but you must have a higher aim than this or you will never be a good writer. (4)

Good writing, these articles and others maintain, has an educational and social purpose for a real community of readers, like those of the *Maine* and *Ohio*. These articles suggest that taking up the practice of writing for agricultural journals allows young writers to compose on familiar subjects with the real purpose of sharing their knowledge with others, a process that will be an effective education in improving their own skills as well. In "Writing" in *Ohio*, James M. Taylor articulates this even more pointedly, arguing that teachers have approached the teaching of writing incorrectly: "The fault lies in the failure to make their knowledge practical. Teaching others to parse and analyze is not teaching to write the English language correctly. Experience proves this" (302). Taylor likens teaching composition by means of rules of grammar to teaching a man to tear down a building and then expecting him to understand how to build it, claiming that "their drill in the school room, while ostensibly professing to teach them to write correctly, has failed in this essential particular" (302). One of the main points of contention is that whatever students have learned to write, they have not learned the most important form: knowledge-based articles for publication in agricultural press. Taylor criticizes schools for creating grammarians, rather than writers, saying:

> In like manner there are any number of our best grammarians, if thorough knowledge of the technicalities of that branch as now generally taught is a test, who would feel bewildered if required to write a notice ten lines in length for publication. (302)

Taylor advocates instead "practically useful training" in any branch of study, writing included, and while his comments are directed at the education of children and young adults, the implication is clear: children, like their parents, need to use participation in agricultural journals as a way to supplement the limited education offered in schools. This additional education, for both the "young folks" and the farmers, is needed so that they can become members of an advanced agricultural community.

Style and Language in the Farmers

Apart from suggesting that their audiences will get better at writing through practice, *Maine Farmer* and *Ohio Farmer* restrict most of their practical advice on other elements of writing to brevity and language. Articles written primarily by editors make clear how the nature of the scientific agricultural community they have defined shapes the associated discoursal expectations. Underscoring the fact that they value compositions based in knowledge and facts, articles like "Study Brevity—Give Us Facts" in *Maine* and "The Editor's Shears" and "The Editor's Pencil" in *Ohio* enjoin prospective writers to tailor their compositions to their audience by making their statements more concise. The writer of "Study Brevity," presumably the editor, states simply:

> It will be better for you, and much easier for us, if you will make it a point to condense your statements as much as possible, giving only the main facts and conclusions. Avoid long introductions; say what you have got to say, and stop. This "stopping" part is a grand thing, if everybody only knew just when to put it in operation. (1)

The author of "Study Brevity" does not give much in the way of strategies for how to "stop" or "condense," but the writer of "Editor's Shears" and "Editor's Pencil" makes a similar point, offering more specific advice on accomplishing the task. The editor provides an example of an article recently submitted to the journal, making clear that this article, or part of it, will in fact be published, but wants readers to observe that

> the writer makes the mistake that most young writers make—and some old ones, too—of wasting a lot of effort, paper and ink, in trying to introduce the subject. When they get through with this and get down to business—practical business—telling what they themselves know, about raising corn, or whatever it is, they are all right. ("Shears" 498)

Suggesting to potential journal writers that their true skill lies in "telling what they themselves know," rather than crafting a "glittering introduction," the editor also makes clear to readers why this particular audience values brevity—and not, apparently, introductions:

> What we want to impress upon young writers is the fact that no glittering introduction is wanted in a practical article. Pitch right into the subject. Tell what you yourself know of importance bearing on the subject in the briefest possible manner and *stop* when you have told it. ("Shears" 498; italics in the original)

Writing, for both these journals, is to be practical, rather than glittering—an ideal that matches the editor's plea that "it's not rhetoric the people want but facts" ("Farm Experience" 293).

"The Editor's Pencil," citing "The Editor's Shears" and "The King's English" series as attempts to help readers refine their language and adopt brevity, offers further explanation for the desire for conciseness, framing the request in terms of publication labor and audience expectations:

> What our readers and ourselves want on practical topics, is specific facts from the writer's experience, and brief conclusions from them, all given in clear, terse English. This we have tried to enforce in recent editorials, "The King's English," and "The Editor's Shears." The editor's pencil *must*, in the interests of our readers and our advertisers, dash through all superfluous and general matter in contributors' articles, and come at once to the essential and specific. (24; italics in the original)

This article goes on to specifically outline why brevity is "in the interests of our readers and our advertisers," but the other articles outline a few of the outcomes of brevity as well, among them the fact that it will allow more writers to publish their work, leading to greater variety in the journal. "Hints to Young Writers" in *Maine Farmer* further emphasizes the value of brevity for agricultural audiences, explaining that "long articles, however well written, are often passed over, when brief ones are read, and better remembered" (1). The writer of "Editor's Pencil," at the same time, asks writers to put themselves in the place of the publisher and "let the writer change the standpoint and think this: 'every inch of space takes money'" (24). "Study Brevity" asks writers to "write often, but write short" (1); the value of the state-local journal is that it touches on (or attempts to touch on) all subjects related to farm economy and boasts that it presents multiple viewpoints, something these articles suggest is partly accomplished by having many brief articles.

"Writing short" has implications for journal readers too. It is not just, as "Study Brevity," "Editor's Shears," "Farm Experience," and numerous other writing-related articles point out, that journal readers desire specific knowledge and factual articles; knowledge of the life realities of the audience should help readers understand the call for brevity as well. The writer of "Editor's Pencil" requests that readers keep this in mind as they compose:

> What I am writing now will be seen by nearly a quarter of a million pairs of eyes. If because I do not write cleanly, condense properly, begin at the beginning or stop at the end of what I really have of value to convey—if I thus waste one minute of the time of each reader, then I have caused a total loss of about 150 days. (24)

The readers of *Maine* and *Ohio* are busy—as the articles on reading and writing repeatedly acknowledge. For "Editor's Pencil," the costs of literary digression are steep: it wastes time and money on the part of readers, as well as ink and paper on the part of the writer. In short, unlike the *Journal*, which encouraged contributors to be brief as a reflection of special budgets in the magazine, the editors of *Maine* and *Ohio* assert that the desire for brevity is related to the conditions of the community for which a farmer is writing.

The author of "Editor's Pencil" shows future writers how they may avoid this waste by giving a lesson in ways to condense. Presenting an introduction sent in by a correspondent, the editor notes the places where the writer strays into unnecessary discussion, and then shows different ways to fix the text: "two courses lay before the editor—to cut out this Introduction entirely, as superfluous, or to condense its thought somewhat as follows . . ." (24). The lesson is echoed in *Maine Farmer*'s "Hints to Young Writers," where attempting to make language more concise is presented as a matter of revision that, like any other aspect of writing, will gradually become easier with practice. Readers are advised:

> If you could do so, that is, if you could spend the time (and if you mean to write no time could be so well spent) it would be a grand thing for you to re-write your articles and reduce them in length one-half. In a little time this practice would give you a habit of directness in thinking and writing that would be of great service to you. (1)

Just as so many articles address the reluctance or insecurity they imagine some of their readers feel about writing for publication, so too the articles focused on brevity make clear that "there is no touch of sarcasm or even blame in what we say" ("Editor's Pencil" 24). Many writers could benefit, so "Editor's Pencil" claims, from trying to be more concise; "Editor's Shears" offers an anecdote about how "President Canfield of our State university tells a good joke of himself," giving a speech that would have benefited from the "editor's shears."

The belief that imperfect writing was not something to be embarrassed about also appears in *Maine*'s and *Ohio*'s treatments of language and grammar. The editor of *Ohio*, in his plea for audience members to contribute, explains that it is important for farmers to participate in sharing agricultural knowledge regardless of their comfort level with writing, claiming that "one common excuse is they cannot express themselves properly, but this is a poor one. The most effective writers and speakers use the simplest language" ("Farm Experience" 293). Other portions of that journal, as well as *Maine*, expand this claim about effective writers; articles like "Hints to Correspondents" and "Neglected Tool" suggest that their contributors should view the journal as another forum like the Grange or a textual version of "talk over the fence," a practice cast as being critical to farm management, and in this way they should seek to write in language they already use as farm professionals.

"Neglected Tool" argues this clearly in its request to readers: "Write in your own way—use the plain words you would in talking, for they are the best" (369). Likewise, "The Editor's Strainer" suggests that reluctant writers imagine they are discussing topics with a friend, advising:

> Tell it as you would to a friend whom you wished to inform, interest, or instruct. But tell it concisely for space is precious, and with great care, for you are telling it to three hundred thousand friends instead of one. (164)

These articles reference the fact that skilled farmers' words are valued in open discussion, and that they will have the same value in print, whether or not the writers have followed all rules of grammar. In doing so, the articles also frame the language of the press as an extension of the active, scientific agricultural community and their own illustration of the new farmer. In fact, throughout these journals, the reason offered for this particular view of language is that the knowledge, debate, or advice contained within the article outweighs its stylistic value; writers need to be clear and understandable:

> Be careful in stating facts or in reporting the results of any experiment to make your meaning clearly understood. We are quite frequently compelled to throw aside otherwise interesting and no doubt important statements, simply because they are unintelligible to us. ("Study Brevity" 1)

"Editor's Strainer," continuing to suggest that the textual discussion contained in the journal is another form of "over the fence" or Grange talk, explains that the writer's "own language" is best:

> Don't try to show off. Be yourself and no one else. If you have nothing worth telling, do not try to tell it. If you have, tell it in your own language, simply, clearly, quietly, forcibly if the subject calls for force. (164)

As articulated most clearly in "Neglected Tool," "good spelling, grammatical sentences and high-sounding words never make a good article alone." According to the editor:

> We would rather have one article crammed full of good sense and useful knowledge, with every word misspelled, and every sentence a violation

of grammar rules, than to have all the nicely rounded sentences ever written, if they were devoid of these requisites. (369)

"Institute Workers," another reply to the discussion of grammar and "King's English," is even more strongly critical of favoring style over content; W. N. Cowden criticizes a former contributor, XYZ, for publishing the grammar violations of unnamed state speakers. Cowden asserts that "she doubtless refers to the provincialisms common to all parts of the state," arguing that such forms of ridicule are "over fastidious" and that

> it is facts and instructions that the people want and should have, and the better the dress in which the facts and instruction are clothed, the more acceptable; but often these are none the less beautiful or useful because in home-spun. (249)

This is not to suggest, *overall*, that spelling and grammar are not mentioned as concerns—spelling, in fact, is frequently held up as the one area where writers should be able to aim for correctness. However, nearly all discussions of grammar and language concerns are framed as ways readers can voluntarily "improve" themselves and not as impediments to writing for the public. Cowden concludes her criticism of XYZ's emphasis on grammar by noting that

> this is no apology for bad grammar, or illogical arrangement or bad pronunciation, but only a protest against a wholesale charge against a class that do a great amount of hard work and endure a large amount of exposure and do a great deal. (249)

Similarly, the second article of the "King's English" pair mentions incorrect spelling and minor grammar errors, saying, "These are defects, of course, but you all know that, and will naturally do the best you can," and adding that only more major writing and content issues will prevent publication: "Any editor will overlook them [misspellings] gladly if the article is full of meat and is comparatively free from the more serious defects mentioned" (30). "Editor's Strainer," the last in the "Editor" series of articles on grammar, outlines in greatest length the journal's perspective on offering advice on style and mechanics. Here the editor responds to the "good press" generated by the previous articles and explains:

> A paper like The Ohio Farmer has a large number of correspondents who can and do furnish the kind of matter needed—practical information—but who have no special desire to improve their style, but simply to convey

their thought clearly and briefly. Their articles are always welcome, and our suggestions and mild criticisms are not intended for them at all, any further than they desire to benefit by them. They are intended chiefly for those who wish to improve their literary style. (164)

Thus, much as potential writers are reassured of the value of the message they could convey to the journal, they are also told not to worry over grammatical rules when they write.

Both *Maine* and *Ohio* continue to address issues of grammar as a way to further assuage the fears of reluctant writers, giving advice on correctness mixed with assurances both that the value of their composition is not dependent on grammar and that they can easily improve the grammatical correctness of any article they have written by following the magazine's advice. "Hints to Correspondents," for instance, claims that "as to the rules of writing, the greatest amount of trouble we find is in the writer's attempting to observe too many of them"; the fact that the writer "desperately" wants to make certain words emphatic or is "so fearful" about borrowing words without credit, according to this editor-instructor, leads them into making more errors than they would have made if they had had confidence in the clarity of their own words (408). What follows the editor's observation, then, is a lesson in grammar rules and mistakes to avoid, instructing readers in the use of citation, italics, commas, and capital letters: "As a rule, use capital letters to begin words only at the starting of a sentence, names of individuals, towns, rivers, places, months of the year, days of the week, etc." (408). "Hints to Writers" and the "King's English" series give similar advice, warning writers to be wary of overusing dashes and semicolons and not to use alliteration, which "is the vice of newspaper headliners and the disgust of all good taste" ("King's English" 10). Repeatedly, writers are reminded that "a little attention to this matter will make a decided improvement with those willing to learn" ("Hints to Correspondents" 408). The editor reassures, "We do not write this in a spirit of criticism, but simply to benefit our readers who may desire to improve themselves in this direction" ("Hints to Writers" 78).

It is clear, however, that the editor places the expertise of his hopeful writers in the realm of content and wishes them to either learn to improve their linguistic style or avoid such rules altogether, and not simply because it "shows greater ignorance." He requests of readers:

> Do not strew in commas broadcast; if they and the other punctuation points cannot be used according to given rules, please leave them out

entirely, for it is easier for an editor to place one here and there than to strike out a dozen or two in every sentence. ("Hints to Correspondents" 408)

Just as writers should not waste "150 days" of readers' time with lengthy digressions, so too they should not waste the effort of the editor with convoluted punctuation usage; the writer's time is better spent on addressing the goals for his or her composition. Here as well, the differences in roles assumed by the editor and farmer are apparent. The farmer-writer's authority in the community resides in his agricultural expertise, while the editors suggest that their own expertise resides primarily in facilitating that community's discussion. Like the editors of the *Journal* and the *Bazar*, the farming magazine editors wielded significant power in defining what writing was acceptable and even controlling the illustration of who the farmer-writer should be. Nonetheless, in these articles teaching and encouraging readers to become writers, editors connect their lessons to a compelling literacy identity capable of allowing writers to participate, contribute, and enact change.

Farmers as Professionals and Teachers

In arguing that farmers have a responsibility to their local farming community and their profession to contribute written accounts of their experiences and knowledge of agriculture, magazines like *Ohio* and *Maine* provided writers not only with content to write about but also an outcome to write toward. In *Maine*, Monroe states simply that "farms are schools" and "farmers are teachers" (1); he is speaking of the possibilities for agricultural education at home in the form of reading and practical experience. However, in their assertion that farmers needed to compose articles "crammed full of good sense" that would "be a benefit to all," the editors of these two magazines extended Monroe's argument: farmers teach through their writing. To become a writer for *Ohio* or *Maine* was to become a professional with the authority to act as teacher, of many rather than a few.

Connected to the periodicals' generous treatment of their readers' insecurities about the rules of writing was a deep sense of respect and an acknowledgment of authority: readers were simultaneously students of writing and professionals in their field. Magazine editors were not alone in this perspective, moreover; contributors like Quercus Alba and Red Oak made parallel assertions about the authority farmers held on agricultural matters and the necessity of their sharing that education with others. Alba claims that "there are farmers who with their pens, can, in an hour, impart to the young farmer as much on a certain subject as they can learn in a lifetime of study and experience" (1), and Oak urges experienced farmers to "speak for the sake of justice and a higher degree of right education in farming" (1). For *Ohio*, *Maine*, and farming periodicals in general calling for the written contributions of readers, farmers possessed valuable knowledge that outweighed the literary abilities of the editors and publishers of the agricultural press. Editors could fix grammar but could not supply the desired content of a farming paper, as W. W. Stevens made clear in *Farmers' Home Journal*: "Most editors of agricultural papers are more theoretical than practical and are hardly competent to give the inquiring farmer information in detail" (561). Members of the reading audience, then, needed to become published writers because, as the editor of *Southern Planter* maintains in "Farmers as Writers and Executors," "there is no greater obligation or necessity among farmers than that they should teach and learn of each other" (413). The editors of *Ohio* and *Maine*, then, sought to offer readers advice in advanced literacy to help them become more effective communicators and teachers. In this, *Maine* and *Ohio* joined the *Bazar* and the *Journal* in crafting a literacy identity and in fostering literacy practices that presented audiences with the ability to become active participants in spheres the periodicals believed were especially suited to their readers.

Conclusion: Subscribing to a Professional Writing Community

I argued in the introduction that magazines deserve attention in literacy and composition studies because of their wide circulation and their presence in the lives of a population larger and more diverse than that visible in college classrooms. I argued that periodicals, especially women's magazines and farm journals, sought to supplement the literacy education provided in schools by offering instruction in the specific kinds of reading and writing practices their readers would use in their social, familial, and working lives. Periodicals, as the preceding chapters have explored, deployed new definitions of advanced literacy and sold literacy identities to readers. The discussion so far has primarily concerned the efforts and writing of editors and, for the farm journals, of a relatively small collection of farm writers. In this respect, editors and publishers acted as influential literacy sponsors outlining the definitions and pedagogies of literacy not only promoted by the magazine but also considered fundamental to their reading audience. While all of these periodical sponsors visibly asserted their own authority as writers, they also promoted discourse-specific writing practices, whether for women's clubs, magazine columns, or agricultural professionals, and sought to empower readers by emphasizing the value of their contributions.

The obvious difference among these periodicals was the gender identity of the named primary audience—although this divide was not so clean among actual readers. However, in their creation of a set of periodical-specific literacy practices and identities, nineteenth-century editors demonstrate that gendered approaches to literacy learning were more nuanced and interrelated than today's readers might assume. Certainly, for *Maine* and *Ohio*, the primary audience and literacy identity were male and, unsurprisingly, were tied to a profession and public, even political participation. In contrast, both the *Bazar* and the *Journal*, overall, emphasized a female identity still rooted in the domestic or private sphere. *Maine* and *Ohio* did not assume that readers needed new literacy skills to enlarge or move away from old definitions of the domestic sphere; the *Bazar* and *Journal* did. And yet all these journals did believe that readers were entering new communities or markets, and that doing so required them to learn new literacy practices.

More specifically, both the *Bazar* and the *Farmer*s asserted that the fulfillment of their readers and the welfare of the region and even nation depended on audiences forming focused, collaborative, intellectual communities. The nature of such communities was, of course, very different, but the approach was the same and gave readers the sense that their own literacy endeavors would have meaning for themselves and for others. All these magazines, correspondingly, fostered a sense of professionalization for their publications as well as their readers. Editors of the *Bazar*, the *Journal*, and the *Farmer*s believed that their readers felt that they had not yet entered the professional realm increasingly visible in the emerging consumer culture, and these editors used the literacy practices they advocated as a way to professionalize readers. I do not want to collapse differences in the kinds of professionalization magazines offered to women and men or the social and economic power connected to those differences. Rather, I would argue that the overlapping strategies deployed by magazines naming both male or female and urban or rural identities imply that the turn to professionalization and the creation of like-minded communities held a powerful appeal for turn-of-the-century audiences, and that editors tapped into this appeal.

While the importance of popular journals in the history of literacy and composition is visible in the advice and perspectives on literacy articulated by editors, it is even more visible in the way readers responded to literacy identity constructions emphasizing professionalization and took ownership over their participation with the periodical. It is not possible to know how each individual reader used and thought about these periodicals, but letters and contributions to the magazines offer evidence of both how a varied turn-of-the-century reading audience connected with the different possibilities for literacy and how professionalization was possible in a public rather than an academic venue. Indeed, information provided by the periodicals on the extent and nature of reader participation suggest that turn-of-the-century readers valued their ability to create and write for a community within a major professional publication and were correspondingly willing to negotiate the terms and limits set by editors. Ultimately, readers used their participation with these periodicals not only to claim a professionalized status within a community of writers, but also to bestow habits of literacy and professionalization on one another.

Negotiating Participation

It is easy to examine the authority wielded by the creators and editors of this collection of periodicals and imagine a homogenous community of readers, directly mirroring the magazine-inspired audience identity, that had little autonomy in determining how they would interact with magazine or the literacy practices editors sponsored. Certainly, the content of the periodical was subject to editorial control, as has been visible at times in the previous chapters. However, for all that editors attempted to portray a clear, if flexible, identity for readers, the popularity of the publications and the extent of their circulation meant that many *Journal*, *Bazar*, and *Farmer* readers had lives, identities, and appearances that did not conform to the personae outlined by editors.

This collection of magazines, then, demonstrates more than just the value of creating platforms that support diversity and blend a range of values and goals; reader participation with *Ohio*, *Maine*, the *Bazar*, and the *Journal* illustrates how well editors were able to embrace a multifaceted audience by offering possibilities for new literacy experiences and a sense of professionalization within a community. Likewise, considering these seemingly disparate magazines in connection with one another illustrates the importance of historians and researchers reading periodicals as texts speaking to a hybrid audience—an audience composed of not merely the individuals or communities overtly invoked by editors, nor even just the list of subscribers, but rather those subscribers and borrowers who negotiated limits and identities outlined by editors to buy into all of the periodical or only the parts that granted access to at least one role they wished to assume or explore. That so many readers did participate reveals how much a diverse audience valued its ability to subscribe to new venues for literacy and professionalization.

In *Literate Zeal*, Janet Carey Eldred considers the advent of *Mademoiselle* in the 1930s, outlining how the magazine's literary goal was shaped by its sense of audience. In this discussion, Eldred argues that

> the rhetorical work editors were doing—it is still the rhetorical work editors do—was constitutive: they were naming a niche, a group with significant numbers and buying power, and then inviting readers to identify with it, to grow the market. (119)

The rhetorical work Eldred sees in *Mademoiselle* and the *New Yorker* has its roots in the work done by Bok, Sangster, and the editors of *Maine* and *Ohio*. Eldred is in part pointing to the discrepancies between the audiences editors invoked and the actual audiences who read the magazines and perhaps even ultimately identified with particular departments. Significantly, though, Eldred also indicates the extent to which editors were not naming or classifying their readers, but creating and selling potential identities that readers might find attractive. For this reason, it would be a mistake to believe that the identity constructions I have been exploring directly mirrored the readers or that readers necessarily felt that they were confined to these roles. Rather, the roles of the professional farmer of the *Farmers*, the *Bazar* clubwoman, and the *Journal* consumer expert, as well as the literacy practices editors attached to them, reflected cultural aspirations, values, and fears with which a varied audience found it could identify, to varying degrees.

Moreover, the reality that audiences overlapped—that many *Journal* subscribers could have, and did, also read the *Bazar* or the *Farmers*—suggests that what the editors sponsored was one option for literacy identity among the many offered by various periodicals, schools, clubs, and other community and work-related institutions. The noticeable popularity of the particular group of periodicals, and identities, I have been exploring here further suggests that the specific brands of practices and identities presented by these editors were especially meaningful for turn-of-the-century Americans, perhaps in part because of the sense of community and professionalism connected to them.

Nevertheless, even as readers subscribed to, and claimed ownership of, these magazines and their corresponding literacy constructions, their identification with the periodical should best be understood not as entire, but as part of a mix. Although she is focused more on the self-representation and misrepresentation of a specific writer, Laura Laffrado, in her article on Fanny Fern's essays, speaks to the multifaceted identity constructions in print in the nineteenth century, which readers both identified with and identified against as partial, not absolute, representations of their public and private selves. After tracing the range of readers' responses to and misrepresentations of Sara Payson Willis's alter ego, "Fanny Fern," Laffrado notes that Willis saw herself as "a 'chameleon female' *because* she is so often misrepresented. Misrepresentations are vital elements of her linguistic self-representation, and thus any one self-representation, any 'true' self-representation, is impossible—as impossible as permanently describing a chameleon as any one color" (86; italics in the original). In her writing,

Fern takes on and compares representations of herself, allowing Willis to craft an ambiguous, even contradictory literary persona.

Considering both Willis and her literary contemporaries more broadly, then, Laffrado contends that these women writers "thus recognized the essay as a genre where a self could be revealed, even confessed to, without that self becoming the one permanent public and private self that the author would then have to inhabit" (91). I would argue that just as writers such as Willis used the popular press to explore components of self, rather than "one permanent public and private self," so readers also responded to editors' (and contributors') presentation of a literacy identity as a partial representation, or misrepresentation, of themselves. The popularity of *Journal*, *Bazar*, and farm publications is a testament, therefore, to readers' ability to interpret the literacy practices and identity promoted by the magazine as a reflection of one possible self or partial self.

Furthermore, while the periodical platform may define the terms and limits of literacy interactions and identities in print, readers themselves determine to what uses they will put the advice given in print and how fully they will "subscribe" to the magazine's literacy offerings. Readers could, and no doubt often did, read against the grain and apply magazine content in ways editors did not imagine or intend. In *Intimate Practices*, for example, Anne Ruggles Gere presents evidence of how Mormon clubwomen and the Improvement Club of New York recycled and critiqued content from the *Ladies' Home Journal* for their own purposes, arguing that "using what Daniel Miller calls consumption after purchase, clubwomen frequently transformed the *Journal* into forms quite different from what Bok intended" (98). Such practices would not have been restricted to the *Journal*; acknowledging that editors and publishers set the terms of the magazine's literacy sponsorship should not correspondingly indicate that readers always or passively accepted such terms. Readers could use, reject, or adapt editors' advice in their reading and writing experiences outside the magazine, such as in clubs, societies, and correspondence, and also had no obligation to accept and participate in the periodicals unless they wished to support or contribute to communities present in its pages. They could, in short, use and even combine the magazine-sponsored literacy identities for various purposes and roles.

Still, the popularity of the publications and the volume of reader participation attest to the fact that readers desired to enter into a literate exchange with a periodical community, and that the *Ladies' Home Journal*, *Harper's Bazar*, and the agricultural journals were an important part of their lives. The previous chapters explored the significance editors placed on reader engagement; indeed, the literacy activities they so strongly advocated required readers to interact with the magazine and with other members of the reading audience—*Ohio* bluntly campaigned for audience members to write to and for them, the *Bazar*'s columns relied on groups of clubwomen communicating with and making use of their study and organization advice, and Bok staffed large departments of editors to read and respond to reader letters in his mission for the *Journal* to become indispensable to American women.

Clearly, editors sought an engaged reading audience who would want to write, and statistics offered by the magazines—on the number of readers who contributed letters or articles or who participated in magazine departments and programs, such as the *Bazar*'s "Home Study Club" or the *Journal*'s "Free Scholarship" program—reveal the desire of readers to engage with the periodicals. Letters sent to E. B. Cutting of the *Bazar*'s "Home Study Club" demonstrate not only that the writers obviously want advice for their clubs, but also that they have been following Cutting's responses to other letters and outlines for other clubs. A survey of the column further revealed that in a four-year period, 264 women had letters published in the column, and more sent letters that were not printed. Moreover, while it is difficult to ascertain how many of the writers for the farm publications were farmers who had been encouraged to write by editors, in 1893 *Ohio* boasted that it currently had "157 names of writers with whom we keep a regular book account, paying them for contributions, most of whom we have 'discovered'" ("A Few Facts" 142). The editor clarifies, however, that this list of paid contributors did not include the additional writers whose letters appeared in various columns, such as the "Woman's Department," suggesting that far more than 157 members of the audience contributed to the *Farmer* in a year.

Bok's thorough statistical assessment of his magazine and its readers likewise provides some sense of the number of readers who participated in the *Journal*. In 1890, the first year of the program, four hundred women participated in the *Ladies' Home Journal* scholarship contest by soliciting subscriptions for the magazine, and while all were paid for their efforts, three earned scholarships. Although Bok does not reveal the number of participants later on, he does advertise that by 1897, the *Journal* had given three hundred scholarships. Readers also interacted with the *Journal* by corresponding with either Bok or the many editors of his advice departments, as discussed in chapter 2. In his autobiography, in fact, Bok boasts of the success of his service departments, claiming that before long, the letters streamed in by the tens of thousands during a year. The editor still encouraged, and the total ran into the hundreds of thousands, until during the last year, before the service was finally stopped by the Great War of 1917–18, the yearly correspondence totalled nearly a million letters. (Bok, *Americanization* 174)

Although these letters did not appear in the printed magazine, they are nonetheless indicative of significant and sustained participation with the periodical, its editors, and identity constructions.

It is equally clear, too, that at times readers claimed responsibility for shaping the content of columns and programs within the periodicals, demonstrating the extent to which some readers and contributors felt they could negotiate the terms for literacy set by the editors. A particular example of how reader participation visibly reshaped magazine content—and indeed, its terms of literacy sponsorship—is seen in the *Journal*'s "free scholarship" endeavors for those who sold subscriptions. The magazine at first offered readers a fairly limited list of options: enrollment in extension courses or home economics courses as scholarship prizes. Later, it responded to readers' requests by expanding the scholarship program to include courses at a number of fine arts schools in the East. Ultimately, again responding to suggestions from the audience, Bok advertised a list of eight hundred colleges and universities for both men and women that would accept *Journal* scholarships. In this way, readers demanded, and were ultimately given, sponsorship that extended beyond conservative, domestic coursework to include the possibility of a college education. However, even more women wrote to the editors requesting that the program be again extended to allow women not inclined to seek a college degree to build a home library by earning "free books" in exchange for solicited subscriptions. Bok responds to the popularity of these requests in the December 1894 issue by advertising the "Library Bureau," which will

> seek to organize among the hundreds of thousands of *Journal* readers a "Home Library League." Through this channel readers will not only be able to purchase any and every published book at the lowest possible price, but they will also be freely supplied with any information which they may desire about literary matters. ("New Departure" 33)

It is here, in the evolution of the scholarship program, that periodicals such as the *Journal*, the *Bazar*, *Ohio*, and *Maine* reveal some of the ways readers used periodicals to discuss, negotiate, and even sponsor other literacy practices, particularly self-study or course work in extension programs, colleges, and institutes. Chapter 4 explored some of the perspectives farming journals offered on education in general and the need for practical and contextually grounded education for agricultural communities. In addition, much as the *Journal* uncovers its readers' desires to build a personal library or enroll in reading courses, fine arts courses, or even college, so too do farm journals such as *Ohio* contain information on their readers' literacy efforts outside of the periodicals. In particular, agricultural publications featured advertisements for and references to readers participating in reading courses and "extension" programs through land-grant universities such as Cornell. In fact, the connection among the agricultural press, the Country Life movement, and the development of extension courses became increasingly predominant toward the end of the century, as Nancy K. Berklage discusses in "The Establishment of an Applied Social Science: Home Economists, Science, and Reform at Cornell University, 1870–1930." Linking the development of home economics to the growth of extension programs—programs based primarily through agricultural colleges and land-grant universities that allowed students to take courses "by extension," usually through the mail—Berklage notes the correlation between extension programs and the Country Life movement, citing rural historians' critique that "home economics reinforced domestic ideologies that were detrimental to rural women" (186). While the implications for extension work and home economics courses in rural communities are complex, Berklage and the journals themselves simultaneously make clear that many women in rural areas were motivated to participate in such courses.[1]

Investigations of the *Journal*, *Bazar*, and farm publications thus have uncovered not just a single, editor-sponsored set of literacy practices and gendered identity constructions, but also a collection of readers' desires and purposes. It is equally clear that while audiences responded well to the primary identity sponsored by these periodicals, readers did not confine themselves to the singular and potentially limiting, if powerful and appealing, literacy identity offered by the periodicals. Rather, the history of *Maine*, *Ohio*, the *Bazar*, and the *Journal* might be better described as the interaction between editors and large hybrid audiences in the task of promoting representations of a range of literacy practices, purposes, and identities. Moreover, the popularity of the publications and the volume of reader participation attest to the fact that many readers desired and valued their ability to enter into a literate exchange on a professional, wide-circulation platform. Through letters sent to editors and writing featured in the correspondence columns, readers of all these magazines demonstrated the value they placed in their own interaction within the magazine, underscoring the responsibility they felt for helping "compose" the text. These contributions demonstrate readers' belief that participation in the magazine conferred a sense of professionalization to writers, and also that contributors themselves, rather than just editors, could sponsor professional literacy skills among other readers.

Claiming a Professional Writing Community

It is in the correspondence columns and the audience-supplied content of the *Bazar*, the *Journal*, and farm journals that readers make clear that what they value most about the publications is their ability to sponsor participation, not only in clubs and courses outside the magazine content, but within the magazine as well, within the community of readers. Some readers of the *Journal* and *Michigan*, especially, feel strongly enough about the value of reading and participating that they outline efforts to circulate and distribute periodicals beyond official subscriptions. The *Journal* women of "Just among Ourselves" attest to the value of reading and participating with the women's publication by requesting that subscribers help circulate the magazine among those unable to afford subscription costs. They coordinate the redistribution of old copies of the periodical:

> For the lonely families far out on our western plains there are many kind thoughts, and I hope the thoughts will be the inspiration of many worthy deeds. "Uncle Sam" will have to carry numerous packages of papers and magazines which have been saved from destruction and sent on journeys of usefulness. (May 1891, 26)

The department editor supports the practice, explaining:

> In my own house, I have for years gathered weekly newspapers and sent them to friends in isolated places, who, being deprived of society, long for the companionship which comes through reading, and yet by reason of the exigencies of life, cannot spend money to buy books or papers.

Editors, of course, sought to increase sales by reminding readers of the quality of the publication and urging them to recommend the magazine to others. However, the discussions in "Just among Ourselves" and the "Woman's Department" columns of *Michigan* and other farm journals note readers' own attempts to promote and enable more persons to have access to the magazines, thereby extending their audience community.

Explaining why it is important for women to read and join the conversation of the farm magazines, an *Ohio* reader asserts, "We should strive to keep ourselves well informed, and to cultivate as well as strengthen the mind" because "a farmer's wife is much more a partner in her husband's business than wives generally are" ("What Farmers' Wives Read" 30). It is clear, here and in the "Just among Ourselves" column, that what readers hope to extend to other potential readers is not just the editor-written magazine content, but also the opportunity for others to enter into the community. More pointedly, the *Ohio* contributor begins to offer a reason why: interaction with the periodical is an intellectual endeavor leading toward a possibility for professionalization.

Significantly, too, this community-building activity appears almost exclusively in the women's and domestic columns of the agricultural journals. It is possible that as women were primarily responsible for purchasing magazine subscriptions for the family—even for the agricultural publications predominantly catering to male farmers—they were also more likely to pass copies along to neighbors. It is equally likely that for male readers of agricultural journals, the discussions and social connections visible in the periodical were supported and supplemented by their activities with Grange organizations; rural female readers, on the other hand, would have been more reliant on the periodical to gain access to discussions of agricultural matters and foster social connections with other women in farm communities. Women's letters, in both the farm periodicals and the women's magazines, repeatedly point to the connection they feel with the other women writing in the correspondence columns and their use of the magazine as a resource for information. Readers such as the contributors to "Just among Ourselves," then, take seriously the task of further distributing among their peers the communal and literacy opportunities offered by the periodical.

Correspondingly, letters and articles both male and female readers submitted to correspondence columns and journals as a whole clearly speak to readers' belief that their magazines were more valuable because of the mixed authorship; that, in fact, the *Farmer*s, the *Journal*, and the *Bazar* were more useful and applicable to readers' lives because these platforms combined the contributions of regular editors, a mix of writers, and readers as well. It is equally apparent, moreover, that readers valued the ability to take part in this written conversation and see their interactions in a major publication as a type of education in professional writing. In an issue of *Maine Farmer*'s "Woman's Department" column, one reader comments on her appreciation of the column and the publication, explaining:

> I am a reader of the Farmer and take an interest in the Woman's Department; have read it with pleasure and benefit; have often wished I could cheer and encourage others as they have helped me with the interchange of thought and experience. ("Women's Rights" 1)

Her remarks on not simply the value of the journal but specifically the pedagogical value of reader-contributed portions are echoed by other readers of the farm journals and women's magazines. Throughout their letters and contributions, readers reveal the importance of magazines in their literate lives, particularly in their ability to participate in it.

Integrated into articles on dairy farming and letters requesting study guides of Spanish culture or discussing current arguments about women's rights are statements on the benefit the reader has derived from reading the contributions of other readers. In the January 1897 issue of *Maine Farmer*, one reader, Carolyn, notes, "You can get some useful ideas by reading the woman's column, and gain experience in writing by short articles for it" ("A Word to the Wise" 3). At the same time, in the *Journal*'s "Just among Ourselves," Mrs. C.H.B. asserts, "I have been a reader of your much esteemed pages for three years, and always enjoyed so much your letters from the readers," then expresses her belief that readers' contributions are thoughtful and useful and are meant to be used as an impetus for further discussion (July 1890, 22). She begins her own contribution by explaining:

> I was just looking over my January number and re-read the open letter to Annie Curd. Now I do not wish to enter into a contest with either Annie Curd or E. A. Spofford, for, doubtless, I would be badly worsted by either of them, for I see they both have their subject at heart and seem to understand it well. (July 1890, 22)

Both Carolyn and Mrs. C.H.B. thus point to a shared belief that reading and writing for the publication is educational; that entering this kind of written community is valuable in and of itself; and that this interaction is cyclical in that it also helps writers learn the habits and skills of magazine writing. Further, it is equally clear that Carolyn and Mrs. C.H.B. take the reader-writers seriously as professional magazine contributors. That Mrs. C.H.B. and other contributors reference rereading other readers' letters—potentially months after the initial publication—further emphasizes the value they place on reader contributions as examples of legitimate magazine discourse.

Ultimately, many of the reader contributors to the *Bazar*, the *Journal*, and the farm publications see themselves as professionals helping compose the magazine. Thus in the correspondence departments, and for the farm journals all agricultural departments, writers acknowledge that composing magazine content is part of a shared endeavor and encourage other readers to participate and take responsibility for composing the column. Many of the young contributors to *Maine Farmer*'s "Young Folks' Column" admit to wanting to see their name in print, such as Addie:

> I have had a nice invitation to write something for the young folks' column, and as I would like to see my name in the paper, I will see what I can do about it. I see that most all of the little girls write about their school and the work they can do, but I will tell you about my pet horse, Jennie. (Jan. 1885, 4)

However, most contributors make clear that part of the reason they wish to join the published conversation—either in a correspondence column or through articles in the ongoing discussion of agricultural matters—is not simply because, like Addie, they wish to see their name in the paper, but because they assume responsibility for constructing and continuing the reader conversations that make the magazine so valuable. In the agricultural journals, editors continually encourage readers to write, as I explored in chapter 4, and, occasionally, articles open with a statement about the value of many voices adding to debates over farm practices. Moreover, throughout the *Journal*'s "Just among Ourselves," the *Bazar* correspondence columns, and the "Woman's" departments in the farm magazines, also correspondence-based columns, letter writers encourage the efforts of previous writers and exhort more readers to join the conversation. In *Maine*'s "Woman's Department," Cleo echoes statements made by other reader-contributors by asserting:

> I believe if we were individually to make the same resolve, "I can if I try" in regard to the writing of articles for this column there will be no need of clipping from other papers and no necessity for another. ("Thoughts on Our Column" 4)

Furthermore, she uses the community atmosphere to address particular writers, admonishing them for their disappearance from the community, asking if "Clarissa Potter [has] become so deeply foundered, in the sea of matrimonial bliss, as not to be able to keep her head above the many domestic duties" so that she can write to the "Woman's Department" (4).

Like other correspondents, Cleo situates the work of contributors as part of the necessary business of the magazine and argues that the content and success of the column are dependent on readers' willingness to participate.

Significantly, it is the contributors who advance editors' calls to write by arguing that audience members have a responsibility to their community. Cleo further encourages reluctant members of the reading community by praising the skills of the audience and also noting the purpose reader contributions serve for a larger community:

> Isn't there as much talent and power of writing among our Maine women of the farm, as in other States? Are the farmers wives and daughters of this good State becoming so degenerated that they cannot even take up a pen, to write a word in defence of themselves, and their rights? (4)

Contributors of articles to the agricultural discussions in journals such as *Ohio* are even more vocal about the responsibility of readers to write for the "advancement" of the profession. J. Moldenhawer argues in *Ohio*:

> The difficulty is to convince our farmers of this fact [to participate in the press], but just as a preacher is never responsible for results but only for his efforts, which must be hearty and genuine, so the "pen and ink butter and cheesemakers," as well as the agricultural editors, can only be held responsible for whatever hard work and careful writing they do in order to convert a farmer from his old routine ways. (263)

Other readers, such as the following contributor to the *Journal*, reinforce the importance of reader contributions to the community by asserting that the magazine (and correspondence column) is built on its reputation for allowing readers to speak and contribute. This reader describes her desire to contribute to "Just among Ourselves" by stating:

> So many pleasant nooks and corners in The Ladies' Home Journal tempt one to enter and chat with their pleasant occupants and "presiding queens," that I hesitate which to select, taking it for granted that those who come on business will not be refused admittance to their sanctums nor denied an interview with their inmates and visitors. So, by your leave, I select "Just Among Ourselves" and, as I tell my tale of woe, I can but wonder if my sisters are in like perplexity. ("One Given to Hospitality" 32)

Here a reader articulates her belief that the column is in part defined by the fact that contributors "will not be refused admittance to their sanctums" and suggests that this very policy has justified her desire to participate. In doing so, contributors again take on the authorizing role of an editor, suggesting the degree of professionalization some readers believed they achieved through their interactions with the periodicals.

Other writers acknowledge this sense of responsibility to participate in a shared conversation by noting how the words of others have prompted their own composition. A "Pittsfield Farmer" outlines his previous desire to contribute before launching his own perspective on an issue that had been under discussion for a while, claiming that he had

> been desirous of writing to The Farmer for some time, but could not nerve up to the point before some one else would write about the subject I was intending to write about, or ask the same question—as an instance, the Bohemian oat question. We farmers need such schemes well and often aired. ("The Factory System" 108)

Frank Amon similarly situates his motivation for contribution in the belief that debates in the magazine should be intelligently considered and offer multiple perspectives. He asserts:

> It is not, as you perhaps know, much to one's credit to question the values of opinions of capable men who freely give of them to the readers of a paper so popular as the Ohio Farmer has now become, but should they feel sensitive because I write differing from them at times, please say to them, that I am a believer in the dissemination of ideas suggestive, as well as of records of practical knowledge and expressions of individual judgment. (147)

Whether they are contributing to a correspondence or advice-based column or publishing a full article, writers from the reading audience affirm a shared value of open debate and conversation in this forum, where all contributions are considered worthwhile for their ideas and efforts. In this way, too, the authorizing power of the periodical shifts away from just the editors and toward the contributors. As contributors, readers are able to enter a popular, professional realm of writing to the extent that they can even sponsor the continued literacy and professionalization of other readers.

Subscribing to and Sponsoring Multiple Literacies

Ultimately, perhaps the most valuable contribution periodicals can make to our histories of literacy and composition is here in the partially self-sponsoring, professionalizing platforms they offered for literacy to the general population. Although formal education, especially higher education, was still somewhat limited at the turn of the century for women, persons of color, and those who simply could not afford the time or tuition, periodicals such as the *Bazar*, the *Journal*, and farm publications represent popular nonacademic sites where readers could still seek out advanced, community-specific literacy skills and even a sense of validation and professionalization. The literacy skills that editors sponsored, and that contributors sponsored among themselves, was marked not by progress toward a degree conferred by an institution, but by visible participation in, and subscriptions to, a magazine community.

The forums in this particular collection of magazines were not the only sites of periodical-based literacy experiences for these audiences, however. Many magazines beyond this collection allowed readers to contribute, though almost exclusively in correspondence columns. In addition, readers could and would have been involved in local organizations that necessitated literacy skills and circulated materials both internally and publicly. The *Bazar* devoted explicit attention to the clubs and societies formed by women, many of which circulated texts among members and other women's clubs. Both Kelley and Gere trace U.S. women's clubs' work in circulating their own writing, demonstrating that "a system of circulating texts among clubs—even before the formation of national organizations—enabled clubwomen to share their literacy practices with one another," and "national organizations formalized and extended this textual circulation" (Gere, *Intimate Practices* 8). In addition, the farming periodicals often included reports from farmers' clubs and agricultural societies. Thus the contributions made by readers to the *Bazar*, the *Journal*, *Maine*, and *Ohio* are neither uninformed by other influences nor the only option available to their writers. These journals, then, are ultimately a few examples of the sort of literate activity turn-of-the-century Americans engaged in outside of the classroom setting that allowed them to have a visible, tangible voice within a community, or communities, of their choosing.

In the end, the popularity of this particular collection of magazines is perhaps testament to the appeal of a site that fostered a sense of community among readers and allowed them to participate and contribute in multiple ways, not unlike the kind of literate interaction available through digital sites and apps today. The fact, moreover, that these periodical audiences were diverse and overlapped one another also suggests that just as we explore different interests and selves in different areas of life and different sites online, so did turn-of-the-century magazine readers and writers seek the ability to subscribe to multiple literacy possibilities.

At the same time, as mixed-authorial texts, popular magazines have something to teach us. For although the literacy identities and skills circulated here had clear limitations, these journals did create spaces where readers felt that their knowledge and language were valued, where they were offered instruction on entering a textual community, and where they felt they could achieve some level of professionalization. Donehower, in "Rhetorics and Realities," analyzes what has historically been a problematic relationship between rural communities and outside literacy sponsors, an imbalanced relationship that tended to support only three responses: assimilation, appropriation, or rejection (62). She argues instead for exchanges where outside literacy sponsors and rural students seek "mutual identification" by understanding "the ways their lives are and might be interlinked" and where learning is "a genuine cultural exchange that recognizes the possibility of mutual beneficence among all parties" (73). I would argue that the content of the *Journal*, the *Bazar*, and the agricultural journals reveals readers responding in multiple ways: assimilating, appropriating, and rejecting. The sponsoring editors of these journals—both the farm periodicals and the women's magazines—are simultaneously outside sponsors and internal members of readers' home communities; they visibly position themselves as publishing experts and authorities, but they nonetheless claim an interest in readers' local and personal affairs and seek to adapt literacy practices and roles to suit the needs of their audience. However, editors are not the only sponsors present in these publications; reader-contributors also support and participate in the discourse conventions and identities appearing in the publications. In this way, editors and contributors join their individual expertise to negotiate practices and identities for literacy, offering a possibility for current compositionists and literacy scholars to consider.

The work of editors and contributors in farm journals suggests we might continue to consider places where the boundaries between sponsor and sponsored are blurred, where participants may take advantage of one form of sponsorship while simultaneously sponsoring others. In such a way, these journals may prompt us to consider not just how institutions can be sponsors, but also how spaces of sponsorship may allow participants and creators to blur boundaries between teacher and student. As educational sites, journals suggest that distinctions between outside and local, expert and novice, are not always as important as what the site itself may afford: allowing all participants to speak, valuing different voices, and constructing texts that mix the work of editors and readers, teachers and students. Ultimately, what distinguishes these periodicals is not their creation of a site for literacy learning that fully matches contemporary pedagogical ideals. Rather, periodicals demonstrate the way sites composed of mixed agendas and voices can still prompt valuable and rewarding work for students of writing.

NOTES
WORKS CITED
INDEX

Notes

Introduction: Literacy by Subscription

1. In *Quare Women's Journals,* Stone and Pettit discuss their efforts to establish a settlement school in the Kentucky mountains, commenting on how popular and useful magazines were for the communities they served (Stoddart). Similarly, in *An Ohio Schoolmistress,* Hardy notes the importance of magazines in her students' and her own literacy development, as does Golden in *Red Moon Called Me.*

2. *Harper's Bazar* did not adopt its contemporary spelling, *Harper's Bazaar,* until 1929.

3. *Michigan Farmer* continues to be published today.

1. Literacy Identities: Defining Magazine Writers

1. At times Bok is appalled at the confidences given to him; in his recurring column, "At Home with the Editor," he frequently discusses the topics raised in letters he has received and, at one point, warns mothers not to force their daughters "by indifference or neglect, to come to me or to any other man or woman on earth for advice which she should receive from you" (May 1891, 10).

2. One paragraph of the Brooklyn Woman's Club profile reads thus:

> The presidents have always been strong women, the pictured quartette being typical of the company who have in turn held the gavel over this fine assembly. Mrs. Ellen T. Brockway is a charter member of the club, and has always been prominent in its committee-work, besides her distinguished

service as its leader. Mrs. Amelia K. Wing is a longtime member, winning her way to its head by rightful qualities. Mrs. Marianna W. Chapman, the immediate predecessor of Mrs. Backus, is a woman of dignified, gracious presence that is supplemented with a clear-headed, gentle calm, inherited from her Quaker ancestors. Mrs. Helen H. Backus, the present president, is also an ex-president, having preceded Mrs. Chapman to the limit of her continuous eligibility to the office. Mrs. Backus is a woman of high intelligence and scholarly education, and gifted besides with a rare genius for presiding that will make her substitute extremely difficult to find. (98)

3. Features such as "Education at Home," "Teaching a Little One to Read," "Before They Go to School," and "Edward Howard Grigg's Talks: Moral Training of the Child" speak to mothers, representing them as pivotal actors in nurturing children's literacy and selecting appropriate reading material.

4. Importantly, *Ohio* also offers images and profiles of its female "Household Writers." These biographies mirror those of their male counterparts, including the women's education, farm and household experience, and writing.

2. Buying and Selling Literacy: The Ladies' Home Journal

1. Throughout his autobiography, Bok speaks of himself in the third person:

Before long, the letters streamed in by the tens of thousands during a year. The editor still encouraged, and the total ran to hundreds of thousands, until during the last year, before the service was finally stopped by the Great War 1917–1918, the yearly correspondence totaled nearly a million letters. (Bok, *Americanization* 174)

2. Bok does not offer the name of the editor of the new bureau.

3. Much of the work these physician-editors did was not visible in the magazine. What did appear was first the "Young Mother's Calandar" in 1904 and then the "Young Mother's Home Club" in 1906, where "Emelyn Lincoln Coolidge, M.D. of The Babies' Hospital, New York," discussed health and other issues related to raising children. Likewise, a question-and-answer column called "Pretty Girl Questions by Emma Walker, M.D." appeared in 1906–7. In addition to working at "The Babies' Hospital" and writing for the *Journal*, Dr. Coolidge also wrote a book, *The Mother's Manual*, which was part of the Women's Home Library series that Margaret Sangster, editor of *Harper's Bazar*, edited.

4. The magazine advertises that any girl who brought in over one thousand subscriptions would be able to "secure the lowest prize," suggesting that the number of winners each year was flexible (there were three the first year, in 1890)—though what Bok meant by "lowest prize" and the full details of how much funding the scholarships entailed is not offered. Contestants who were not able to reach the one-thousand-subscription quota were paid a return of 25 cents per subscription in 1890.

5. In fact, other magazines did contain personable editors, such as "Father Forrester" in the children's magazine at midcentury. However, this form of editorial expression was not common until later in the nineteenth century, and numerous periodical histories make note of Bok in discussing the beginning of the trend.

6. In the first issue of the column "At Home with the Editor," Bok assures readers that executive work will be left on the editor's desk and his addresses to his readers shall be composed at home:

> These pleasantly familiar talks, which monthly I enjoy on this page with my readers, shall come from within the precincts of my own home. There, by my own fireside, I shall be better able to imagine myself seated at your hearthstone. There, in my favorite chair, cheered by the glow of the evening home lamp, and with those around me who are man's best friends, I know I shall feel closer in sympathy with your interests and thoughts. Since home is the watchword of our Journal, why is not the editor's home the best place from which he should talk to his readers? (10)

7. In the 1900 *The National Cyclopedia of American Biography*, Mabie's work as an author and editor is discussed. He is also described as an educator and lecturer: "as a public lecturer on literary and social questions he has a wide audience. He is, in fact, one of our most influential American educators, working outside the curriculum" (J. T. White 10:43).

8. As the only way to distinguish among these column entries is by their dates, here and throughout, when the date is not first mentioned in the text, it will appear in the parenthetical citation.

9. Among other things, a "good novel" is marked by the fact that it is "interesting but it must also be sound, sane, well-constructed and well-written." He clarifies that "a sane story is both sincere and true to life" (15).

10. Interestingly, the magazine contains rather few stand-alone articles on letter writing. Most of the letter-writing advice is offered through the "Side Talks with Girls" column and its editor, Ruth Ashmore, and also in the "My Girls" column by Margaret Sangster, the editor of *Harper's Bazar*.

In this way, the discussions of writing letters are strangely compartmentalized within the magazine.

11. The first two issues of "Just among Ourselves" were edited by an "Aunt Catherine." Catherine, however, never offered her true identity, and she was swiftly replaced by Abbott as "Prudence." The tone and style of the column in the first two months, moreover, was consistent with Abbott's technique. Given that Bok himself had briefly headed a column, "Just between Ourselves," that functioned in much the same way as "Just among Ourselves" ultimately did, it seems likely that "Catherine" was simply a placeholder for a column intended for Abbott. The Abbotts, who wrote for and edited the *Outlook*, were already connected to Bok through their work with Mabie.

12. This is a bit of an understatement, given the number of subscriptions required to win: over a thousand.

3. Joining the Club: Clubwomen, Magazine Readers, and Scholars

1. As was common in magazines at the time, quite a number of the articles have no listed author, making it difficult to know how many writers are contributing to the larger discussion on education. It is possible that some of these articles were written by Sangster or Jordan, which may partially explain the continuity of ideology.

2. In his autobiography, Bok discusses his criticism of clubs and the subsequent *Journal* article written by President Cleveland that supported his view; when a club published a statement of its resolution to boycott the *Journal*, Bok attempted to bring a lawsuit against it. He later admits that even when he turned from "destructive" to "constructive" criticism of the clubs' methods, "they were too angry with him even to admit that his suggestions were practical and in order" (301).

3. At the same time, however, the discourses of professionalism increasingly used by academics depreciated the quality and seriousness of the study clubwomen undertook, denying it the authority attached to colleges; Gere sees this as systematic of English studies' moves toward disciplinarity, saying that "to professionalize English studies, then, would-be academics had to discredit clubwomen's literary projects in favor of their own; they stigmatized the literacy practices of women's clubs to enhance those of professors" (214).

4. Describing the growth of clubs in 1892, Anna B. McHahan, of the Friends in Council club of Quincy, Illinois, asserts that "they gave us the

habit of expressing ourselves on paper; they taught us not to fear the sound of our own voices; they made us acquainted with each other's mind and thoughts" (qtd. in Martin 92).

5. No information is available on the identity of E. B. Cutting, in the magazine or elsewhere. Cutting's knowledge of women's clubs—their meetings and their study habits—suggests that it is drawn from personal experience. I am working, therefore, on the assumption that Cutting is a woman.

6. Cutting assures them that their club "shows a fine sentiment" and will enjoy the reading, before suggesting they study Victor Hugo, Bismarck, and Robert Browning and compare "how the master passion conquered a novelist, a statesman, and a poet" (Sept. 1908, 913).

7. In this same issue, moreover, Cutting, as well as the contributors themselves, reminds readers that serious reading should also be a pleasure. One reader, for instance, explains, "At my home in Ohio there are few trees and a wide expanse of the sky, and I am anxious to know something about the stars that I see night after night." Cutting responds by wishing to aid her in "having a real companionship with the stars themselves" and recommends a book "which makes a charming relationship between the nomenclature of the stars and literature" (Oct. 1908, 1034).

4. Special Invitation to Write: Magazine Readers as Contributors

1. Like other farming journals, *Michigan* publishes the writing of audience members throughout all sections of the paper and does not restrict the comments of contributors to specific correspondence columns. Moreover, while some articles are signed, as is this one, with a city of origin, presumably denoting that the writer is a contributor rather than an editor, other articles are left unsigned. Thus it is not always clear who is writing what articles. Here and throughout, I always note where an article is presumably written by a contributor.

2. In "Latent Abilities: The Early Grange as a Mixed-Gender Site of Rhetorical Education," Carolyn Ostrander examines women's active participation in and contribution to Grange rhetoric. While the journals I study include writing from female readers, they clearly imagine and speak to a predominantly male (farmer) audience.

3. Few of these articles are signed. The articles I consider here that offer advice on grammar and style, and encourage readers to contribute to the journal, are all written from the perspective of one of the magazine editors.

It is equally true, however, that articles published in these journals, those related to farming rather than writing matters, do not consistently name an author either, some offering no name and others giving name and city or county.

Conclusion: Subscribing to a Professional Writing Community

1. Another fantastic resource for work on the history of home economics is Cornell University's Mann Library *Home Economics Archive: Research, Tradition, History* and its Rare and Manuscript Collections site, "From Domesticity to Modernity: What Was Home Economics?"

Works Cited

Abbott, Mrs. Lyman. "Just among Ourselves." *Ladies' Home Journal* 7.8 (1890)–24.9 (1907). *American Periodicals Series Online*. Web. 1 Sept. 2011.

Adams, David Wallace. *Education for Extinction: American Indians and the Boarding School Experience, 1875–1928*. Lawrence: UP of Kansas, 1996. Print.

Alba, Quercus. "Writing for the Public." *Maine Farmer* 45.40 (1877): 1. *American Periodicals Series Online*. Web. 1 Sept. 2011.

Amon, Frank. "Notes and Suggestions." *Ohio Farmer* 22.10 (March 1873): 147. *American Periodicals Series Online*. Web. 9 May 2013.

Annie. "A Call." *Maine Farmer* 49.45 (1881): 4. *American Periodicals Series Online*. Web. 1 Sept. 2011.

Bailey, Liberty Hyde. *The Country Life Movement in the United States*. New York: Macmillan Company, 1911. *Gutenburg.org*. Web. 10 April 2013.

Bailey, Nettie. "The Significance of the Woman's Club Movement." *Harper's Bazar* 39.3 (1905): 204–9. *American Periodicals Series Online*. Web. 1 Sept. 2011.

Baldwin, Mary R. "The Busy Woman's Reading." *Harper's Bazar* 31.8 (1898): 164–65. *American Periodicals Series Online*. Web. 1 Sept. 2011.

Barton, David, and Mary Hamilton. "Literacy Practices." *Situated Literacies: Reading and Writing in Context*. Ed. David Barton, Mary Hamilton, and Roz Ivanic. London: Routledge, 2000. 7–15. Print.

Beetham, Margaret. *A Magazine of Her Own? Desire and Domesticity in the Woman's Magazine, 1800–1914*. New York: Routledge, 1996. Print.

Berklage, Nancy K. "The Establishment of an Applied Social Science: Home Economists, Science, and Reform at Cornell University, 1870–1930." *Gender and American Social Science: The Formative Years*. Ed. Helene Silverberg. Princeton, NJ: Princeton UP, 1998. 185–231. Print.

Berry, Francesca. "Designing the Reader's Interior: Subjectivity and the Woman's Magazine in Early Twentieth-Century France." *Journal of Design History* 18.1 (2005): 61–79. Print.

Bok, Edward. *The Americanization of Edward Bok*. New York: Charles Scribner's Sons, 1921. Print.

———. "At Home with the Editor." *Ladies' Home Journal* 8.3 (1891):10–12.12 (1895): 14. *American Periodicals Series Online*. Web. 1 Sept. 2011.

———. "Helps to Literary Success." *Ladies' Home Journal* 7.7 (1890): 12 and 7.8 (1890):14. *American Periodicals Series Online*. Web. 1 Sept. 2011.

———. "The Magazine with a Million." *Ladies' Home Journal* 20.3 (1903): 16. *American Periodicals Series Online*. Web. 1 Sept. 2011.

———. "Mr. Bok's Literary Leaves." *Ladies' Home Journal* 6.12 (1889): 11. *American Periodicals Series Online*. Web. 1 Sept. 2011.

———. "A New Departure." *Ladies' Home Journal* 12.1 (1894): 33. *American Periodicals Series Online*. Web. 1 Sept. 2011.

———. "Words for Young Authors." *Ladies' Home Journal* 7.4 (1890): 13. *American Periodicals Series Online*. Web. 1 Sept. 2011.

———. "Writing for the Dollar." *Ladies' Home Journal* 8.2 (1891): 18. *American Periodicals Series Online*. Web. 1 Sept. 2011.

Bourdieu, Pierre. *Language and Symbolic Power*. Cambridge, MA: Harvard UP, 1991. Print.

boyd, danah. "Why Youth Heart Social Network Sites: The Role of Networked Publics in Teenage Social Life." *Youth, Identity, and Digital Media*. Ed. David Buckingham. Cambridge: MIT Press, 2008. 119–42. Print.

Brandt, Deborah. *Literacy in American Lives*. New York: Cambridge UP, 2001. Print.

Brown, Anna Robertson. "The Girl Who Goes to College: Before She Goes." *Ladies' Home Journal* 10.8 (1893): 14. *American Periodicals Series Online*. Web. 1 Sept. 2011.

———. "The Girl Who Goes to College: After She Gets There." *Ladies' Home Journal* 10.9 (1893): 22. *American Periodicals Series Online*. Web. 1 Sept. 2011.

Brown, Geo. H. "Writing for the Paper." *New England Farmer* 63.16 (1884): 1. *American Periodicals Series Online*. Web. 1 Sept. 2011.

"The Business Letter." *Harper's Bazar* 31.37 (1898): 782. *American Periodicals Series Online.* Web. 1 Sept. 2011.

"A California Housekeeper on Chinese Servants." *Harper's Bazar* 13.19 (1880): 290. *American Periodicals Series Online.* Web. 1 Sept. 2011.

Caplan, Eric. *Mind Games: American Culture and the Birth of Psychotherapy.* Berkeley: U of California P, 1998. Print.

Carolyn. "A Word to the Wise." *Maine Farmer* 65.13 (1897): 3. *American Periodicals Series Online.* Web. 1 Sept. 2011.

Carr, Jean Ferguson, Stephen L. Carr, and Lucille M. Schultz. *Archives of Instruction: Nineteenth-Century Rhetorics, Readers, and Composition Books in the United States.* Carbondale: Southern Illinois UP, 2005. Print.

Chambers, Michael Allen. *Traditional Values and Progressive Desires: Tensions of Identity in the Rhetoric of the Granger Movement in Illinois, 1870–1875.* Diss. University of Maryland, 2008. College Park: UMI, 2008. Print.

Chowdry, I. N. "Reading for Farmers and How Some Farmers Read." *Ohio Farmer* 83.14 (1893): 262. *American Periodicals Series Online.* Web. 8 May 2016.

Clapp, N. A. "Farm Home Reading." *Michigan Farmer* 51.13 (1907): 385. *American Periodicals Series Online.* Web. 1 Sept. 2011.

Cleo. "Thoughts on Our Column; Woman's Department." *Maine Farmer* 41.9 (1897): 4. *American Periodicals Series Online.* Web. 9 May 2013.

"Club Women's Seriousness." *Harper's Bazar* 31.52 (1898): 1112. *American Periodicals Series Online.* Web. 1 Sept. 2011.

"A College Girl's Experience as a Wife." *Ladies' Home Journal* 22.11 (1905): 42. *American Periodicals Series Online.* Web. 1 Sept. 2011.

Cowden, W. N. "Institute Workers." *Ohio Farmer* 91.12 (1897): 249. *American Periodicals Series Online.* Web. 1 Sept. 2011.

Cowdry, I. N. "Reading for Farmers and How Some Farmers Read." *Ohio Farmer* 83.14 (1893): 262. *American Periodicals Series Online.* Web. 1 Sept. 2011.

"Current Comment." *Ohio Farmer* 99.16 (1901): 350. *American Periodicals Series Online.* Web. 1 Sept. 2011.

Cushman, D. Q. "A Few Thoughts." *Maine Farmer* 54.2 (1885): 2. *American Periodicals Series Online.* Web. 1 Sept. 2011.

———. "Original Occupation." *Maine Farmer* 55.40 (1887): 1. *American Periodicals Series Online.* Web. 1 Sept. 2011.

Cutting, E. B. "Our Home Study Club." *Harper's Bazar* 42.9 (1908)–46.10 (1912). *American Periodicals Series Online.* Web. 1 Sept. 2011.

———. "Suggestions for Home Study." *Harper's Bazar* 42.8 (1908): 781–83. *American Periodicals Series Online*. Web. 1 Sept. 2011.

———. "Women and Home Reading." *Harper's Bazar* 42.2 (1908): 154–57. *American Periodicals Series Online*. Web. 1 Sept. 2011.

Damon-Moore, Helen. *Magazines for the Millions: Gender and Commerce in the* Ladies' Home Journal *and the* Saturday Evening Post, *1880–1910*. Albany: SUNY Press, 1994. Print.

Danbom, David B. *Born in the Country: A History of Rural America*. Baltimore: Johns Hopkins University Press, 1995. Print.

———. "Rural Education Reform and the Country Life Movement, 1900–1920." *Agricultural History* 53.2 (1979): 462–74. Print.

de Castell, Suzanne, and Allan Luke. "Defining 'Literacy' in North American Schools: Social and Historical Conditions and Consequences." *Journal of Curriculum Studies* 15 (1983): 373–89. Print.

Dixey, Wolstan. "Poets and Editors." *Ladies' Home Journal* 7.7 (1890): 12. *American Periodicals Series Online*. Web. 1 Sept. 2011.

Donehower, Kim. "Rhetorics and Realities." *Rural Literacies*. Ed. Kim Donehower, Charlotte Hogg, and Eileen E Schell. Carbondale: Southern Illinois UP, 2007. 37–76. Print.

Donehower, Kim, Charlotte Hogg, and Eileen E Schell, eds. *Reclaiming the Rural: Essays on Literacy, Rhetoric, and Pedagogy*. Carbondale: Southern Illinois UP, 2012. Print.

———. *Rural Literacies*. Carbondale: Southern Illinois UP, 2007. Print.

Dye, Nancy S. Introduction. *Gender, Class, Race, and Reform in the Progressive Era*. Ed. Noralee Frankel and Nancy S. Dye. Lexington: UP of Kentucky, 1991. 1–9. Print.

Dyke, Charles Bartlett. "The Training of Teachers for Indian Schools." *Journal of Proceedings and Addresses of the Thirty-Ninth Annual Meeting . . .* National Educational Association. Chicago: U of Chicago P, 1900. 696–98. Print.

"The Editor's Pencil." *Ohio Farmer* 90.2 (1896): 24. *American Periodicals Series Online*. Web. 1 Sept. 2011.

"The Editor's Shears." *Ohio Farmer* 89.24 (1896): 498. *American Periodicals Series Online*. Web. 1 Sept. 2011.

"The Editor's Strainer." *Ohio Farmer* 95.8 (1899): 164. *American Periodicals Series Online*. Web. 1 Sept. 2011.

"The Editor's Table." *Michigan Farmer* 31.22 (1897): 422. *American Periodicals Series Online*. Web. 1 Sept. 2011.

"The Educational Bill." *Maine Farmer* 56.15 (1888): 2. *American Periodicals Series Online*. Web. 1 Sept. 2011.

Eldred, Janet Carey. *Literate Zeal: Gender and the Making of a New Yorker Ethos*. Pittsburgh: U of Pittsburgh P, 2012. Print.

"The Endings of Letters." *Harper's Bazar* 17.5 (1884): 75. *American Periodicals Series Online*. Web. 1 Sept. 2011.

Enoch, Jessica. *Refiguring Rhetorical Education: Women Teaching African American, Native American, and Chicano/a Students, 1865–1911*. Carbondale: Southern Illinois UP, 2008. Print.

Ewell, S. H. "Does Education Tend to Promote Morality?" *Michigan Farmer* 33.21 (1898): 411. *American Periodicals Series Online*. Web. 1 Sept. 2011.

"The Factory System." *Ohio Farmer* 61.7 (1882): 108. *American Periodicals Series Online*. Web. 9 May 2013.

"Farmers as Writers and Executors." *Southern Planter* 45.8 (1884): 413. *American Periodicals Series Online*. Web. 1 Sept. 2011.

"Farm Experience." *Ohio Farmer* 58.19 (1880): 293. *American Periodicals Series Online*. Web. 1 Sept. 2011.

"Fashionable Letter-Writing." *Harper's Bazar* 16.25 (1883): 389. *American Periodicals Series Online*. Web. 1 Sept. 2011.

"A Few Facts." *Ohio Farmer* 84.8 (1893): 142. *American Periodicals Series Online*. Web. 1 Sept. 2011.

"For the Farmer." *Maine Farmer* 12.1 (Jan 1844): 1. *American Periodicals Series Online*. Web. 1 Sept. 2011.

"Free Education Prize Winners." *Ladies' Home Journal* 8.4 (1891): 10. *American Periodicals Series Online*. Web. 9 May 2013.

Fry, John J. "'Clear Thinking—Right Living': Midwestern Farm Newspapers, Social Reform, and Rural Readers in the Early Twentieth Century." *Agricultural History* 78.1 (2004): 34–49. Web. *JSTOR*. 12 April 2013.

G.C.S. "The Young Farmers' Corner." *Ohio Farmer* 103.5 (1903): 93. *American Periodicals Series Online*. Web. 1 Sept. 2011.

Gee, James Paul. *Social Linguistics and Literacies: Ideology in Discourses*. London: Falmer Press, 1990. Print.

Gere, Anne Ruggles. *Intimate Practices: Literacy and Cultural Work in U.S. Women's Clubs, 1880–1920*. Carbondale: Southern Illinois UP, 1997. Print.

———. "Kitchen Tables and Rented Rooms: The Extracurriculum of Composition." *College Composition and Communication* 45.1 (1994): 75–92. Print.

Gilbert, Z. A. "Progress in Agriculture." *Nineteenth Annual Report of the Secretary of the Maine Board of Agriculture for the Year 1874*. Augusta, ME: Sprague, Owen, and Nash, Printers to the State, 1874. 220–30. Print.

"The Girls' Club: With One Idea: To Make Money." *Ladies' Home Journal* 20.11 (1903): 40–24.12 (1907): 72. *American Periodicals Series Online.* Web. 1 Sept. 2011.

"Girls of Whom We Are Proud." *Ladies' Home Journal* 9.8 (1892): 12. *American Periodicals Series Online.* Web. 1 Sept. 2011.

Gold, David. *Rhetoric at the Margins: Revising the History of Writing Instruction in American Colleges, 1873–1947.* Carbondale: Southern Illinois UP, 2008. Print.

Gold, David, and Catherine L. Hobbs. *Educating the New Southern Woman: Speech, Writing, and Race at the Public Women's Colleges, 1884–1945.* Carbondale: Southern Illinois UP, 2013. Print.

Golden, Gertrude. *Red Moon Called Me: Memoirs of a Schoolteacher in the Government Indian Service.* San Antonio, TX: Naylor, 1954. Print.

Goodburn, Amy M. "Girls' Literacy in the Progressive Era: Female and American Indian Identity at the Genoa Indian School." *Girls and Literacy in America: Historical Perspectives to the Present.* Ed. Jane Greer. Santa Barbara: ABC-CLIO, 2003. 79–102. Print.

Gordon, Edward E., and Elaine H. Gordon. *Literacy in America: Historic Journey and Contemporary Solutions.* Westport, CT: Praeger, 2003. Print.

Gordon, Lynn D. *Gender and Higher Education in the Progressive Era.* New Haven, CT: Yale UP, 1990. Print.

Graff, Harvey J. *The Literacy Myth: Literacy and Social Structure in the Nineteenth-Century City.* New York: Academic Press, 1979. Print.

———. "The Literacy Myth at Thirty." *Journal of Social History* (2010): 625–61. Print.

Hale, Emma M. "Letter-Writing for Busy People." *Ladies' Home Journal* 13.5 (1896): 24. *American Periodicals Series Online.* Web. 1 Sept. 2011.

Haller, John S., Jr. *The History of New Thought: From Mind Cure to Positive Thinking and the Prosperity Gospel.* West Chester, PA: Swedenborg Foundation Press, 2012. Print.

Hardy, Irene. *An Ohio Schoolmistress: The Memoirs of Irene Hardy.* Ed. Louis Filler. Kent, OH: Kent State UP, 1980. Print.

Hawes, S. J. "The Educational and Social Responsibilities of the Grange." *Maine Farmer* 66.31 (1898): 8. *American Periodicals Series Online.* Web. 1 Sept. 2011.

"Hints to Correspondents." *Ohio Farmer* 49.26 (1874): 408. *American Periodicals Series Online.* Web. 1 Sept. 2011.

"Hints to Writers." *Ohio Farmer* 69.6 (1886): 94. *American Periodicals Series Online.* Web. 1 Sept. 2011.

"Hints to Young Writers." *Maine Farmer* 40.23 (1872): 1. *American Periodicals Series Online*. Web. 1 Sept. 2011.

Hobbs, Catherine, ed. *Nineteenth-Century Women Learn to Write*. Charlottesville: UP of Virginia, 1995. Print.

"Home Chats with Farmers' Wives." *Michigan Farmer* 33.6 (1898): 112. *American Periodicals Series Online*. Web. 1 Sept. 2011.

"How Six Girls Worked Their Way through College." *Ladies' Home Journal* 21.9 (1904): 22. *American Periodicals Series Online*. Web. 1 Sept. 2011.

"How Six More Girls Worked Their Way through College." *Ladies' Home Journal* 21.10 (1904): 22. *American Periodicals Series Online*. Web. 1 Sept. 2011.

Illouz, Eva. *Saving the Modern Soul: Therapy, Emotions, and the Culture of Self-Help*. Berkeley: U of California P, 2008. Print.

"Immigration's Effect upon Women." *Harper's Bazar* 33.38 (1900): 1347. *American Periodicals Series Online*. Web. 1 Sept. 2011.

Ivanic, Roz. *Writing and Identity: The Discoursal Construction of Identity in Academic Writing*. Philadelphia: John Benjamins Publishing Company, 1998. Print.

Johnson, Joan Marie. "'Drill into Us . . . the Rebel Tradition': The Contest over Southern Identity in Black and White Women's Clubs, South Carolina, 1898–1930." *Journal of Southern History* 66.3 (2000): 525–62. Print.

Johnson, Nan. *Gender and Rhetorical Space in American Life, 1866–1910*. Carbondale: Southern Illinois UP, 2002. Print.

———. *Nineteenth-Century Rhetoric in North America*. Carbondale: Southern Illinois UP, 1991. Print.

Joliffe, Lee. "Women's Magazines in the 19th Century." *Journal of Popular Culture* 27.4 (1994): 125–40. Print.

Jordan, Elizabeth. "With the Editor." *Harper's Bazar* 42.2 (1908): 192. *American Periodicals Series Online*. Web. 1 Sept. 2011.

"Just among Ourselves." *Ladies' Home Journal* 8.6 (1891): 26. *American Periodicals Series Online*. Web. 9 May 2013.

Kelley, Mary. *Private Woman, Public Stage: Literary Domesticity in Nineteenth-Century America*. New York: Oxford UP, 1984. Print.

"The King's English." *Ohio Farmer* 88.1 (1895): 10. *American Periodicals Series Online*. Web. 1 Sept. 2011.

"The King's English." *Ohio Farmer* 88.2 (1895): 30. *American Periodicals Series Online*. Web. 1 Sept. 2011.

"The King's English—Once More." *Ohio Farmer* 88.6 (1895): 130. *American Periodicals Series Online*. Web. 1 Sept. 2011.

Laffrado, Laura. "'I Thought from the Way You *Writ,* That You Were a Great Six-Footer of a Woman': Gender and the Public Voice in Fanny Fern's Newspaper Essays." *In Her Own Voice: Nineteenth-Century American Women Essayists.* Ed. Sherry Lee Linkon. New York: Garland Publishing, 1997. 81–96. Print.

Leonard, Priscilla. "The Laws of Letter Writing." *Harper's Bazar* 38.11 (1904): 1125–27. *American Periodicals Series Online.* Web. 1 Sept. 2011.

"Letters." *Harper's Bazar* 15.23 (1882): 354. *American Periodicals Series Online.* Web. 1 Sept. 2011.

"Letter-Writing." *Harper's Bazar* 8.18 (1875): 282. *American Periodicals Series Online.* Web. 1 Sept. 2011.

Lewis, G. P. "Farmers Should Write for the Agricultural Papers." *American Agriculturalist* 7.12 (1848): 371. *American Periodicals Series Online.* Web. 1 Sept. 2011.

———. "Farmers Should Write for the Agricultural Papers." *Maine Farmer* 16.21 (1848): 1. *American Periodicals Series Online.* Web. 1 Sept. 2011.

Lightner, A. B. "A Farmer's Notions about Agricultural Journals." *Southern Planter and Farmer* 37.8 (1876): 561. *American Periodicals Series Online.* Web. 1 Sept. 2011.

Lindey, Sara. "Boys Write Back: Self-Education and Periodical Authorship in Late Nineteenth-Century Story Papers." *American Periodicals* 21.1 (2011): 72–88. Print.

Logan, Shirley Wilson. *Liberating Language: Sites of Rhetorical Education in Nineteenth-Century Black America.* Carbondale: Southern Illinois UP, 2008. Print.

Mabie, Hamilton. "Mr. Mabie on Self-Culture." *Ladies' Home Journal.* 23.11 (1905): 20. *American Periodicals Series Online.* Web. 1. Sept. 2011.

———. "Mr. Mabie's Literary Talks." *Ladies' Home Journal.* 19.4 (1902)–21.3 (1904). *American Periodicals Series Online.* Web. 1 Sept. 2011.

Mann, Horace. *Fifth Annual Report of the Massachusetts Board of Education.* Boston: Board of Education, 1841. Print.

Marchalonis, Shirley. "Women Writers and the Assumption of Authority: The *Atlantic Monthly*, 1857–1898." *In Her Own Voice: Nineteenth-Century American Women Essayists.* Ed. Sherry Lee Linkon. New York: Garland Publishing, 1997. 3–26. Print.

Martin, Theodora Penny. *The Sound of Our Own Voices: Women's Study Clubs, 1860–1910.* Boston: Beacon Press, 1987. Print.

Mattingly, Carol. *Well-Tempered Women: Nineteenth-Century Temperance Rhetoric.* Carbondale: Southern Illinois UP, 1998. Print.

McCracken, I. Moriah. "'I Pledge My Head to Clearer Thinking': The Hybrid Literacy of 4-H Record Books." *Reclaiming the Rural: Essays on Literacy, Rhetoric, and Pedagogy.* Ed. Kim Donehower, Charlotte Hogg, and Eileen E. Schell. Carbondale: Southern Illinois UP, 2012. 121–42. Print.

Miller, Sally M., ed. *The Ethnic Press in the United States: A Historical Analysis and Handbook.* New York: Greenwood Press, 1987. Print.

Miller, Susan. *Assuming the Positions: Cultural Pedagogy and the Politics of Commonplace Writing.* Pittsburgh: U of Pittsburgh P, 1998. Print.

"Mission of the Agricultural Paper." *Ohio Farmer* 94.16 (1898): 290. *American Periodicals Series Online.* Web. 1 Sept. 2011.

Moje, Elizabeth Birr, and Allan Luke. "Literacy and Identity: Examining Metaphors in History and Contemporary Research." *Reading Research Quarterly* 44.4 (2009): 415–37. Print.

Moldenhawer, J. "Dairy Thoughts for the Average Farmer." *Ohio Farmer* 100.15 (1901): 263. *American Periodicals Series Online.* Web. 9 May 2013.

Monroe, G. E. "Agricultural Education at Home." *Maine Farmer* 54.16 (1886): 1. *American Periodicals Series Online.* Web. 1 Sept. 2011.

Mott, Frank Luther. *A History of American Magazines, 1865–1885.* Vol. 3. Cambridge: Harvard UP, 1938. Print.

Mrs. A.E.R. "The Housekeeper." *Ohio Farmer* 62.21 (1882): 338. *American Periodical Series Online.* Web. 9 May 2013.

Mrs. C.H.B. Letter. "Just among Ourselves." *Ladies' Home Journal* 7.8 (1890): 22. *American Periodicals Series Online.* Web. 11 June 2013.

"A Neglected Tool." *Ohio Farmer* 46.24 (1874): 369. *American Periodicals Series Online.* Web. 1 Sept. 2011.

"Neighborhood Literary Societies." *Michigan Farmer* 13.45 (1882): 7. *American Periodicals Series Online.* Web. 1 Sept. 2011.

Ness, Elmer W. "The Young Folks' Column." *Maine Farmer* 55.44 (1887): 4. *American Periodicals Series Online.* Web. 1 Sept. 2011.

"Novel-Readers." *Harper's Bazar* 13.30 (1888): 466. *American Periodicals Series Online.* Web. 1 Sept. 2011.

Oak, Red. "Writing for the Public." *Maine Farmer* 45.51 (1877): 1. *American Periodicals Series Online.* Web. 1 Sept. 2011.

Ohio State Grange. *Centennial History of the Junior Grange in Ohio.* Salem, OH: Lyle Printing and Publishing, 1988. Print.

"One Given to Hospitality." *Ladies' Home Journal* 10.5 (1893): 32. *American Periodical Series Online.* Web. 11 June 2013.

"On Letter Writing." *Harper's Bazar* 32.38 (1899): 800. *American Periodicals Series Online.* Web. 1 Sept. 2011.

"On Writing." *Maine Farmer* 49.7 (1881): 4. *American Periodicals Series Online*. Web. 1 Sept. 2011.

Ostrander, Carolyn. "Latent Abilities: The Early Grange as a Mixed-Gender Site of Rhetorical Education." *Reclaiming the Rural: Essays on Literacy, Rhetoric, and Pedagogy*. Ed. Kim Donehower, Charlotte Hogg, and Eileen E Schell. Carbondale: Southern Illinois UP, 2012. 107–20. Print.

"Our Girls." *Harper's Bazar* 43.2 (1910)–45.2 (1911). *American Periodicals Series Online*. Web. 1 Sept. 2011.

"Our Girls' Exchange." *Harper's Bazar* 45.3 (1911)–46.7 (1912). *American Periodicals Series Online*. Web. 1 Sept. 2011.

"Our Public Schools." *Maine Farmer* 48.6 (1880): 2. *American Periodicals Series Online*. Web. 1 Sept. 2011.

Patterson, Martha H. *The American New Woman Revisited: A Reader, 1894–1930*. New Brunswick, NJ: Rutgers UP, 2008. Print.

"Points in Letter-Writing." *Harper's Bazar* 28.32 (1895): 646. *American Periodicals Series Online*. Web. 1 Sept. 2011.

Prescott, Gerald. "Wisconsin Farm Leaders in the Gilded Age." *Agricultural History* 44.2 (1970): 183–99. Print.

Preston, Alice. "What Would You Do? A Page of Girls' Questions." *Ladies' Home Journal* 24.2 (1907): 31. *American Periodicals Series Online*. Web. 1 Sept. 2011.

"Reading for Pleasure." *Harper's Bazar* 23.13 (1890): 230. *American Periodicals Series Online*. Web. 1 Sept. 2011.

Roich, Katharine. "The College-Bred Woman in Her Home." *Ladies' Home Journal* 16.8 (1899): 14. *American Periodicals Series Online*. Web. 1 Sept. 2011.

Rooks, Noliwe M. *Ladies Pages: African American Women's Magazines and the Culture That Made Them*. New Brunswick, NJ: Rutgers UP, 2004. Print.

Rose, Mike. *Lives on the Boundary*. New York: Penguin Books, 1989. Print.

Royster, Jacqueline Jones. "History in the Spaces Left: African American Presence and Narratives of Composition Studies." *CCC* 40 (1999): 563–84. Print.

———. *Traces of a Stream: Literacy and Social Change among African American Women*. Pittsburgh: U of Pittsburgh P, 2000. Print.

"Rural School Problem." *Michigan Farmer* 31.21 (1897): 402. *American Periodicals Series Online*. Web. 1 Sept. 2011.

Sangster, Margaret. *An Autobiography*. Whitefish, MT: Kessinger Publishing Company, 2004. Print.

———. "My Girls: Uses and Abuses of Reading." *Ladies' Home Journal* 18.10 (1901): 32. *American Periodicals Series Online*. Web. 1 Sept. 2011.

———. *Winsome Womanhood*. New York: Fleming H. Revell Company, 1900. Print.

Scanlon, Jennifer. *Inarticulate Longings: The Ladies' Home Journal, Gender, and the Promises of Consumer Culture*. New York: Routledge, 1995. Print.

Schultz, Lucille M. "Letter-Writing Instruction in 19th Century Schools in the United States." *Letter Writing as a Social Practice*. Ed. David Barton and Nigel Hall. Philadelphia: John Benjamins Publishing Company, 2000. 109–30. Print.

Sherman, William L., and Paul Theobald. "Progressive Era Rural Reform: Creating Standard Schools in the Midwest." *Journal of Research in Rural Education* 17.2 (2001): 84–91. Print.

Smiles, Samuel. *Self-Help*. London: John Murray, 1859. Print.

S.N.B. "The Education of Our Boys." *Michigan Farmer* 15.34 (1884): 1. *American Periodicals Series Online*. Web. 1 Sept. 2011.

Snyder, Beth Dalia. "Confidence Women: Constructing Female Culture and Community in 'Just among Ourselves' and the *Ladies' Home Journal*." *American Transcendental Quarterly* 12.4 (1998): 311–25. Print.

"A Social Need." *Harper's Bazar* 20.48 (1887): 810. *American Periodicals Series Online*. Web. 1 Sept. 2011.

Soltow, Lee, and Edward Stevens. *The Rise of Literacy and the Common School in the United States: A Socioeconomic Analysis to 1870*. Chicago: U of Chicago P, 1981. Print.

"Some of Our Contributors: Men Who Write for Us." *Ohio Farmer* 98.21 (1900): 373–74. *American Periodicals Series Online*. Web. 1 Sept. 2011.

Soper, Grace W. "Occupations of Women College Graduates: II." *Harper's Bazar* 21.2 (1888): 18–19. *American Periodicals Series Online*. Web. 1 Sept. 2011.

Starr, Martha A. "Consumption, Identity, and the Sociocultural Constitution of 'Preferences': Reading Women's Magazines." *Review of Social Economy* 62.3 (2004): 291–305. Print.

Steinberg, Salme Harju. *Reformer in the Marketplace: Edward W. Bok and* The Ladies' Home Journal. Baton Rouge: Louisiana State UP, 1979. Print.

Stevens, W. W. "Writing for the Paper." *Farmers' Home Journal* 47.2 (1886): 561. *American Periodicals Series Online*. Web. 1 Sept. 2011.

Stoddart, Jess, ed. *The Quare Women's Journals: May Stone and Katherine Pettit's Summers in the Kentucky Mountains and the Founding of Hindman Settlement School*. Ashland, KY: Jesse Stuart Foundation, 1997. Print.

Street, Brian. *Social Literacies: Critical Approaches to Literacy in Development, Ethnography, and Education*. London: Longman, 1995. Print.

"Study Brevity—Give Us Facts." *Maine Farmer* 38.51 (1870): 1. *American Periodicals Series Online*. Web. 1 Sept. 2011.

Swales, John. *Genre Analysis: English in Academic and Research Settings*. Cambridge, MA: Harvard UP, 1990. Print.

Taylor, James M. "Writing." *Ohio Farmer* 60.19 (1881): 302–3. *American Periodicals Series Online*. Web. 1 Sept. 2011.

Taylor, Isobel M. "Letters—Written and Received." *Harper's Bazar* 30.39 (1897): 810. *American Periodicals Series Online*. Web. 1 Sept. 2011.

Thomas, Angela. "Blurring and Breaking through the Boundaries of Narrative, Literacy, and Identity in Adolescent Fan Fiction." *A New Literacies Sampler*. Ed. Michele Knobel and Colin Lankshear. New York: Peter Lang, 2007. 137–65. Print.

Thompson, Eleanor Wolf. *Education for Ladies, 1830–1860: Ideas on Education in Magazines for Women*. New York: King's Crown Press, 1947. Print.

Tonkovich, Nicole. "Rhetorical Power in the Victorian Parlor: Godey's Lady's Book and the Gendering of Nineteenth-Century Rhetoric." *Oratorical Culture in 19th-Century America: Transformations in the Theory and Practice of Rhetoric*. Ed. Gregory Clark and S. Michael Halloran. Carbondale: Southern Illinois UP, 1993. 158–83. Print.

U.S. Census Bureau. "No. HS-21. Education Summary—High School Graduates, and College Enrollment and Degrees, 1900 to 2001." *United States Census Bureau*, 2012. Web. 2 Jan. 2012.

Voorhees, Henry. "Agricultural Education Not a Success." *Michigan Farmer* 32.5 (1897): 80. *American Periodicals Series Online*. Web. 1 Sept. 2011.

W. "Book Farming." *Maine Farmer* 12.49 (1844): 1. *American Periodicals Series Online*. Web. 1 Sept. 2011.

Weber, Rose-Marie. "Even in the Midst of Work: Reading among Turn-of-the-Century Farmers' Wives." *Reading Research Quarterly* 28.4 (1993): 292–302. Print.

Welch, Margaret Hamilton. "Club Women and Club Work." *Harper's Bazar* 30.42 (1897)–32.42 (1899). *American Periodicals Series Online*. Web. 1 Sept. 2011.

"What and How Shall We Read?" *Maine Farmer* 54.2 (1885): 2. *American Periodicals Series Online*. Web. 1 Sept. 2011.

"What Farmers' Wives Read." *Ohio Farmer* 58.2 (1880): 30. *American Periodicals Series Online*. Web. 2013.

White, J. T. *The National Cyclopedia of American Biography*. Vol. 10. New York: James T. White and Company, 1900. Print.

White, Kristin Kate. "Training a Nation: The General Federation of Women's Clubs' Rhetorical Education and American Citizenship, 1890–1930." Diss. Ohio State University, 2010. Print.

Wiley, Franklin B. "The Literary Beginner." *Ladies' Home Journal* 19.3 (1902): 36–19.11 (1902): 26. *American Periodicals Series Online*. Web. 1 Sept. 2011.

"Will Education Do All?" *Maine Farmer* 52.23 (1884): 2. *American Periodicals Series Online*. Web. 1 Sept. 2011.

Williams, Bronwyn. "Literacy, Power and the Shaping of Identity." *Identity Papers: Literacy and Power in Higher Education*. Ed. Bronwyn Williams. Logan: Utah State UP, 2006. 1–13. Print.

"The Winter's Educational Campaign." *Michigan Farmer* 46.18 (1904): 326. *American Periodicals Series Online*. Web. 1 Sept. 2011.

"Woman's Department." *Maine Farmer* 55.8 (1887)–56.7 (1887). *American Periodicals Series Online*. Web. 1 Sept. 2011.

"Women and Men: The Alphabet as a Barrier." *Harper's Bazar* 29.21 (1896): 438. *American Periodicals Series Online*. Web. 1 Sept. 2011.

"Women's Rights." *Maine Farmer* 50.15 (1882): 1. *American Periodicals Series Online*. Web. 9 May 2013.

"Women's Work for Their Cities." *Harper's Bazar* 43.8 (1909): 766. *American Periodicals Series Online*. Web. 1 Sept. 2011.

"Young Folks' Column." *Maine Farmer* 53.9 (1885): 4. *American Periodicals Series Online*. Web. 9 May 2013.

Index

Italicized page numbers indicate figures.

Abbott, Mrs. Lyman, 74–79, 172n11
Adams, David Wallace, 5, 24
advertisements, 30, 49, 76, 113
advice, 34–35, 41–42; book selection, 58–59; on how to conduct group study, 107–8; invention, 134–35; letter writing, 67, 74–75, 89–93, 115; by readers, 114–15
advice manuals, 90, 92
African Americans, 7, 17, 24, 94
agricultural colleges, 14, 124–25, 137
"Agricultural Education Not a Success" (Voorhees), 45–46
agricultural press. *See* farm journals
agricultural profession, 10, 13, 19, 120; contributing to, 38–43, 45–46, 149–50; as science, 123, 126, 128, 131; societies, 121–22. *See also* farm journals
American Agriculturalist, 39
American Farmer, 121
American Indians, 11, 24
Americanization of Edward Bok, The (Bok), 49, 50, 55–56
American New Woman Revisited, The: A Reader, 1894–1930 (Patterson), 116
American womanhood, 31–32
arbitration, 97

Archives of Instruction (Carr, Carr, and Schultz), 21, 60, 64–65, 70
"At Home with the Editor" (Bok), 30, 31, 52, 57, 169n1 (chap. 1), 171n6
Atlantic Monthly, 72, 74
audiences, 8–9; collective identity, 25–26; family-based, 9, 32, 123; gender-specific, 20, 151–52; hybrid, 18, 153–54, 158; men, 17, 27, 40, 41, 47, 63; middle- and upper-middle-class women, 17, 27–28, 32, 60–61, 87, 89–90; multiple, 47–48, 153–54, 164–66; reader awareness of, 113–14; rural, 121–22, 127, 134; urban, 4, 7, 16, 31, 47, 94, 122–23, 126, 152. *See also* literacy identity; participation
authority: authoritative tone, 54, 58–59, 65; of editors, 102–3, 109; experts, 53–55; gender and, 72, 74; women's clubs, 94, 109–11

Bailey, Liberty Hyde, 126
Bailey, Nettie, 83, 97–98
Baldwin, Mary R., 34–35, 87, 88
Barton, David, 19–20
Beetham, Margaret, 37–38
Berklage, Nancy K., 158
Berry, Francesca, 35, 37

Bok, Edward, 11, 16, 19, 23; autobiography, 30, 49, 50, 156–57, 170n1; conservative ideals of womanhood, 50, 81, 96; editorial persona, 53, 57; as immigrant, 9–10, 52–53; multiple audiences and, 47; service mission, 52; topic choices, 24–25; *Articles:*: "Helps to Literary Success," 69, 71; "The Magazine with a Million," 27; "Mr. Bok's Literary Leaves," 69; "Words for Young Authors," 73–74; "Writing for the Dollar," 70, 72–73
"book farming" / "paper farming," 42–43, 46, 127, 128, 130
book reviews, 59, 62
Born in the Country (Danbom), 125, 126
Bourdieu, Pierre, 20, 28
Brandt, Deborah, 20, 126–27
Brooklyn Woman's Club, 32, 33, 169–70n2
Brown, Anna Robertson, 80–81
Brown, Geo. H., 133
businessmen, 53
"Busy Woman's Reading, The" (Baldwin), 34–35, 87, 88

capital, education as, 38, 65–66
Carr, Jean Ferguson, 21, 60, 64–65, 70
Carr, Stephen L., 21, 60, 64–65, 70
census reports, 7
Centennial History of the Junior Grange in Ohio, 122
Chambers, Michael Allen, 38, 43, 128, 130, 133
class, 42–43; middle- and upper-middle-class women, 3–4, 12, 17, 24, 32, 60–61, 87, 89–90; target audiences, 17, 27–28, 87, 89–90
Cleveland, Grover, 172n2
"Club Women and Club Work" (Welch), 32–34, *36*, 84–85, 93–96, *95*, 98–99
collective identity, 25–26, 130
college: agricultural, 14, 124–25, 137; articles on, 11, 12, 32, 80; scholarship competitions, 55–56, 79–82

"College-Bred Woman in Her Home, The" (Roich), 12, 32
comment columns, 5–6, 112–13, 140–42, 160–61, 173n1
communities of readers and writers, 8, 21, 25–26, 30–38; creating a community of women, 93–100, 152; effective literacy, 21–22; needs of, 144–45; professional writing community, 159–64; textual, 67, 112–15, 130, 135, 138, 160, 163
composition textbooks, 21, 64–65, 70, 89
compulsory education laws, 6–7
"Confidence Women: Constructing Female Culture and Community in 'Just among Ourselves' and the *Ladies' Home Journal*" (Snyder), 77
conservative ideals, 50, 56, 61, 81, 90, 96
consumerism, 19, 35, 37; book selection advice, 58–59; consumption after purchase, 155; editorial persona and, 57–58; gendered literacy identity, 30, 49–50, 56, 62, 67–68, 151, 158; women as writers, 67–69
"Consumption, Identity, and the Sociocultural Constitution of 'Preferences': Reading Women's Magazines" (Starr), 30
content of magazines, 30, 46, 64, 78, 91–94, 162, 166; farm journals, 121–22, 128, 134, 147–50; shaping, 93, 101–4, 114–15, 157
contexts for literacy, 7–8, 25, 44–45
contributions, 22, 23–24, 26, *40*; composition process, 139–40; to farm journals, 38–43, 45–46, 119–50; *Harper's Bazar*, 112–15; readers as editors, 162–63; readers as educators, 160–61; reciprocal relationships, 127; teaching readers to become farmer-writers, 134–42; of young readers, 140–42. *See also* farm journals
Cornell University, 158

correspondence courses, 54
Country Life Commission, 13, 126
Country Life movement, 9, 10, 13, 121, 126, 158
critical thinking skills, 12
cultural capital, 20, 38
Curtis, Cyrus, 50
Curtis Publishing Company, 30, 50
Cutting, E. B., 3, 6, 7, 32, 100–112, 156, 173nn5–7

Damon-Moore, Helen, 49, 50, 54, 56, 57, 81
Danbom, David B., 125, 126
de Castell, Suzanne, 24
delivery systems, 20–21
design and decoration, 35, 37
"Designing the Reader's Interior: Subjectivity and the Woman's Magazine in Early Twentieth-Century France" (Berry), 35, 37
Dixey, Wolstan, 72, 73, 76, 78
"Does Education Tend to Promote Morality?" (Ewell), 45
domain-specific literacy practices, 19–20
Donehower, Kim, 120–21, 166
Dresser, Horatio, 55
"'Drill into Us . . . the Rebel Tradition': The Contest over Southern Identity in Black and White Women's Clubs, South Carolina, 1898–1930" (Johnson), 115–16
Dye, Nancy S., 9

editors, 11–12; construction of literacy identity and practices, 25–26; editorial persona, 53, 57–67; farm journals, 123, 142–50; female, 52, 56, 67, 84; literacy practices promoted by, 3, 8–9; as mentors, 101–3; negotiating market and editorial control, 67–79; negotiation with reader-writers, 77–79; *Articles and Columns:*: "At Home with the Editor," 30, 31, 52, 57, 169n1 (chap. 1), 171n6; "The Editor's Pencil," 142–45; "The Editor's Shears," 142–43, 145; "The Editor's Strainer," 146, 147–48; "With the Editor" issue, 99. *See also* advice; contributions; letters to the editor
Educating the New Southern Woman (Gold and Hobbs), 81
education, 10–12; basic, 4–5; as capital, 38, 65–66; critique of formal schooling, 8, 14–16, 135, 141–42; for immigrants, 44–45; intellectual life for women, 87–93; for older women, 87; outcome for women, 81; practical, 136–37; reader contributions as, 160–61; standardized, 9–10; teacher understanding of students, 23–24; at turn of the century, 3–8. *See also* higher education
"Educational and Social Responsibilities of the Grange, The" (Hawes), 39
"Educational Bill, The," 45
Educational Bureau (*Ladies' Home Journal*), 55
Education for Extinction (Adams), 5
Education for Ladies, 1830 to 1860 (Thompson), 10
"Education of Our Boys, The" (S.N.B.), 14
effective literacy, 21–22
Eldred, Janet Carey, 56, 153–54
Enoch, Jessica, 4, 5, 24
"Establishment of an Applied Social Science, The: Home Economists, Science, and Reform at Cornell University, 1870–1930" (Berklage), 158
Ethnic Press, The (Miller), 18
"Even in the Midst of Work: Reading among Turn-of-the-Century Farmers' Wives" (Weber), 13
Ewell, S. H., 45
experts, 53–55, 71, 166
extension courses, 13, 121, 126, 158

Farmer's Home Journal, 121, 123
farming, two conceptions of, 42–43
farm journals, 7, 18, 117–18, 166; "book farming," 42–43, 46, 127, 128, 130; bureaucratic practices, 127–28; circulation, 122; defining *Farmer* farmer, 128–34, *129*; definitions of good writing, 120–21; editors, 123, 142–50; education discussed in, 12–13, 124–25, 141–42; farmers as professionals and teachers, 149–50; invention advice, 134–35; knowledge, sharing of, 131–33; language and grammar, 145–47; literacy identity and, 38–39, 120; local school issues, 9, 10, 24; "old, veteran farmer" and new writer-farmer, 132–33; pedagogy, 120–21, 127, 135, 140; readers as contributors, 119–50; reciprocal relationship with contributors, 127; state-based, 16–17, 25, 121, 122; style and language in, 142–49; turn-of-the-century publications, 121–28; "Woman's Department," 156, 159–63; writers, 38–43, 45–46. See also contributions
Farm Progress, 121
Feminina, 35, 37
femininity, 35–38
Fern, Fanny (Sara Payson Willis), 154–55
Fifth Annual Report of the Massachusetts Board of Education (Mann), 5
4-H clubs, 127–28
Fry, John J., 122

Gender and Rhetorical Space in American Life, 1866–1910 (Johnson), 89, 92
Gender, Class, Race, and Reform in the Progressive Era (Dye), 9
General Federation of Women's Clubs, 96, 115
Gere, Anne Ruggles, 22, 109–11, 155, 165; *Intimate Practices*, 94, 96; "Kitchen Tables and Rented Rooms: The Extracurriculum of Composition," 2

Gilbert, Z. A., 123
"Girls' Literacy in the Progressive Era: Female and American Indian Identity at the Genoa Indian School" (Goodburn), 11
"Girl Who Goes to College, The" (Brown), 80–81
Godey's Lady's Book, 10
Gold, David, 57, 81
Goodburn, Amy M., 9, 11
good of the nation, 3–5
Gordon, Edward E., 2, 4, 5, 6–7, 24
Gordon, Elaine H., 2, 4, 5, 6–7, 24
Gordon, Lynn D., 9, 11
Graff, Harvey, 2, 4, 5, 6, 7, 24, 45
Granger movement, 13, 14, 38, 128–30

Hale, Sarah, 10
Hamilton, Mary, 19–20
Harper and Brothers, 83
Harper Collins Publishing, 83
Harper's Bazar, 3, 6, 9, 83, *85*, 154; advocating intellectual life for women, 86–93; agenda, 84–86, 98, 115; audience, 18–19, 27, 30, 32, 47–48; community and agency in, 112–15; creating community of women, 93–100, 152; critique of education, 23; fashion plates, 86; legitimizing role, 110–11; letter-writing advice, 89–93, 115; names of clubwomen, 33–34; reader contributions, 112–15; "With the Editor" issue, 100; women's education, 10–11; Articles:: "A California Housekeeper on Chinese Servants," 44; "Club Women's Seriousness," 98; "Fashionable Letter-Writing," 90–91; "The Laws of Letter Writing," 89, 92; "Letters," 89; "Letters—Written and Received," 92, 93; "Mistress and Maid," 44; "Novel-Readers," 35; "On Letter Writing," 92; "Points in Letter-Writing," 92–93; "Reading for Pleasure," 87–88; "The Significance of the

Woman's Club Movement," 97–98; "A Social Need," 44; "Women and Home Reading," 100; "Women and Men: The Alphabet as a Barrier," 44; *Columns::* "Books and Readers," 101; "Club Women and Club Work," 32–34, 36, 84–85, 93–96, 95, 98–99; "Home Study Club," 3, 17, 19, 30, 32, 84–85, 88–89, 93, 96, 100–112, 154; "Our Girls' Exchange," 85, 91, 93, 112–15. *See also* women's clubs

Harper's Magazine, 69, 83

Hawes, S. J., 39

higher education: agricultural colleges, 14, 124–25, 137; critique of, 14–15, 53, 124–25; extension courses, 13, 121, 126, 158; lack of focus on purposes of, 56, 67, 71–72, 81–82; for women, 10–12; women's clubs and, 109–11. *See also* education

histories of composition and literacy, 1–3

History of American Magazines, 1865–1885, A (Mott), 13, 38

Hobbs, Catherine, 21–22, 57, 81

Hogg, Charlotte, 120–21

home economics, 158

"Home Study Club" (*Harper's Bazar*), 3, 17, 30, 32, 84, 100–112, 154; advice on how to conduct group study, 107–8; collaboration, 85, 100, 103–6, 113; community of women, 93, 96; journals, 107–8; members as writers, 88–89

household management, 32, 35

Howard, Matilda Williams, 32–33

hybridity, 90, 112, 126; of magazines, 18, 21, 56, 111–12, 153, 158

identity. *See* literacy identity

identity-as-difference approaches, 28

ideologies, 20–21, 96

Illinois Granger movement, 130, 133

illiteracy, 3–5, 24–25, 43–45

Illouz, Eva, 55

immigrants, 4, 7, 24, 44–45; Bok as, 9–10, 52–53

impression management, 89

Improvement Club of New York, 155

Inarticulate Longings: The Ladies' Home Journal, Gender, and the Promises of Consumer Culture (Scanlon), 10, 49, 56

industrialization, 4–5

intellectual life for women, 86–93; as domestic, 87–88

Intimate Practices (Gere), 94, 96

"'I Pledge My Head to Clearer Thinking': The Hybrid Literacy of 4-H Record Books" (McCracken), 126

"'I Thought from the Way You *Writ*, That You Were a Great Six-Footer of a Woman': Gender and the Public Voice in Fanny Fern's Newspaper Essays" (Laffrado), 72, 153–54

Ivanic, Roz, 29

James, William, 55

Johnson, Joan Marie, 115–16

Johnson, Nan, 5, 89, 92

Joliffe, Lee, 20

Jordan, Elizabeth, 84, 86, 100

"Just among Ourselves" (Abbott), 17, 27, 51, 74–79, 172n11; limited range of options, 69; negotiation between reader-writers and editors, 77–79; textual community, 67, 113, 159, 160, 163

Kelley, Mary, 57, 71–72, 81, 94, 97, 106, 165

"Kitchen Tables and Rented Rooms: The Extracurriculum of Composition" (Gere), 2

Knapp Curtis, Louisa, 50, 54

Ladies' Home Journal, 1, 8, 9, 29, 49–82, 51, 155; audience, 18–19, 32, 47–48; "Aunt Patience," 56, 74–75; authoritative tone, 54, 58–59, 65; circulation,

Ladies' Home Journal (continued)
16, 124; competing discourses, 56–57; definitions of literacy, 43–44; departments, 51, 57–58; as educational institution, 54; influence of, 16, 49, 84; letters to the editor, 30, 52, 64, 70, 74–75, 156–57; national market, 52–57; negotiating market and editorial control, 67–79; purchasing subscriptions for literacy, 79–82; scholarship competitions, 55–56, 79–82, 156–57, 171n4; service-oriented departments, 53–55; subscription collection programs, 52–57; women as consumers and sellers of literacy, 19, 35, 37, 49, 67–69; women as writers for, 67–69, *68*; women's education, 10–11; *Articles::* "The College-Bred Woman in Her Home," 12, 32; "A College Girl's Experience as a Wife," 12; "Girls of Whom We Are Proud," 55; "Helps to Literary Success," 69, 71; "How Six Girls Worked Their Way through College," 80; "Letter-Writing for Busy People," 67; "The Literary Beginner," 69, 70–71; "Literature Not a Bed of Roses," 69; "Mr. Bok's Literary Leaves," 69; "Mr. Mabie on Self-Culture," 64; "Side Talks with Girls," 81; "The Snobbery of Education," 53; "What Would You Do? A Page of Girls' Questions," 76–77; "Words for Young Authors," 73–74; *Columns::* "At Home with the Editor," 30, 31, 52, 57, 169n1 (chap. 1), 171n6; "The Girls' Club: With One Idea: To Make Money," 81; "Just among Ourselves," 17, 27, 51, 67, 69, 74–79, 113, 159, 160, 163, 172n11; "The Library Bureau," 53–54, 67, 157; "Pretty Girl Questions by Emma Walker, M.D.," 54, 56; "Side Talks with Girls," 53. *See also* "Mr. Mabie's Literary Talks" (Mabie)

Ladies' Journal, 50
Ladies Pages: African American Women's Magazines and the Culture That Made Them (Rooks), 17, 18
Laffrado, Laura, 72, 154–55
Lawrence, Mortimer, 123
Leonard, Priscilla, 89, 92
letters to the editor, 30, 52, 64, 70, 74–75, 154, 156–57
letter writing, 15; advice, 67, 74–75, 89–93, 115; audience, consideration of, 92–93; exclusionary rhetoric in advice, 89–90
"Letter-Writing Instruction in 19th Century Schools in the United States" (Schultz), 89–90
Lewis, G. P., 39, 42
lifestyle-specific literacy practices, 18, 25–26
literacy: advanced, 8, 16, 58, 63, 72, 85, 101, 117–18; autonomous interpretations, 46; contexts, 7–8, 25, 44–45; defined by magazines, 15, 25, 43–48; gendered understanding of, 84; multiple, 164–66; women as consumers and sellers of, 19, 35, 37, 67–69
"Literacy and Identity: Examining Metaphors in History and Contemporary Research" (Moje and Luke), 28
literacy crisis, 1, 4, 24–25
literacy histories, 24
literacy identity, 18–19, 25–29; conservative, 50, 56, 61; construction of, 25–26; farm magazines and, 38–39, 120; gendered consumer, 30, 49–50, 56, 62, 67–68, 151, 158; multiple, 47–48, 51, 56, 81–82, 153. *See also* audiences
Literacy in America: Historic Journey and Contemporary Solutions (Gordon and Gordon), 2, 4
Literacy in American Lives (Brandt), 20
literacy learning, 1–5; by subscription, 16–22
literacy myth, 2, 24, 47

Literacy Myth, The: Literacy and Social Structure in the Nineteenth-Century City (Graff), 2, 4, 5, 6
literacy practices, 25–29; domain-specific, 19–20; extension courses, 13, 121, 126, 158; lifestyle-specific, 18, 25–26; sharing experiences, 35, 38, 103–6; shift from elocution to literary appreciation, 64. *See also* reading practices
literacy rates, 7, 24–25
literacy sponsors, 20–21, 126–27, 151, 157, 164–66
"Literary Beginner, The" (Wiley), 69, 70–71
"literary domestics," 71–72, 81
literary market, 37, 43–44. *See also* publishing industry
Literate Zeal: Gender and the Making of a New Yorker Ethos (Eldred), 56–57, 153–54
Logan, Shirley Wilson, 2
Luke, Allan, 24, 28

Mabie, Hamilton Wright, 37–38, 57–67, 69
Mademoiselle, 153–54
Magazine of Her Own, A? Desire and Domesticity in the Woman's Magazine, 1800–1914 (Beetham), 37–38
magazines: construction of literacy, 7–8; femininity, construction of, 37–38; hybridity of, 18, 21, 56, 111–12, 153, 158; literacy defined by, 15, 25, 43–48; Progressive education and, 8–16; sharing, 27, 77, 159
Magazines for the Millions: Gender and Commerce in the Ladies' Home Journal *and the* Saturday Evening Post, *1880–1910* (Damon-Moore), 49, 50, 54, 56, 81
"Magazine with a Million, The" (Bok), 27
Maine Farmer, 9, 14, 16–17, 19, 121, 123; circulation, 28; critique of education, 23; readers as contributors, 120; *Articles:*: "Book Farming," 127; "Hints to Correspondents," 134, 146, 148; "Hints to Young Writers," 144–45; "On Writing," 139, 141–42; "Our Public Schools," 141; "Study Brevity—Give Us Facts," 142, 144; "What and How Shall We Read?," 137–38; "Woman's Department," 160–61, 162–63; "Writing for the Public," 131; "Young Folks' Column," 140–41, 162

Mann, Horace, 4–5, 6
Marchalonis, Shirley, 72, 74
marketing strategy, 12, 16, 49, 82, 97
market research, 30
marriage, education and, 11
Martin, Miss Irwin, 33
Martin, Theodora Penny, 94, 96, 109, 110, 111
Mason, Harriet, 122
Mattingly, Carol, 97
McCracken, I. Moriah, 126, 127–28
mechanics, 21–22, 71, 73–74
medical instruction, 54
memoirs, 3
mentors, 44, 46, 101–2, 104
Michigan Farmer, 16–17, 117, 123, 135; higher education, view of, 124–25
middle-class audience, 3–4, 12, 17, 24, 27–28, 60–61, 87, 89–90
Miller, Daniel, 155
Miller, Sally M., 18
Miller, Susan, 2
"mind cure" movement, 55
Moje, Elizabeth Birr, 28
moral and social values, 4–6, 9, 19–20, 44–45, 134
Mormon clubwomen, 155
motherhood, 54
Mott, Frank Luther, 13, 38
"Mr. Mabie's Literary Talks" (Mabie), 37–38, 51, 57–67, 69, 171n7; "Five Marks of a Really Good Novel," 62; "good" literature, 61–62; "How to Form the Reading Habit," 62; on newspapers, 62–63; "Six Rules for Those Who Read," 66–67

New Century Club of Philadelphia, 32
New England Farmer, 121, 123, 133
newspapers, 62–63
new woman, 61, 86, 90, 116
New Yorker, 154
Nineteenth-Century Rhetoric in North America (Johnson), 5
Nineteenth-Century Women Learn to Write (Hobbs), 21–22
novels, 35, 62, 171n9

"Occupations of Women College Graduates" (Soper), 11
Ogden, Anna, 112
Ohio Farmer, 5, 7, 9, 14, 16–17, 19, 121, *129*; circulation, 28; contributors, 39–41, *40*, 119–20, 130, 156; "Mission of the Agricultural Paper," 136–37; Women's Department, 122; *Articles::* "The Editor's Pencil," 41–42, 142–45; "The Editor's Shears," 142–43, 145; "The Editor's Strainer," 146, 147–48; "Farm Experience," 45, 119–20, 128, 132, 134, 138; "A Few Facts," 41, 156; "The King's English" series, 130, 144, 147, 148; "Men Who Write for Us," *40*; "A Neglected Tool," 41, 42, 131–33, 138, 146–47; "Some of Our Contributors," 23, 41; "What Farmers' Wives Read," 160; "Writing," 142; "The Young Farmers' Corner," 138–39
Ohio State Grange, 122
Ostrander, Carolyn, 173n2
"outside" culture, 22

participation, 56; literacy sponsors, 20–21; negotiating, 153–59; professional writing community, 159–64
Patrons of Husbandry, 13
Patterson, Martha H., 116
pedagogies, 2, 6, 13, 17, 23, 151, 161; critique of, 14–16, 141; in farm journals, 120–21, 127, 135; women's clubs as models, 84–85, 93–94, 100–101
penmanship, 33, 93

Pennsylvania Farmer, 123
pictures and image content, 30, 32
"Poets and Editors" (Dixey), 73
polite conventions, 34
postbellum identity, 116
practical knowledge, 15–16
Prescott, Gerald, 122
Preston, Alice, 76–77
Private Woman, Public Stage: Literary Domesticity in Nineteenth-Century America (Kelley), 71–72, 81, 94, 97, 106
professionalization, 22, 42, 127, 152–53, 159–66. *See also* agricultural profession
"Progressive Era Rural Reform: Creating Standard Schools in the Midwest" (Sherman and Theobald), 13
Progressive ideals, 9, 11, 123
psychoanalysis, 55
public schools, 6–7, 15, 52–53, 141
publishing industry, 20, 69; book reviews, 59, 62; navigating, 59–67. *See also* literary market

racial identity, 116
reading clubs, 3, 38, 65–66
"reading people," 34–35
reading practices, 32, 34–37, 58, 62–63; collaborative, 100, 103–6, 112–13; economic value, 65–66; for farmers, 135–38; instruction in, 57–67; as national project, 60; polite conventions, 34; "profitable," 62; reflection, 104–9; "Six Rules for Those Who Read," 66–67; time management, 63–64. *See also* literacy practices
Reclaiming the Rural: Essays on Literacy, Rhetoric, and Pedagogy (Donehower, Hogg, and Schell), 120–21
Refiguring Rhetorical Education (Enoch), 5
Reformer in the Marketplace: Edward W. Bok and The Ladies' Home Journal (Steinberg), 50, 52–53, 55, 57
rhetorical skills, 21–22

"Rhetorics and Realities" (Donehower), 166
Rise of Literacy and the Common School in the United States, The (Soltow and Stevens), 15
Roich, Katharine, 12, 32
Rooks, Noliwe M., 17, 18
Roosevelt, Theodore, 13
Royster, Jacqueline Jones, 24
"Rural Education Reform and the Country Life Movement" (Danbom), 126
Ruralist, 13
Rural Literacies (Donehower, Hogg, and Schell), 120–21
rural literacies, 9–10, 13, 38–39, 120–21, 127–28. *See also* farm journals

Sangster, Margaret, 34, 83–84
Saturday Evening Post, 49
Saving the Modern Soul: Therapy, Emotions, and the Culture of Self-Help (Illouz), 55
Scanlon, Jennifer, 10, 49, 56
Schell, Eileen E., 120–21
scholarship competitions, 55–56, 79–82, 156–57, 171n4
Schultz, Lucille M., 21, 60, 64–65, 70, 89–90
self, construction of, 37–38
Self-Help (Smiles), 55
self-help literature, 55
self-hood, 29
self-representation, 154–55
separate spheres, 11, 50, 57; *Harper's Bazar*'s expansion of, 86–87; intellectual life as domestic, 87–88; professional domesticity, 61, 63; social agendas and, 97; writing as way out, 56, 71–72
servants, 12, 32, 44
Sherman, William L., 9, 13
sites of literacy, 1–2, 20–21
Smiles, Samuel, 55
Snyder, Beth Dalia, 77

social capital, 44
social relationships, 32, 35, 87–88; farm community, 38; home study clubs and, 102–3; letter writing and, 91–93
Soltow, Lee, 15
"Some of Our Contributors" (*Ohio Farmer*), 23
Soper, Grace W., 11
Sound of Our Own Voices, The: Women's Study Clubs, 1860–1910 (Martin), 94, 96, 109
Southern Planter, 121, 123, 136, 150
Starr, Martha A., 30, 32, 35
Steinberg, Salme Harju, 50, 52–53, 55, 57
Stevens, Edward, 15
St. Louis Star, 13
Street, Brian, 46
student writers, 29
subscription collection programs, 52–57, 159; scholarship competitions, 55–56, 79–82, 156–57
suffrage, 86
surveys, 30

Taylor, Isobel M., 92, 93
Taylor, James M., 15, 142
textbooks, 21, 64–65, 70, 89
textual communities, 67, 112–15, 130, 135, 138
Theobald, Paul, 9, 13
Thompson, Eleanor Wolf, 10
time management, 63–64
Tonkovich, Nicole, 10
Traditional Values and Progressive Desires: Tensions of Identity in the Rhetoric of the Granger Movement in Illinois, 1870–1875 (Chambers), 38, 43
"Training a Nation: The General Federation of Women's Clubs' Rhetorical Education and American Citizenship, 1890–1930" (White), 94, 96
"Training of Teachers for Indian Schools, The" (Dyke), 5

Tribune and the Farmer, 50
True Womanhood, 63
Truth, Sojourner, 21
Twitchell, George, 123

"unlettered" people, 34
upper middle class, 87, 89–90

Voorhees, Henry, 45–46
voters, literacy and, 5–6

Weber, Rose-Marie, 13
Welch, Margaret Hamilton, 32–33, 36, 91, 109. *See also* "Club Women and Club Work" (Welch); *Harper's Bazar*
Well-Tempered Women: Nineteenth-Century Temperance Rhetoric (Mattingly), 97
White, Kristin Kate, 94, 96, 110, 111
Wilder, Laura Ingalls, 13
Wiley, Franklin B., 70, 76, 78, 79
"Will Education Do All?," 45
Willis, Sara Payson, 154–55
Winsome Womanhood (Sangster), 83–84, 87
women: as consumers and sellers of literacy, 19, 35, 37, 67–69; employees of magazines, 30, 54; shifting roles, 27
"Women and Home" (*Tribune and the Farmer*), 50
Women's Christian Temperance Union, 97
women's club movement, 19, 84, 94, 111, 115

women's clubs, 10, 14, 22, 30, 83–118; academics and, 172n3; Bok and, 50; circulating texts among, 165; club of magazine readers, 100–112; club-women as mentors, 44; creating community of women, 93–100; criticism of, 96, 98; fulfillment found in, 96–97; General Federation of Women's Clubs, 96; *Harper's Bazar*'s influence on, 93–94; higher education and authority, 109–11; ideology of citizenship, 96; procedure, 109; profiles of clubwomen, 32–33; social agendas, 96; southern, 116; study clubs, 84, 94–95, 99–100. *See also Harper's Bazar*
women's rights, 96
"Women Writers and the Assumption of Authority: The *Atlantic Monthly*, 1857–1898" (Marchalonis), 72, 74
working class, 5
Working Mother, 30
Working Woman, 30, 32
"Writing" (Taylor), 15
writing: as act of identity, 29; for club work, 89; journals, 107–8; needs of community, 144–45; novice writers, 35; payment for, 113, 115. *See also* contributions; letter writing
Writing and Identity: The Discoursal Construction of Identity in Academic Writing (Ivanic), 29
"Writing for the Public" (Oak), 42–43, 46

yellow journalism, 60
yeoman class, 130

Alicia Brazeau is the director of the writing center at the College of Wooster, where she also teaches courses in composition and writing pedagogy. Her work has appeared in *College English* and *Children's Literature Association Quarterly*.